MOBILE MAR
MASTERCLASS

APP STORE OPTIMIZATION

A STEP-BY-STEP GUIDE TO BOOSTING YOUR APP'S ORGANIC DOWNLOADS

OLIVER HOSS

App Store Optimization:

A Step-By-Step Guide to Boosting Your App's Organic Downloads

Copyright © 2019 by Oliver Hoss

All rights reserved.

Published by: Oliver Hoss, www.oliverhoss.com

Hildanusstrasse 6, 3013 Bern, Switzerland

Editing: Dr. Vonda, www.book-editing-services.com

Cover Design: Jennifer C. Toomey, www.jenctoomey.com

ISBN (Print, Paperback): 978-3-952-5095-0-0

ISBN (E-Book, PDF File): 978-3-952-5095-1-7

TABLE OF CONTENTS

LIST OF TABLES

LIST OF FIGURES

INTRODUCTION

When Apple's *App Store* opened its digital doors in 2008, it offered only 500 different iOS apps to its customers.[1] A mere three months later, Google launched its store called *Android Market* with just 50 apps.[2]

One decade later, users can choose from more than 1.9 million iOS apps, and 1,000 new ones are added each day. On Google Play, 2.8 million apps are available, and this number grows by 4,500 per day.[3]

While this enormous variety is fantastic for users, it is a nightmare for app publishers, especially for those, who enter the market with their first app. It has never been harder to gain users.

Occasionally an app becomes a viral success without any marketing efforts. A famous example was *Flappy Bird*. The arcade game by a Vietnamese indie developer was downloaded more than 50 million times, and it generated daily ad revenues of up to $50,000.[4]

Unfortunately, success stories like this are rare.

Many app publishers rely on buying traffic to grow their user base. But as more companies move towards mobile each year, this approach gets more and more expensive.[5] For this reason, independent developers in particular must focus on another source for new users: Organic traffic.

Organic users are free, and scaling their number is possible for everyone. All you need to get organic users is knowledge about App Store Optimization, or ASO.

This knowledge is multi-faceted. App Store Optimization is one of the most challenging fields of Mobile Marketing. It touches many topics, and thus it requires different skills to master ASO:

- It requires a basic technical understanding of the app stores' algorithms.
- It needs creativity to design visual creatives and catching texts that attract and amaze users.
- It requires analytical skills to evaluate the outcome of optimization efforts and draw the right conclusions from it.

- It takes empathy to understand users' behavior and to deal with their feedback.

- It requires the will to learn and to keep track of technical developments that impact the app stores.

- And last but not least, it requires the stamina to keep researching and testing, even when the results are not as good as expected.

Many myths exist around App Store Optimization, and there is much content on the Internet trying to demystify it. One thing is indisputable though: If you want to make your app a success, there is no way around App Store Optimization.

Why this book?

You can find tons of information about App Store Optimization online. Hundreds of content creators write articles and blog posts, create videos or share their insights on social media on a daily basis.

So why is this book necessary?

Well, most of the available content pieces face at least one of the following problems:

First, they are scattered all over the place. Most companies in the mobile industry have their own blogs and newsletter cycles. Also, many individuals use their private social media accounts to publish information. Keeping track of all these sources would be a full-time job. And as a developer, you have better things to do.

The second reason arises from the first. As the content is scattered, it lacks a central thread connecting the single content pieces. Especially for newcomers, a missing underlying concept makes it difficult to understand the full meaning of ASO.

Third, most authors do not have a neutral view on topics. They are employees of ad networks, agencies or other companies with an agenda. And they want to be successful in their jobs and earn money. That means their opinions are biased. They will promote their business field as the single most important factor in mobile marketing, and of course, they will never tell you anything that could harm their business. Although this behavior is understandable, it prevents a well-balanced view of ASO.

Fourth, authors need to keep themselves relevant and in readers' minds. Again, the number of content producers is huge, and many of them (and respectively their companies) are competitors. So to stand out, they face constant pressure to publish new content. But writing is just one of many aspects of their job. They can invest only limited time in producing content. In-depth research is in most cases not possible because it consumes too much time. As a result, most of the one-page articles, white papers, and case studies do not cover a topic in detail. They give general advice like "research your keywords" or "optimize your screenshots". But they fail to deliver detailed tutorials about how to do it.

The purpose of this book is to solve these issues. During my career, I have read hundreds of articles, blog posts, e-books, and white papers. I have seen tutorial videos, participated in webinars, and had personal conversations with people in the industry. This book summarizes the takeaways from these activities, and it presents them to you from the neutral point of view of someone who struggled with ASO just like you do.

I filtered the useful information, concepts, and best practices out of the tons of content, and I connected them with a central thread. And of course, I added my personal experience from doing ASO.

The result is the most comprehensive ASO book in the industry.

Is this book for you?

This book is for independent developers who are about to release their first app on iTunes or Google Play.

It is for people who work for app studios that struggle to get their apps flying.

It is for marketing professionals who want to expand their knowledge to the app sector.

It is for employees of established businesses dipping their toe into the mobile world for the first time.

It is for students, aiming to become marketers, product managers or developers in the mobile industry.

And it is for everyone else who is curious about apps, the app stores, and mobile technology.

What will you learn?

We will begin by defining the basic vocabulary and metrics you need to understand Mobile Marketing. Based on that knowledge, we will discuss how iTunes and the Google Play Store work. You will learn about your app's product page and the pieces of information it contains. You will understand which purpose each element has, and how you can optimize it to serve this purpose. I will introduce you to multiple techniques to make your product page a better experience for potential users, and I will show you a lot of tools that will help you with your daily ASO work.

This book will give you all the information you need to develop your own ASO strategy and make your app a success. It is perfect for you if you are entirely new to ASO, because it will take you through the process step by step. But it will also give you many new ideas if you already have a basic understanding of the industry.

By buying this book, you took the first step toward a successful app business. Let us continue on this journey, shall we?

Additional Resources

To understand the content in this book, especially in the chapter about videos, please visit my website and check out the additional resources there:

www.mobile-marketing-masterclass.com/aso/resources/

The restricted content can be accessed by using this password:

@cc3ss-2019

PART I

ASO THEORY

CHAPTER 1
THE BASICS

Whenever we enter a new field of business or research, we come across words that we do not understand or cannot classify into the new context. This issue is especially real for technical fields. App Store Optimization is no exception. To understand the techniques of ASO, you need a basic knowledge of its vocabulary. Thus let me define the basic terms and concepts, so we are on the same page.

What is ASO?

First and foremost, here is the fundamental question: What is App Store Optimization?

ASO is the process of optimizing an app's product page in the app stores. The purpose of ASO is to maximize the app's visibility and improve the conversion rate, with the goal of increasing the number of organic downloads.[6]

This definition contains the final goal of ASO: Increasing the number of downloads. But it also includes two subgoals that contribute to the final goal:

- Creating Visibility
- Improving the Conversion Rate

These subgoals are the two big challenges of ASO. All your efforts contribute to one of them. We will talk in depth about how to create visibility in part II and about Conversion Rate Optimization in part III of this book.

Definition: Apps

Let us talk about apps for a minute. An *app* (short for *application*) is a "computer program that is designed for a particular purpose."[7] I am sure you know the term in the context of smartphones and tablets. But it is common in the context of desktop computers, smart TVs, wearables (smart watches), and other electronic devices, too. However, only apps for smartphones and tablets are relevant for this book.

We will limit our research further by the devices' operating systems (OS). That is the "software that allows a user to run other applications on a computing device."[8]

iPhones and iPads run on *iOS*. Samsung, Huawei, and many other manufacturers use Google's OS called *Android* on their phones and tablets. A tiny number of devices operate on other systems like *Windows Phone OS*, *Blackberry* or *Symbian*. As these other systems make up less than 1% of all devices, we will ignore them for our research. All considerations in this book are about iOS and Android apps.

We can also categorize apps by their price model. There are three common models used across all app stores:

Premium Apps

To download and use *Premium apps* (or *Paid apps*), users must pay a price upfront. Famous examples are *Threema*[9], a messenger app focusing on users' privacy, or the mobile version of the multi-player game *Minecraft*[10].

Free Apps

In contrast, users do not have to pay for free apps. They can enjoy all functions without limitations. *Facebook Messenger*[11] is a typical free apps.

Freemium Apps

Finally, many apps are free of charge at the time users download them, but they come with locked features or limited content. To unlock this content and enjoy the app to its full potential, users have to pay. These apps are *Freemium Apps*, with freemium being a combination of the words *free* and *premium.*

A piece of premium content is called in-app purchase (short: IAP). IAPs are 100% virtual. The entire buying process takes place online, including the order, the payment, and the distribution. A shirt or another physical product that you order via a shopping app is not an IAP.

IAPs can be for example:

- Consumable currency that allows users to speed up game mechanics, for example, *Gems* in *Clash of Clans*[12].

- A pack of recipes for a cooking app that is permanently available after the purchase like in *Veggie Weekend*[13].

- A subscription that hides ads like in the *USA today* app[14].

Definition: App Stores

Apps are distributed via app stores. The app store on your phone is a pre-installed shopping app that allows you to buy other apps. It is bound to one operating system: either iOS or Android.

If users look for iOS apps, there is only one official place to find them: Apple's *iTunes*.

For Android apps, the number of app stores is bigger. *Google Play Store* is the most popular. But several smaller stores like the *Samsung Store* or the *Amazon App Store* also provide Android apps. In some countries like China, the situation is even more confusing. While Chinese users cannot access Google Play, there are many alternative stores such as *Myapp*, *Baidu*, *Xiaomi* or *Oppo*. Besides those, there are hundreds of others focusing on users of distinct demographics or in certain regions, or on owners of specific devices.

As iTunes and Google Play have the biggest global market share, we will focus on them and ignore alternative stores.

Definitions: Product Page & Metadata

Every app in the stores has a *product page* (or *store listing*). The product page is a showcase to present what the app does and how it looks. It summarizes all the information about your app that users can get before downloading it, including texts and visual creatives such as screenshots and videos. These pieces of information are called *metadata*.

Check out the examples for product pages on iOS and Google Play on the next page.

Fig. 1: Product Page on iPhone
(Source: adapted from Gordon 2018)[15]

Fig. 2: Product Page on Google Play
(Source: adapted from Gordon 2018)[16]

On-Page Metadata

As the app owner, you can manipulate some of the metadata elements. These elements are called *on-page metadata* or *on-metadata*. You can access and manipulate it via *iTunes Connect* or the *Google Play Console*.

Here is a list of the on-page metadata:

Metadata	Type	iOS	GooglePlay
App Title	Text	30 characters	50 characters
Subtitle	Text	30 characters	—
Short Description	Text	—	80 characters
(Long) Description	Text	4,000 characters	4,000 characters
Promotional Text	Text	170 characters	—
Keyword Field	Text	100 characters	—
In-App Purchases	Text Text Visual	Title: 30 characters Description: 45 char. Icon	Title: 55 characters Description: 80 char.
App Icon	Visual	1	1
Screenshots	Visual	up to 10	up to 8
Feature Graphic	Visual	—	1
Video	Visual	up to 3	1
Developer Name	Text	1	1
App Category	Text	up to 2	1

Tab. 1: On-Page Metadata Elements on iOS and Google Play
(Source: adapted from Gordon 2018)[17]

Off-page Metadata

In contrast to on-metadata, *off-page metadata* (or *off-metadata*) is not editable. It includes, for instance:

- reviews and ratings by users,
- the app's data weight,

- information about available languages,
- the age rating that indicates whether your app is appropriate for children or not,
- and so forth.

Again, you cannot edit off-metadata. The store mechanics compose it. That does not mean that it is impossible to change it, though. By cleaning your app's code, you can reduce its data weight. And by adjusting in-app content, you can get a better age rating. But you cannot manipulate metadata to show a wrong data weight or an age rating of your choice.

For ASO, on-metadata is more important than off-metadata because you have full control over it.

Definition: Conversion Opportunities

Just as brick-and-mortar bookstores use various techniques to promote their books, app stores use different methods, called *conversion opportunities*, to present apps. Every time people come across your metadata in the app store, you have the opportunity to convert them into users for your app. In general, we can differentiate between three types of conversion opportunities: browsing, active search, and the product page.[18]

Each opportunity is linked to specific user behavior. They differ in the amount of information (or metadata) that users see. You need to make sure that people have a great experience, no matter how they discover your app. Thus you must optimize your metadata for all conversion opportunities.

Browsing

Browsing the app store is like strolling through the aisles of the bookstore without a concrete goal. People stop at a shelf, scan some book titles, and skim through cover texts until they find something interesting.

In the app stores, users check out features. Features are prominent placements on the store's homepage. They are comparable to stand-up displays next to the door of the bookstore that are visible to everyone coming in.

On iOS, only limited metadata shows up for these features. In most cases, users see the title, the subtitle, the app icon, and the price. The exception is the *Story*. It is an editorial piece that promotes information about one app. Every day, the store's editorial team creates two Stories: The "App of the Day" and the "Game of the Day." Both include a large promotional graphic, screenshots, the preview video, or a combination of these.

Another way to browse the app store is to check the top charts. The charts display the most popular and the most successful apps for the user's country, just like a bestseller list pinned to the wall next to the bookstore's counter. iOS charts display app titles, subtitles, icons, and prices.

The "Home"-page of Google Play shows different segments of apps. Some segments, such as "Recommended for you" are tailored for individual users. Others promote apps connected to popular topics like fitness or cryptocurrencies.

On Google Play, browsing people see even less information than on iTunes: Only icons, titles, and prices appear. In the charts, the average star ratings are shown additionally.

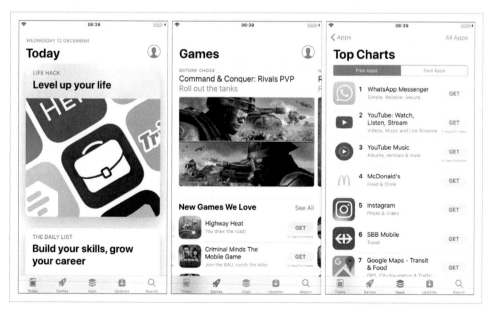

Fig. 3: Browsing on iOS (Home, Games, Top Charts)
(Source: iTunes)

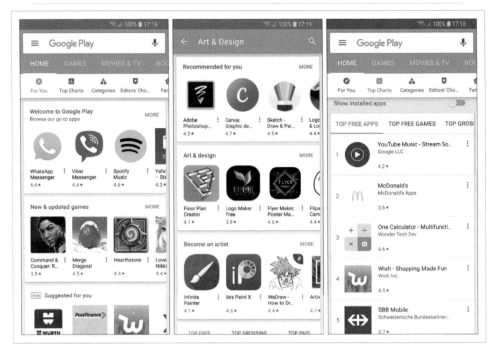

Fig. 4: Browsing on Google Play (Home, Category, Top Charts)
(Source: Google Play)

Active Search

When users perform a search on the app stores, the second conversion opportunity occurs. If people know what they are looking for or at least have a broad idea, they use the search function to find apps that match their needs. The search function is like the clerk who knows all the books in the store, their cover texts, and which categories they belong to.

In search results, iOS users see more metadata than while browsing: app titles, subtitles, app icons, prices, and average ratings. In addition, iPhone users will get the first three preview videos or screenshots of every app, given they are in portrait mode. In case the screenshots are in landscape orientation they will only see one. iPad owners get two portrait creatives or one in landscape orientation.

In search results on Google Play, almost the same elements show up as in browsing: titles, icons, prices, average ratings, and additionally publisher names. In landscape mode, publisher names and rating scores are not visible. There is only one exception: If the search term perfectly matches an app's title, the search result will include the screenshot gallery.

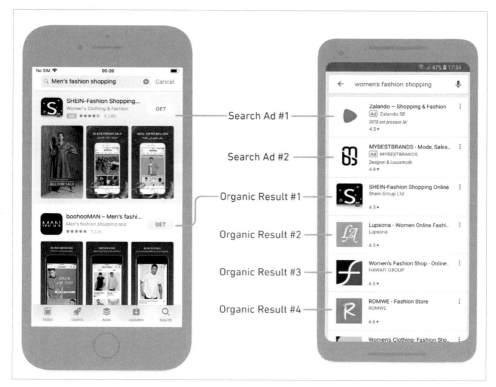

Fig. 5: SERPs on iTunes and Google Play
(Source: Author's own illustration)

Full Product Page

Users who arrive on the product page have either clicked a search result or seen the app in features or charts. They also might have followed an external link, for example by clicking a banner ad.

On the product page, users get the complete experience, including all texts, screenshots, and videos.

The Interplay of Conversion Opportunities

Conversion opportunities are linked to each other. For example, there is a strong link between great rankings in search results and making it into the top charts. On average, an iOS app needs to rank for more than 25 keywords to make it into the top 150 of its category. To make it into the top 100, it has to rank for at least 65 keywords.

But it is not only about the number of keywords an app ranks for. It is also about the position they gain on the SERP. The apps on top of the category rank #1 for at least six to seven keywords, and #2 or #3 for nice or ten more terms.[19]

We can take away from this data that success in search will not only generate more visibility, it will also increase the chance of getting an app into the top charts.

To sum up conversion opportunities, have a look at the following table. It shows which metadata elements affect the different conversion opportunities.

	Browsing		Search		Product Page	
	iOS	GP	iOS	GP	iOS	GP
App Title	yes	yes	yes	yes	yes	yes
Subtitle	yes	—	yes	—	yes	—
Short Description	—	no	—	no	—	yes
(Long) Description	no	no	no	no	yes	yes
Keyword Field	no	—	no	—	no	—
In-App Purchases	yes	no	yes	no	yes	yes
App Icon	yes	yes	yes	yes	yes	yes
Screenshots	no	no	yes	(yes)	yes	yes
Feature Graphic	—	no	—	(yes)	—	yes
Video	(yes)	no	yes	no	yes	yes
Average Rating	no	yes	yes	yes	yes	yes

Tab. 2: Metadata Elements in different Conversion Opportunities (Source: Author's own illustration)

Definition: Users

So far, I have used the term *users* several times. By users, I mean persons who own a smartphone or a tablet. They might browse the app store or use its search mechanism. They read through app descriptions, check out screenshots, watch preview videos, and download and use your app. Depending on their activity, I will also call them *viewers*, *readers*, *potential users* or simply *people*.

In any case, I mean the same: people who could be your customers if you manage to convince them to download your app.

Nevertheless, it makes sense to distinguish two groups of app store users, because they behave differently. Based on this behavior, you can approach them at different conversion opportunities.[20]

Explorers

Once an app has raised their interest, explorers check out all the information available. They read through the whole description and check every screenshot. They watch the preview video and read other users' reviews. Explorers care about details and take their time to make a reasonable download decision.

Based on this behavior, the product page is the conversion opportunity to win over explorers.

Deciders

In contrast, decisive users want a fast solution. They judge an app very quickly based upon their first impression and on little information. It takes them only a few seconds to decide whether they want to download or not.

Deciders do not visit the product page. They download apps directly from features, charts or SERPs. Thus, search results are crucial to win over deciders. The metadata on which these users base their download decision are:

- the app title and subtitle
- the icon
- the preview video (or the poster frame if the video does not autoplay)
- the gallery screenshots

CHAPTER 2
THE MOBILE MARKETING FUNNEL

No matter in which category users belong and how they come across your app, they all have to follow a specific journey. This journey takes them from noticing your app for the first time to downloading it (and beyond).

The *Mobile Marketing Funnel* is a concept that breaks this journey down into three stages with six single steps. The idea behind the funnel is simple: Only if people complete one step after another will they complete their journey and become loyal users.[21]

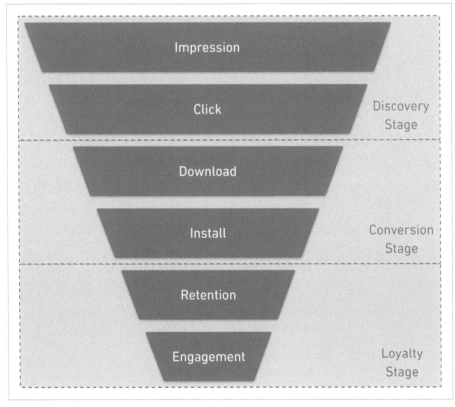

Fig. 6: The Mobile Marketing Funnel
(Source: adapted from TUNE)[22]

People who fail to complete one step will not complete the following steps either. That means that the number of users will shrink from step to step.

The graphic illustrates this pattern: Each box stands for the number of users that complete the single steps. The impression box is on top, the click box below and the other boxes follow underneath. Every box is smaller than the one above it. The graphic looks like a funnel and gives the concept its name.

The Mobile Marketing Funnel is a framework for your marketing actions. If you address people properly at every step of the journey, you will increase the chance that they become valuable users.

The Discovery Stage

Before people can use your app, they need to know that it exists. They need to become aware of your app, its features, and its capability to solve their problems. This discovery process includes two steps:

Step 1: The Impression

The first step in users' journey is an ad impression or, more precisely, the exposure to an impression. Actually, it is not a step, because it is not an action that users initiate voluntarily. It is rather a trigger to start the journey.

When marketers talk about impressions, they mean "the point in which an ad is viewed once by a visitor, or displayed once on a web page."[23] In other words, it is the moment when an ad catches a viewer's eye.

In the context of ASO, every piece of metadata qualifies as an ad, for instance, a screenshot on the SERP or an app icon in the top charts.

Step 2: The Click / Product Page Visit

If users consider an app interesting and want to learn more about it, they click the ad. That is their first voluntary action. The click initiates the second step of the user journey: visiting the product page.

The term *click* is common for this part of the user journey. But depending on the tools and people you work with, you might come across other names for the same action:

- In Apple's *Search Ads* tool, it is called *tab*. This term emphasizes the mobile character of this action, in contrast to what users of desktop computers do with a mouse.

- In the *Analytics* section of *iTunes Connect*, you will discover the term *page view*. This name points out the result of the action: visiting the product page.

The names differ, but they all refer to the second step of the user journey: clicking the ad and moving forward to the product page of the promoted app.

The Conversion Stage

After inspecting the metadata, it is now up to users to decide whether the app will help them solve their problem or not. If they think that it will, they will convert from potential into actual users. This conversion happens in two steps too.

Step 3: The Download

The third step is the *download* of the app. The click on the download button is the positive result of the decision-making process. It indicates that users want to test the app. For premium apps, the click also indicates users' willingness to pay. After the payment process, the download of the app's file package (the *APK file* on Android or *IPA file* on iOS) to the device starts.

Step 4: The Install

As soon as the download is complete, the device will automatically open the APK file (or the IPA file) and install the app. Thus it seems logical to think of the download and the *install* as one combined step.

But from a technical point of view, they are not. Here is why: The app store counts downloads at the moment when users click the download button. That is true even if the download is disrupted or the installation fails because the device is out of storage.

Installs are counted only when users launch the app for the first time. So it requires an additional action to get from the download to the install. An install indicates that users actually launched the app. A download does not. For this reason, I consider the download and the install two different steps in the user journey.

The Loyalty Stage

The user journey was pretty linear until now: Impression – Click – Download – Install. But after the first opening of the app, users might behave completely different from each other. Some users are focused and goal-oriented. They try to figure out the solution to their problem as soon as possible. Others start playing around. They test this feature, click that button, and explore the app without a clear purpose.

No matter how users interact with your app in the first place, only those who like it will use it on a regular basis.

Step 5: Retention

Retention is the first step toward a deeper relationship between users and the app (and by extension the app owner). Only if people return to an app after opening it for the first time, they can become loyal users. If they do, that is called retention.

Step 6: Engagement

If users return to an app regularly, they will start engaging with it on a deeper level. Finally, they become loyal users. As every app is different, many actions can indicate users' *engagement*:

- returning to the app more frequently
- staying longer (= longer session times)
- giving ratings and reviews in the app stores
- interacting with the developers or support teams
- interacting with other users via social features
- buying IAPs or physical articles from the app

CHAPTER 3
THE ROLE OF ASO

We defined ASO as a package of measures with the goal of "increasing the number of organic downloads." When looking at the Mobile Marketing Funnel, we see that the download is the third step. That means that ASO measures address only the first three steps of the funnel. Beyond the download, ASO has no more impact.

ASO has the final goal of increasing download numbers. But the single measures usually address only one of the two subgoals of ASO: either creating visibility or improving the conversion rate.

Measures for creating visibility address the first step in the Mobile Marketing Funnel: creating impressions. Or in other words, it is about creating conversion opportunities.

The second subgoal is to convert people from seeing your app to downloading it. It is about realizing the conversion opportunities you created before. Measures for this purpose address the second or the third step of the Mobile Marketing Funnel: creating clicks and downloads. We can summarize all of these actions under the term *Conversion Rate Optimization*, or *CRO*.

Key Performance Indicators

For the long-term success of ASO, it is crucial to evaluate the impacts of your work. For this purpose, you need reliable metrics that you can measure easily. These metrics are called *Key Performance Indicators*, or *KPIs*.

Impressions

For the first step of the funnel, the total number of impressions is the most important KPI. Your actions aim at increasing this number.

Clicks

To bring users to the second step, you need to make them click and visit your product page. Thus the total number of clicks is an interesting KPI. But even more important is the ratio: the number of clicks divided by the number of impressions. This ratio is called *click-through rate (CTR)*. Measures addressing the click level should increase the CTR.

CTR = Number of Clicks / Number of Impressions

Downloads

Finally, you must convert product page visitors into users who download your app. The total number of downloads is worth monitoring. But again, the relative metrics are more interesting. The *conversion rate (CVR)* tells you which percentage of product page visitors becomes users. If your efforts are successful, it will rise.

CVR = Number of Downloads / Number of Clicks

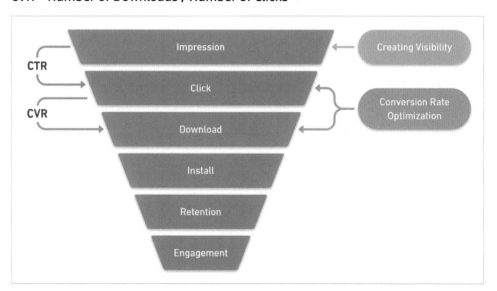

Fig. 7: How ASO Measures impacts the Mobile Marketing Funnel
(Source: Author's own illustration)

How to calculate KPIs

Apple and Google provide the numbers you need to judge your success. For some KPIs, you need to do additional calculations though.

KPIs on iTunes Connect

In the *App Analytics* section on iTunes Connect, you find the total numbers of impressions, product page visits, and downloads ("App Units"). Make sure to use the filters to break them down by traffic source (*Search* or *Browsing*). Be aware that *Search* data includes the downloads generated by *Apple Search Ad* campaigns. So if you run these campaigns while optimizing your product page, you will mess up your data.

Apple delivers neither the CTR nor the CVR, but they give you all the total numbers you need to calculate these rates.

KPIs on Google Play

Google Play provides the total numbers of product page visitors (= clicks) and downloads for *Search* and *Explore*. The latter is Google's synonym for *Browsing*. For *Search*, you can narrow down the data even further, to the keyword level. So you are able to see which keywords deliver the most downloads, at least for the most valuable keywords.

Unfortunately, you cannot see how many people see an impression of your app's assets on Google Play. For this reason, it is difficult to judge the visibility of your app correctly. You need to rely on the number of product page visitors as an indicator of visibility. In addition, you should track your app's ranking in the SERPs for your most relevant keywords (more on this topic later in this book).

Comparing Data over Time

When comparing numbers over time, you need to commit to a period as the baseline for your analysis. It seems logical to use monthly numbers and compare, for instance, May downloads against April downloads. But that is not the best solution for several reasons:

- Some months are longer than others. For example, May has 31 days, but April has only 30 and February even less. In longer months, the total monthly numbers are naturally higher. That makes a fair comparison impossible.

- Seasonal impacts like religious holidays or sports events can distort numbers as well. Filtering out these distortions based on monthly numbers is very difficult.

- App usage depends on the weekday. People use apps with a professional context from Monday morning to Friday afternoon. On weekends, they spend more time on leisure apps, including games. But the number of weekdays and weekends per month differs. In 2018, April had 21 weekdays and nine Saturdays and Sundays. May had 23 weekdays and only eight weekend days. These differences impact monthly numbers significantly.

For those reasons, weekly numbers are a better choice than monthly numbers on a short-term basis, because they always have the same number of weekdays and weekends. Bank holidays are the only factor causing distortions.

For long-term analysis, I recommend comparing monthly data year-over-year, for instance, May 2017 versus May 2018.

PART II

CREATING VISIBILITY

CHAPTER 4
HOW TO CREATE VISIBILITY

Now that we have the basics straight, let us tackle the first challenge of ASO: creating visibility. You need to get your app in front of potential users and create conversion opportunities. Only if they see your app can they download it, so you need to create as many impressions as possible.

In general, you can create organic visibility in two ways:

- By getting your app into top charts or features to target browsing users.

- By bringing your app into search results to make users with a specific intent aware of it.

Features and Stories

As mentioned previously, a feature is a very prominent placement in the app store. Many users will see it. Thus features drive vast amounts of impressions.

Getting a feature depends on the goodwill of Apple's and Google's editorial teams. They decide which apps get the valuable placements, and as the number of feature placements is very low, they are picky.

To get a feature, your app must meet several criteria:[24]

- The basic requirement is a great app. It must be original and free of bugs. Also, it should use some of the latest technologies, for example, Google's multi-window support, which allows users to run two apps simultaneously in split screen mode.

- Your app should have a history of strong KPIs: good retention numbers, an impressive average revenue per user, and a great rating.

- Your product page must be awesome. Neither Apple nor Google will send users over to see crappy screenshots or read poorly written app descriptions.

- Your app has to fit into an interesting story, or it has to be relevant for a topic that the store editors want to highlight.

- Finally, you need a personal connection to your store manager. So try to build a relationship with her or him as early as possible. Do not be pushy, though. When you pitch your app, provide all the data (KPIs, Social Proof, etc.), mention its USPs, and explain how it benefits users.

You see, there are a lot of requirements for qualifying for a feature. For new apps, it is tough to meet them all. I do not want to discourage you, but if you are at the beginning of your career in the app industry, do not waste too much time dreaming about features. There are easier ways to get loads of impressions. Keep on reading to learn about them.

Top Charts

The second way to gain visibility is bringing your apps into the top charts. Both stores provide several rankings:

- Category charts contain—as their name suggests—apps of a specific category. There are usually two lists per category: one for free (and freemium) apps and one for premium apps.

- Overall charts show a ranking of all apps, no matter in which category they belong. There is only one exception: For games, both iOS and Google Play present individual charts. Like category charts, separated overall rankings exist for free and premium apps.

- The "Most Successful" charts rank the apps or games that make the most money on the app store.

Like getting a feature, making it into the rankings is hard for a new app. In particular in developed nations, hundreds of thousands of downloads within a few days are necessary to make it to the top. That is especially true for the overall charts. Besides, an app needs high engagement rates to stay there.

There is a simple thing you can do to improve the chances to get into category charts, though: Pick the right categories for your app. As some of them are more competitive than others, you can increase your odds by choosing wisely.

Be aware, though, that picking your app's category is not a completely free choice. Your app must fit into it. Both Apple and Google let their employees review apps manually. If you choose a category that does not match your app at all, chances for rejection are high. But if your app fits into more than one category, pick those that are less competitive, at least at first. Later, you can switch, when uploading an update for your app.

An excellent example of successfully choosing categories is *Twitter*[25]. Until May 2016, Twitter ranked around #5 in the US charts for the Social Networking category. As more and more journalists started using Twitter, the company decided to switch to the News category. Since then, they consistently rank #1 there.[26]

To find out how competitive a category is, check out the download numbers of the apps on top of the category charts. The more downloads these apps have, the more difficult is it to challenge them. So go for the category where fewer downloads are necessary to make it into the top rankings.

Aside from choosing your category, do not worry too much about rankings. We have already discussed the interplay of conversion opportunities. Kick-start your app's success with the third option to create visibility. If you succeed in doing so, your app will make it into the charts soon after.

Search Results

The third and most important option to create impressions is search. About 65% of installs on iOS and 80% on Android are the results of search queries.[27] Showing your app to the users who perform those queries is a great way to gain visibility.

But search is not only the most promising way to get visibility because of volumes, it is also significantly easier to manage than trying to make it into top rankings or features. It requires neither a strong relation to your app store manager nor a significant number of downloads to make it into SERPs.

All you need is knowledge, and the following pages will provide you with all the knowledge you need to master search.

CHAPTER 5

UNDERSTANDING SEARCH

Optimizing for search is the focus of this part of the book. We will discuss in detail how Apple's and Google's search algorithms work and what you can do to use these algorithms in your favor.

But before we start, we will have to clarify some more vocabulary. I am sorry, I know theory is a pain. But believe me, if you understand the theory, you will master the practical work much more easily.

Definition: Keywords

One of the central elements of ASO is the *keyword*. A keyword is "a word or phrase submitted to a search engine in an effort to locate relevant documents or websites."[28]

"Submitting a word to a search engine" is a complicated description of a simple user action: typing a word into the search bar and clicking the "search" button. This process is called a *search query*, because users query (or ask) the search engine something.

Typical app users do not ask the search engine a grammatically correct question, though. Typing "what free-of-charge program can I use to chat with my friends?" takes too much time. Instead, people use simple terms to narrow down their problem or the solution they desire. For the example above, a search query could look like this: "free chat program". This query gives you three relevant pieces of information about users:

• They want a piece of software, not a physical tool.

• They intend to chat, not to voice-call or send emails.

• They are not willing to pay money.

The three simple terms are key to understanding users' intent and helping limit the number of solutions. Thus we call them keywords.

But not every word used in a search query is a keyword. The search query "a free program to chat" does not provide more valuable information than "free chat program", because "a" and "to" do not narrow down the user intent. The same is true for definite articles (the) and for conjunctions (and, for, that). Therefore these terms are not keywords.

Definition: Long-Tail Keywords

You might have noticed that the keyword definition by Collins mentions not only *words* but also *phrases* that are used in search queries. Phrases are combinations of two or more keywords. These combinations are called *long-tail keywords*. In the example above, the three single keywords create one long-tail keyword: "free chat program".

Long-tail keywords are used in up to 80% of all searches in the app stores.[29] So they are significantly more important than single keywords.

Definition: SERP

The search engine's response to a search query is the *Search Engine Results Page (SERP)*.

The SERP is a ranking of apps which—according to the algorithm—match the keywords that users enter for their query. The best match shows up in rank #1, followed by the less exact matches in descending order. The SERP looks different for every keyword (and also for every country, even if the national language is the same).

Many factors influence the rank that an app achieves for a specific keyword. The most important is the weight of the metadata element where the keyword is implemented. But other factors have an impact too, for instance:[30]

- The total number of product page visits.

- The conversion rate of impressions to installs.

- The total number of downloads.

- The download velocity, which is the number of downloads in the recent past.

- The number and the quality of ratings.

- The number and the quality of reviews.
- The engagement of users, including the number of active users and the time that users spent in the app.
- The average revenue per user.
- The number of app uninstalls.

Why Users search

Understanding the psychology behind search queries is key to being successful in keyword research. Every user who performs a search has a specific intent. To target those users who are most likely to download your app, you need to understand these intents.

We can sort any query on search engines (including web, e-commerce platforms, and app stores) into one of three groups. Each one relates to a specific intent.[31]

Navigational Queries

Users who perform a *navigational search query* look for a specific brand which they already know. The intent behind this sort of query is definite. Users have already decided the solution to their problem and only want to know how and where to get to it.

Typical keywords in navigational queries are brand names like "Ikea", "Uber Eats", or "EasyJet". Misspellings of brand names qualify for this category too.

Transactional Queries

A *transactional search query* indicates the will to perform a transaction in the near future. This transaction can be a purchase, a booking, a rental, or a subscription. The intent behind this query is specific as well. But users who perform transactional searches are not limited to only one solution. They are open to every product or service that fulfills their needs.

Long-tail keywords that contain at least two terms are common for transactional searches—one of the terms names the desired product or service while the second word specifies the transaction users want to do. For instance, they could search for "buy wardrobe", "food delivery" or "book flight".

Search queries with a geographical aspect usually have a strong transactional intent too. Someone who searches for "Restaurants in London" probably plans to go out for dinner there.

Informational Queries

Users who perform an *informational search query* look for general information or advice on a topic. They have a problem and want the knowledge or a tool to solve it. The intent behind these queries is less strong than for transactional queries, so a broader variety of solutions may apply.

Keywords for informational queries often include terms such as "how to", "knowledge" or "wiki", but sometimes only a topic. For instance, users could search for "programming", "coding wiki" or "how to build an app".

Defining a Strategy for Search

Users searching on the app store are special because they share a common intent: They want to download an app. Nevertheless, the three categories apply to app store searches as well. Some users look for a specific app. Others are open to any app solving their problem.

Based on the three categories, you can define your strategy for gaining search traffic.

Which Query Types are worth targeting?

Users who perform a navigational query with brand keywords have an obvious intent. They want to find a specific app, and most likely they are not interested in alternative solutions. Thus a brand keyword has value only for the owner of this brand. It is not worth wasting time and effort targeting users who do navigational searches.

By the way, only 9% of all searches on the app stores are navigational queries.[32] The majority of users are driven by a specific task without knowing exactly which app is the solution.[33] In more than 90% of queries, users with informational or transactional intents search for keywords that are not connected to a brand.[34] These are called *generic keywords*.

Transactional searches are the most valuable queries because they reflect users' will to pay for a service or a product. Targeting those people will more likely result in higher revenues.

But users who do informational searches are open to a broader variety of apps. By targeting these queries, you can approach more potential users.

Both categories are worth targeting, but you should focus on transactional queries with long-tail keywords, because they are more valuable. Also, it is easier to get good rankings for transactional keywords.

Setting a minimum Ranking Goal

Most users want to have a quick solution to their problem. They are not willing to invest much time in the search process. Thus they do not investigate every app on the SERP down to rank #100. They focus on the apps on top of the results page instead.

Data from 2016 shows that 30% of downloads from search occur to the apps that rank #1 for a keyword. 17% of installs go to #2 and 12% to #3. Apps that rank worse than #10 gain almost no traffic.[35]

In 2017, Apple introduced iOS 11. The new version came with a major change for SERPs: The number of results users see without scrolling down shrank. That means that apps in lower ranks gain even less traffic now than the study from 2016 indicates.

Thus your goal must be to get into the top results for the keywords you pick.

On iOS, users will see only two apps on the first page of the SERP. If Apple shows a search ad, it is just one organic search result. For more results, users have to swipe down (see the example graphic on page 23). Aim for #3 or better, so they need only one swipe to see your app.

The Google Play SERP shows more results. Users see at least five apps on the first page, including up to two ads. So chances are higher that people will recognize your app, even if it ranks below #3. For important keywords, rank #5 is acceptable. For less critical terms, #10 is also okay.

CHAPTER 6
KEYWORD RESEARCH

To create visibility from searches, you need to find keywords that create more impressions for your app. This involves several tasks:

- Create a framework for your research.
- Find keywords that people actually search for.
- Judge the value of those keywords by predefined criteria.
- Implement the most valuable keywords into your product page's metadata.
- Measure the impact of your efforts.

Step 1: Preparation

The first step in keyword research is brainstorming. Its goal is to compile a collection of basic terms that describe your app. We will call this collection the *semantic core* of your app.

To prepare this brainstorming, you need a spreadsheet with different segments. This sheet will make it easier to channel your thoughts and help create a diverse set of keywords.

Your sheet can be a table on a piece of paper, a whiteboard, or an Excel file. Define your keyword segments, and add one column per segment to the table. Each segment should cover one aspect of your app. It must be narrow enough to allow you to order your keywords properly but broad enough to enable out-of-the-box thinking.

Here are some suggestions for segments. Feel free to add more (or use fewer) if it makes sense for your app.

User Keywords

Terms in the user segment describe your target audience. Find words to define people who will use your app. Think of gender, age, profession, personality, and character. Is your app for men, women, children or elders? Do you target business people, blue collar workers, athletes or artists?

Also think of the roles that users take when using your app. In an educational app, they are students. On a platform for classified ads, they can be buyers or sellers. Which roles will your users take?

User keywords should be nouns.

Problem Keywords

This segment is for terms that describe users' problems. Which issue do they try to solve? What are the questions they want to have answered? Which struggles do they face?

For problem-related keywords, use nouns. Consider long-tail keywords containing nouns and verbs as well.

Action Keywords

Action keywords describe what users do with your app. Do they offer or search something? Do they read, listen or learn? Do they play or work?

Many relevant actions have a connection to the outcome of your app. How do users improve themselves?

Also, include offline activities that follow the usage of your app: After using a food delivery service, people will eat or drink. Someone downloading a fitness app will exercise or run. People who use a dating app will flirt, date or marry.

Action keywords should be verbs or combinations of verbs and adjectives.

Feature Keywords

This segment is for keywords that explain the functions and mechanics of your app. Which features make your app stand out? What is its USP? Does it have social components that are worth mentioning?

Also think about offline alternatives to your app: The alternative to a market-place app might be a garage sale or a flea market. Users of a news app could read magazines. The alternative for a fitness app is a gym or a personal trainer.

Focus on nouns to describe features.

Category Keywords

Category keywords characterize the industry your app belongs to. That includes the offline, online, and mobile aspects.

Break it down from the broad market to the specific niche. Which products and services do companies create in this market? Which business models are common?

Nouns are the best choice for category keywords.

Linked Markets Keywords

Many industries are linked to each other. Users who look up a keyword related to one niche might also consider products or services of a linked market. This keyword section should contain terms to describe these connected offers.

People who book flights might also book hotels. Users who download a fitness app may be interested in sports gear or in information about nutrition. Find out what products might be interesting to your users. Which additional services would be useful for them?

Keywords that describe linked markets should be nouns or combinations of verbs and nouns.

Location Keywords

The location segment is for keywords that specify where people use your app. Some user needs include a geographical aspect. For instance, people who look up restaurants or hotels do not search the world. They focus on one city or district.

Will people use your app at home, in the office or while traveling? Do they need it in urban areas, in the countryside or at the beach? Do they live in specific countries, regions or cities?

Location keywords should be nouns and names.

Step 2: Brainstorming

Got your segments? Great. Now it is time to create your semantic core. Sit down with people you trust and find keywords. Coworkers are good. But people who come from another professional background than yourself are better. Their view on your app is unbiased, so they will bring in ideas you might not think of. So ask family and friends to help. I recommend to work with pen and paper and transfer your final keyword collection to your Excel file after the brainstorming.

Follow these rules for your brainstorming:

- Write your keyword ideas on Post-its so you can reorder them anytime.

- Go through the segments one by one. Try to find at least three or four core keywords for each.

- Be spontaneous. Speak what comes to your mind without overthinking it.

- Do not hesitate to put terms down that are absurd at first glance. Do not reject ideas because of a gut feeling. It is better to judge keywords later, based upon data.

Step 3: Expanding your Keyword List

Now expand the semantic core by adding related words. Like before, assign each new term into the matching segment. On the next pages, I will introduce you to many techniques to find additional keywords. Make sure to check the chapter on Tools & Sources (page 271) to make this step less time-consuming.

Word Associations

Work through your list keyword by keyword. Read out each term aloud, and write down the first words that come to your mind afterward. Again, no self-censorship.

To get even more diverse ideas, talk to friends who have not been involved in the process so far. Read your keywords to them and pin down their associations.

Synonyms

Look up synonyms for the terms you have found. A synonym is another word with the same or a very similar meaning. For instance, the word "car" is a synonym for "automobile".

Suggestions from Reviews

Be aware that users might talk differently about your app than you do. In the end, their point of view matters. Thus you should listen to them and adapt their language.

Examine the reviews users gave to your app. Also, check which terms people use to review your competitors. If journalists and bloggers write about your app, scan their texts for potential keywords too.

Focus on the aspects that reviewers love because these are especially important to them.[36]

Competitors' Keywords

As you are already spying on your competitors' product pages, do not limit your research to reviews. Check which terms they use in their app descriptions and graphics. Have a look into their websites and social media profiles as well.

Creating Long-Tail Keywords

Remember that most people search for long-tail keywords. To leverage this fact, combine single words from different segments with each other. Of course, not all combinations make sense. So be reasonable. Combining terms from the following segments tends to deliver good results:

- Action & Category
- Problem & Location
- Problem & Action
- Action & Features
- Category & Location
- Category & Feature
- Action & Location
- Action & Linked Markets
- User & Action
- User & Location

This list is not finite. Depending on your app and the keyword segments you picked, other combinations may make sense too.

Suggestions from Autocomplete

One of the most valuable sources, especially for long-tail keywords, is the auto-complete function of the app stores. As soon as users start typing into the search bar, this function will suggest up to five search terms. The term with the most significant search volume is usually the first in the list of suggestions.

So go to iTunes (or Google Play), type in your keywords one by one without executing the search, and note the results.

Step 4: Keyword Validation

By the end of your initial research, you should have a list of at least 100 promising keywords.

You cannot use all of them, though. The space for implementing keywords into the product page is limited. That is especially true for the keyword field on iOS. Thus you need to sort out those keywords that cannot help increase visibility.

To judge keywords, validate them by three criteria: Search Volume, Relevance, and Difficulty.[37]

Criteria 1: Search Volume

If your app ranks #1 for a keyword but nobody searches for it, you will not gain any traffic. So you need to take into account the search volume a keyword generates.

The higher the search volume for a keyword is, the better. Be aware that search volume for long-tail keywords is always lower than for single keywords. But that does not mean that single terms are always the better option.

Criteria 2: Relevance

A keyword that produces many searches is great. But if users do not download your app after spotting it on the SERP, these impressions are worthless.

Only if your app is relevant to a keyword will users download it. This relevance is determined by users' perception of whether your app matches their intent or not. If your app appears to be a solution to their problem, they will consider it relevant and download it. If it seems to be no help, users will ignore it.

The app stores' mechanisms take relevance into account when calculating search results. If many people download an app after seeing it on the SERP for a specific keyword, the algorithm will consider the app relevant to this term. As a result, the app will gain a better rank for this keyword.

The higher the relevance of a keyword, the better. As the intent behind long-tail keywords is more obvious than for single keywords, they are usually more relevant as well.

Criteria 3: Difficulty

You can only generate downloads if your app's rank on SERPs is good enough so that users actually see it. We have already formulated a goal regarding this issue (page 42). Apps with bad rankings will not gain much traffic.

As other marketers try to get their apps into search results as well, you will face serious competition. The more apps competing for a keyword's SERP, the more difficult it will be to get your app in the visible ranks. This difficulty is the third factor we need to consider when judging keywords.

The lower the difficulty to gain a good ranking for a keyword, the better. It is usually less difficult to get good ranks for long-tail keywords than for single keywords.

How to judge your Keywords

Measuring how well your keywords fit these criteria is not easy. Neither Apple nor Google discloses search volume numbers on a keyword level. And they do not give away the data on view-to-install ratio, which is necessary to calculate relevance, either.

If you want to do ASO on a professional level, there is no alternative to using a keyword tool in the long run. All of the various tools provide more or less the same functions:

- First, they estimate the search volume for keywords. Be aware that no tool has access to firsthand data from Apple or Google. They all use algorithms to narrow down the actual volumes, so the estimations differ from tool to tool. For English-speaking countries (the U.S., the U.K., Australia, etc.) estimates are usually good. For other languages, the data quality can be questionable.

- Second, every tool counts the number of apps on the SERP for a keyword. This number is usually very precise. Based on this count, the tools estimate the keywords' difficulty. For this purpose, some apply broad clusters, while others use more gradual scales. To get a rough idea about difficulty, all these approaches are fine.

- Third, keyword tools track the SERP rankings of your app and of your competitors' apps. They also show changes over time, so you can evaluate how successful your visibility strategy is.

- Fourth, most tools help you with your research process by suggesting keywords, based on those you already track.

Before choosing the tool, which fits your needs best, test them. Most providers offer a free trial period of at least seven days. Their support teams are very responsive, and they will happily give you a product demo to explain their tool in detail.

When testing a tool, make sure that the provided data makes sense:

- Search volumes for long-tail keywords should, in general, be lower than for the single terms they contain.

- Also, difficulty should be lower for long-tail keywords.

- Check randomly whether a tool displays SERP rankings for specific keywords correctly.

- In some cases, it happens that tools provide only a few different volume values for smaller countries. So if you focus on other markets than the U.S., make sure that data for these countries is granular enough. Otherwise, you will not be able to judge keywords accurately.

Keyword tools are premium services, so you have to buy a monthly or yearly subscription to use all features. Prices vary depending on the number of apps you own and the number of keywords and competitors you want to track.

Always negotiate before you pick your tool. Prices and conditions are not carved in stone. Especially when you plan to buy a yearly subscription, sales teams are willing to discuss discounts. So do not be afraid to ask for price reductions, prolonged trial periods or individually tailored packages to cover your needs. I will introduce some good keyword tools in detail later (page 272).

If you are not willing to pay for a tool, you will not be able to judge your keywords precisely. However, there are manual ways to estimate both volume and relevance broadly.

Measuring Search Volume

To get an idea of the search volume a keyword generates, use this workaround:

- Sign up for *Apple Search Ads*. You can simply log in with the same credentials you use for iTunes Connect.

- Create a campaign for the country you want to target. The details of the campaign are irrelevant, as you will not actually launch it.

- Add the keywords you want to analyze.

For every keyword, you will see a small horizontal bar which represents the search volume. If you use Google Chrome as your web browser, you can display actual numbers instead of the bar as well. Check these extensions from the Chrome Web Store:

- *Apple Search Ads Search Popularity* by *The Tool – ASO Tool*[38]
- *Search Ads Volume Tool for ASO* by *theasoproject*[39]

Measuring Relevance

Measuring relevance is more complicated. As it is a subjective criterion, users judge the relevance of your app for specific keywords differently. Thus it is hard to predict the average user opinion.

Of course, some terms are obviously relevant or irrelevant. Someone who searches for "piano" will not consider a medieval strategy game relevant.

For a keyword whose relevance (or irrelevance) is not that obvious, try this: Search for the keyword in the store. If the SERP shows apps, which you consider competitors, the keyword is most likely relevant for your app. But if all the top results belong to another category than your app, the keyword is probably irrelevant.[40]

There is still a chance that your competitors just have missed a good keyword. So you cannot take the absence of their apps on the SERP as a firm indicator for an irrelevant keyword. Nevertheless, it is a good hint.

Measuring Difficulty

Validating a keyword's difficulty is—in comparison to relevance and volume—easy in theory. Just search for it in the store and count the results. The number of apps on the SERP gives you a good impression of how difficult it is for your app to get on top.

In actual practice, it takes ages to judge every keyword this way, even if you only estimate the number of results roughly.

Weighting criteria

So we have three criteria to judge keywords. It would be great to find many keywords that generate much traffic, are very relevant and are not competitive at all.

I am sorry to ruin this illusion, but this will not happen. Most keywords, you come across, will qualify for only one or two of the three criteria. For instance, high volumes usually accompany high difficulty, because your competitors want to rank for high volume terms too.

So how should you prioritize volume, relevance, and difficulty? Here is some general advice for a start:

Relevance comes first. Always. A keyword with low relevance is useless, no matter how much volume it drives. So focus on highly relevant terms.

Difficulty is second. If you have to choose between two keywords with similar relevance, go for the less competitive.

Volume is the least important. Of course, you need some volume. As said before, if nobody searches for a keyword, you will not gain new users. But keywords with high relevance and low difficulty are valuable even if they only drive low volumes.

Step 5a: Keyword Implementation on iOS

Now you need to implement the most promising keywords into your product page. On iOS, you can use four different placements for this purpose. They differ in the number of characters you can enter and in weight.

Keywords in metadata with high weight will produce a better SERP ranking for your app than keywords in metadata with low weight. There is no way to manipulate weight. It is the same for all product pages and all apps.

Here are the elements that can contain keywords:

App Title

The app title is the element with the highest weight for the search algorithm. An app with a keyword in its title ranks about twice as good as an app using the same term in the keyword field. This power reflects in SERP ranks: 60% of apps in the Top 5 rankings contain the keywords in their title.[41]

Thus it is crucial for your app's visibility to put the most promising keywords into the title. For every keyword in your title, your app should not rank lower than #3. Otherwise, you waste this precious spot of only 30 characters.

Subtitle

The subtitle is the second element of the product page, which is indexed and searchable. It contains up to 30 characters too.

Only people who use iOS version 11 or later will see the subtitle. By June 2018, that was true for about 81% of devices.[42] But search results are the same for devices using older versions too.

The subtitle's weight for the search algorithm is lower than the title's weight. That makes it the second most important metadata element for search visibility. The subtitle can be a list of features, separated by commas, or a grammatically correct phrase. Whatever serves your efforts to increase visibility is fine. Put in promising keywords that have not found a place in the app title.

Keyword Field

With up to 100 characters, the keyword field offers the most space for keywords. This limit includes commas to separate the single terms. Depending on their length, you can put around 10 to 20 keywords into it.

Unlike the title and the subtitle, the keyword field is invisible to users. Nevertheless, the algorithm searches it like all other indexed metadata. Place relevant terms that are left over after filling the title and subtitle in the keyword field.

Description

You might have heard that keywords in your description increase visibility too. That is not true for iOS. The algorithm will not find keywords in your description, so they will not affect SERP ranks.

However, a proper written description helps to convince visitors to your product page to install your app. For this purpose keywords are valuable. But this topic belongs to the discussion about conversion optimization (page 93). For now, we focus on visibility and thus ignore the description.

General Rules

When I defined the term keyword, I mentioned that not every word is a keyword. Avoid terms that are not. Follow these guidelines, so you do not waste time on words that will not help you gain visibility:

• Do not use articles (a, an, the), conjunctions (and, but) or prepositions (by, at, on, with). These do not help understand users' intention and thus are not keywords.

There are exceptions, though. For semantic reasons, prepositions might be necessary for the app title and the subtitle. I will give examples later in this book (page 227).

• Do not use competitors' brand names. When we talked about search queries, you learned that brand keywords are valuable for the brand owner only. Also, Apple's guidelines forbid targeting trademarks you do not own. If you have a shopping app, you can use the brand names of the products you sell, though.

- Do not use the word *app* or the exact name of the category that your app belongs to. The algorithm will give you visibility for those terms, even if you do not use them in your on-page metadata.

- Do not use *free*. If your app is free or freemium, it will get visibility for long-tail keywords including *free* automatically.

- Do not use words or abbreviations with less than three characters. They are not indexed and will not help to gain visibility.

- Use every keyword only once. If you have already implemented a term into your app's title or subtitle, do not duplicate it in the keyword field. There will be no additional effect on rankings or visibility. Only the metadata element with the highest weight counts for the algorithm.

- Do not use both the singular and the plural form of the same keyword. Use the form which is less competitive or generates more volume. The store algorithm will automatically give you some visibility for the version that you do not target. In most cases, using the singular is the best practice, although your app's ranking will be worse for the plural term.

  Be aware that there are exceptions to this rule. It does apply for simple plural forms in English only. You form simple plurals by adding s to the singular, for example: house/houses, friend/friends, car/cars. Irregular plural forms (men, boxes, babies) will not be indexed if you use the singular form as a keyword. In languages other than English, this rule is not valid either.

  Even in English, there is one more exception to the rule: Your app ranks only for long-tail keywords that contain the form which you use in your metadata. If you want to rank for all long-tail keywords that include the singular or the plural, you need to implement both forms into your product page.

How to implement Long-Tail Keywords

Highly relevant long-tail keywords are the most powerful of all keywords. Implementing them into your product page is a bit more complicated than it is for single terms. To master this task, it is crucial to understand how the store mechanism detects long-tail keywords.

Of course, the algorithm searches for exact matches for long-tail keywords. If you put "french cooking" into your keyword field, your app will show up on the SERP for this long-tail keyword.

Fig. 8: Keyword Field Example I
(Source: iTunes Connect)

But the algorithm also splits long-tail keywords into its components and searches for them individually. That means you can put the terms "french" and "cooking" as single keywords into your keyword field. Even with the comma separating them, the algorithm will find them, and your app will rank for "french cooking".

```
Keywords   ?
french,cooking
```

Fig. 9: Keyword Field Example II
(Source: iTunes Connect)

The order does not matter, and it is not important whether or not the terms stand next to each other in the keyword list.

This approach comes with a great advantage: You will gain visibility for the long-tail keyword, but also for every component. In our example, your app will rank for "french cooking" as well as for "french" and "cooking". But that is not all. In contrast to the version without a comma, your app will also gain visibility for the second combination of the single terms: "cooking french".

Because of this advantage, you should always separate terms in the keyword field by a comma, even if they form a long-tail keyword.

Increasing Visibility for Long-Tail Keywords exponentially

Following this rule opens the door to a great variety of keyword combinations. Let us add "recipe" as a keyword. Your keyword field now looks like this:

Keywords ?
french,cooking,recipe

Fig. 10: Keyword Field Example III
(Source: iTunes Connect)

The algorithm will combine all the single keywords. So your app will make it into the SERPs of the three single terms and of three long-tail keywords. Furthermore, the algorithm considers combinations of more than two words. So your app will be ranked for "french cooking recipe" too. In total, it will appear on the SERP for seven different keywords (plus all alternative orders of the long-tail keywords):

- french
- cooking
- recipe
- french cooking
- french recipe
- cooking recipe
- french cooking recipe

With every single term that you add, the number of long-tail keywords, for which your app ranks, grows exponentially. For example, adding "italian" would result in impressions for the following combinations (among others which are less relevant):

- italian
- italian cooking
- italian recipe
- italian cooking recipe

Cross-Metadata Keywords

The store algorithm combines keywords across different metadata elements. So you can put "french" in the app title and leave "cooking" in the keyword field, and your app will still show up on the SERP for "french cooking". As the title has a higher weight for the algorithm than the keyword field, your app's ranking will be even better than it was before.

If you have identified many relevant long-tail keywords that contain a mutual term, put this term into the title to improve your app's SERP rankings for all its long-tail words.

Indexing In-App Purchases

Marketers often overlook IAPs in their keyword research. That is not surprising, as their original purpose was monetization only. But since a major iTunes update in 2017, IAPs have been indexed, and so they can contribute to an app's visibility.

By November 2017, only 3% of all search results were IAPs.[43] More developers have adjusted their IAPs for search since. But if you do it too, you still belong to a minority. And this means you can gain an advantage over competitors who miss this chance.

If you own a freemium app, you need to do two things:

- First, promote your IAPs. The term *promote* is misleading here because it is not a marketing action in this context. Actually, it is Apple's name for a technical process. Read the *iTunes Connect Developer Help* articles for detailed instructions on how to do it.[44] You can promote up to 20 different IAPs. If you have more, focus on those that sell best or create the biggest revenues.

- Second, set up your IAPs' metadata. Each package needs a title of up to 30 characters, a description of up to 45 characters, and an icon.

Here are some suggestions for IAP metadata:

IAP Description

IAP descriptions should be easy reads that communicate the content of the package. Users who do not know your app and its functions yet may see them, so make sure they get what the IAPs are about.[45]

Also, create unique descriptions for each IAP. People must be able to distinguish them and understand how they differ.

IAP Icon

An IAP icon has to be a high-quality PND or JPEG file of 1024 x 1024 pixels. Many users will see smaller versions, though. And on SERPs, your app icon will overlie the bottom left corner of the IAP icon.

So you need to create IAP icons that users can recognize even when scaled down and underlying the app icon.

For the icons of consumable IAPs, it is common to show what the package contains. Especially games use this WYSIWYG ("What you see is what you get") approach to promote their premium currencies. The challenge in this strategy is to not overload the icon. Putting too many elements into it will make it hard to perceive all the content. So keep it simple.

Here are some examples:

The IAP *Unlock Everypony!* unlocks all characters for the game *My Little Pony Rainbow Runners*[46]. The screenshot below shows how it appears on the SERP on an iPhone 7. Although it is a nice piece of game art, it is hard to get all the elements at first glance. That might work for a particular audience, like little girls who are crazy for ponies. But if you want to attract more mature users, you should avoid packing that much content into one icon.

Fig. 11: IAP *Unlock Everypony!* on SERP
(Source: iTunes)

In contrast, the icon of the IAP *Wave Rider* for the game *Jetpack Joyride*[47] is very clear. It shows users what they will get without overwhelming them with too much content.

Fig. 12: IAP *Wave Rider* on SERP
(Source: iTunes)

<u>IAP Title</u>

The title is the most critical element of the IAP metadata because it is the only indexed element. But your app will not only be ranked for keywords in your IAP titles. It will also gain visibility for long-tail keywords composed from terms in the app title and IAP titles.

Let us go back to *Jetpack Joyride* and its IAP *Wave Rider*. The app appears on the SERP for the long-tail keywords "Jetpack Rider" and "Wave Joyride". Both contain one word from the app title and one term from the IAP title.

You can argue that these examples are not very good, because they do not drive high volumes. I agree. But even so, they prove how the algorithm works.

When choosing titles for your premium currency packages, avoid generic terms like *starter pack*, *gold coins* or *gems*. Instead, try to add one or two important keywords. Pick those that create highly relevant long-tail keywords when combined with the terms in your app title. Think of *War Chest* for your strategy game, a *Flirt Package* for your dating app or a *Leg Training Set* for your fitness app.

Localizing Keywords

The space for keywords on your product page is limited: 30 characters in the title, 30 in the subtitle, and 100 in the keyword field (plus IAP titles for freemium apps).

But there is a trick to increase this limit significantly; it was introduced by Moritz Daan in 2016: Localize your product page.[48]

On iOS you can provide up to 28 different localizations:

- Chinese (Simplified)
- Chinese (Traditional)
- Danish
- Dutch
- English (Australia)
- English (Canada)
- English (U.K.)
- English (U.S.)
- Finnish
- French
- French (Canada)
- German
- Greek
- Indonesian
- Italian
- Japanese
- Korean
- Malay
- Norwegian
- Portuguese (Brazil)
- Portuguese (Portugal)
- Russian
- Spanish (Mexico)
- Spanish (Spain)
- Swedish
- Thai
- Turkish
- Vietnamese

Tab. 3: Available Localizations on iOS
(Source: Daan and Kwakyi 2018)[49]

To understand how you can use this trick, we first need to clarify how the app store algorithm handles localizations.

How the Algorithm works

iTunes has different storefronts. Which storefront users see depends on their country of residence. Each storefront has its own team of content editors (and its individual stories and features) and its own top charts. But most importantly, the search results for the same keyword vary from storefront to storefront.

That is because some developers do not publish their app worldwide, but only in selected markets. But the more interesting reason is Apple's indexing mechanism. In each storefront, the algorithm indexes just a few localizations. For example, if users search for a keyword in the United States, the algorithm scans the metadata of the app's English (U.S.) localization. It also searches the Spanish (Mexico) version. If one of those versions contains the keyword, the app will rank for it. But the algorithm will ignore keywords in other localizations. So no matter which keywords the English (U.K.) product page contains, the app will not rank for them in the United States.

The indexed localizations differ from country to country. Check the following table for details:

Store Front	Indexed Localizations
Australia	English (U.K.), English (Australia)
Austria	English (U.K.), German
Belgium	English (U.K.), French, Dutch
Brazil	English (U.K.), Portuguese (Brazil)
Canada	English (Canada), French (Canada)
China	English (U.K.), Chinese (Simplified)
Cyprus	English (U.K.), Greek, Turkish
Denmark	English (U.K.), Danish
Finland	English (U.K.), Finnish
France	English (U.K.), French
Germany	English (U.K.), German
Greece	English (U.K.), Greek
Hong Kong	English (U.K.), Chinese (Traditional)

Indonesia	English (U.K.), Indonesian
Italy	English (U.K.), Italian
Japan	English (U.S.), Japanese
Korea	English (U.K.), Korean
Luxembourg	English (U.K.), German, French
Macau	English (U.K.), Chinese (Traditional)
Malaysia	English (U.K.), Malay
Netherlands	English (U.K.), Dutch
New Zealand	English (U.K.), English (Australia)
Norway	English (U.K.), Norwegian
Portugal	English (U.K.), Portuguese (Portugal)
Russia	English (U.K.), Russian
Singapore	English (U.K.), Chinese (Simplified)
Spain	English (U.K.), Spanish (Spain)
Suriname	English (U.K.), Dutch
Sweden	English (U.K.), Swedish
Switzerland	English (U.K.), German, French, Italian
Taiwan	English (U.K.), Chinese (Traditional)
Thailand	English (U.K.), Thai
Turkey	English (U.K.), Turkish
Ukraine	English (U.K.), Russian
United Kingdom	English (U.K.), English (Australia)
United States	English (U.S.), Spanish (Mexico)
Vietnam	English (U.K.), Vietnamese
Latin America (without Brazil)	English (U.K.), Spanish (Mexico)
Other Countries	English (U.K.)

Tab. 4: Indexed Localizations in iTunes Storefronts
(Source: adapted from Daan 2016)[50]

How to benefit from this Mechanism

In order to increase your visibility, you have to add localizations of your product page which are indexed in your target country. But instead of using keywords that match this new language, put terms in your target language into it.

Let us say you want to increase visibility in the United States. Here is how you do it:

- Add a localization. In our example, that is Spanish (Mexico), because it is the only localization next to English (U.S.) which is indexed in the United States.

- Add Spanish metadata for all elements except the keyword field. The quality of the translations does not matter, as you do not actually target Spanish speakers. *Google Translate* or a similar tool does the job.

- Now insert English keywords that you have not used in the English (U.S.) version of your product page, into the keyword field of your Spanish (Mexico) localization.

That is it. You have doubled the space for English keywords from 100 to 200 keywords. When people search for the terms in your Spanish (Mexican) keyword field, your app will show up in the SERPs.

Depending on the country you target, you can increase your visibility even further. In Switzerland, for instance, the algorithm indexes four different languages. So you can use four keyword fields (or 400 characters) to get more visibility.

Long-Tail Keywords are monolingual

Be aware that the search algorithm does not combine long-tail keywords across multiple localizations. If you use "cooking" in your English (U.S.) product page and "vegetarian" in your Spanish (Mexico) version, your app will not rank for "vegetarian cooking". Long-tail keywords only work if all components belong to the same localization.

The Localization Strategy is a Trade-off

Another problem can arise for apps that are available globally, because localizations are global. So your Spanish (Mexico) metadata will be the same for all countries which index this localization. If you fill the Spanish (Mexico) keyword field with English terms, you will hurt your app's visibility in Latin-American countries. Users who search for Spanish terms there will not see your apps on SERPs.

You always need to weigh the extra traffic in one market against the loss of visibility in other countries.

The Reviewer's Goodwill

The localization strategy is semi-legal. No official rule forbids it, and I have never heard about an app that was rejected for using it. But reviewers at Apple may delete terms from your keyword fields if they do not match the localization. So use it at your own risk.

Localization Strategy

After getting the basics of the localization strategy clear, let us frame some best practices:

- For an app that is available globally, always create all the English localizations (U.S., U.K., Australia, Canada). The simplest way is to copy and paste your metadata. By doing so, you make sure to gain visibility in all English-speaking markets.

- Your research might show that different keywords are valuable in different storefronts. If that is the case, adjust the indexed metadata accordingly.

- If your app is available in only one country (or if you consider only one language important and do not care about visibility for others), always use all indexed localizations (see the table on page 62). Add translated metadata to the on-page elements, including title and subtitle. But use all keyword fields only for terms in your target language.

- For some apps, one term might be a relevant component of lots of long-tail keywords. On your original product page, space can be too limited to add all terms that are necessary to create these long-tail keywords. In this case, duplicate the important single word to your new localization. It might even make sense to delete it from the original version and use the new localization only for long-tail keywords containing this term.

- Exchanging keywords between localizations can help make the most out of the keyword field's character limit. With 98 characters used in one version and 97 in the other, you waste five characters in total. Switch terms and try to make it 100 and 95. Then add one more term of four or five characters. Make sure that you do not rip long-tail keywords apart, though.

Step 5b: Keyword Implementation on Google Play

The Google Play algorithm differs from its iTunes counterpart. It indexes other elements, and it weighs keywords differently. But you have more space for implementing your keywords.

Here are the metadata elements that matter for search on Google Play:

App Title

As on iOS, the Google Play App Title has the highest weight for the search algorithm. Thus it should contain your most valuable keywords. You have 50 characters to fill.

Short Description

The product page on Google Play contains no subtitle. Instead, you can use the short description to add a text of 80 characters.

Regarding weight for the algorithm, the short description is second.

It is not only important for creating visibility, it also affects conversion optimization. We will discuss how to optimize it in detail later (page 95).

Long Description

Writing the long description for Google Play is one of the most challenging tasks in ASO. Like the short description, it serves two purposes: In contrast to the description on iTunes, the Google Play long description is indexed. So it can generate visibility. The algorithm scans the long description for keywords and matches them with the users' search queries. But a well-written long description helps to increase the conversion rate as well.

To combine both, you have to draft your description around your keywords.

In-App Purchases

Google Play indexes IAP metadata too. You can fill the title with 55 characters and the IAP description with 80 characters.

Keywords in the URL

Google Play also indexes the product page URL. The algorithm will find keywords in the URL and rank the app for these terms. *Super Mario Run*[51] was one of the first apps that used this mechanism. Its URL contains the term *zara* for no apparent reason, and the game shows up on the SERP for this word.[52]

Fig. 13: URL of *Super Mario Run*
(Source: Google Chrome)

Another app using this technique is *Last Day on Earth: Survival*[53]. They have three keywords in their URL: zombie, survival, craft. But the actual app title is missing.

Fig. 14: URL of *Last Day on Earth: Survival*
(Source: Google Chrome)

General Rules for Keyword Implementation on Google Play

Like before for iOS, let us define some general rules for keyword implementation on Google Play:

- Do not use competitors' trademarks. Google forbids it. The only exceptions are products that you sell in a shopping app.

- Use a keyword in multiple metadata elements to improve your app's ranking for it. In contrast to iTunes, Google Play adds up the weight. If you put a term in the title and the long description, your app will rank better than a competitor who uses the same keyword only in the title.

- Use a keyword only once in the title. Duplicating a term in the title will not improve your app's ranking. The same goes for the short description.

- Use a keyword up to five times in the long description. Multiple appearances of a term in your description will create a better ranking for your app. But five times is the limit. Using a keyword more often will not result in a better ranking.

- Keep an eye on the keyword density in your long description. Density is the number of appearances of a keyword divided by the total number of words. The higher the density is (or the more often a keyword appears in relation to the overall word count), the better your app will rank.

  Every term that is not a keyword will lower the density for all of your keywords. So cut words that do not have relevance for search or are not necessary for grammatical reasons, especially adjectives, adverbs, and other filler words.

- If both the singular and the plural form of a keyword are relevant for your app, use both. The Google Play algorithm is pretty good at recognizing similar terms and matching them to related searches. Nevertheless, you should not rely on it. It is better to implement a perfect match for searches that include plural forms.

- For in-app purchases, follow the same pattern as on iOS. Use terms that describe the package and form relevant long-tail keywords when combined with words from the app title.

- If you want to add keywords to your URL (or more precisely, to your app's package name), do it before you release it for the first time. It is not possible to change the package name once your app is live. Choose only keywords that you know are highly relevant and create decent search volumes.

Localization

On Google Play, you can provide translations for 77 languages in total. Unfortunately, the iOS localization strategy does not work on Android. As there are no invisible keyword fields, you cannot use keywords that do not match the localization.

Thus there is only one way to increase visibility in a country: Add a language which many people use for search queries there, for instance, Spanish in the United States.

Step 6: Testing and Optimizing

After initially implementing your keywords into your product page, your work is not done. Depending on the SERP rankings for your keywords, you will have to make adjustments to find the optimal spot for each term.

In case, the results are way beyond your expectations, it might even be worth to go back to Step 3 and find new keywords to test.

Optimizing Keyword Placements on iOS

You need to meet two goals:

- Rank at least #3 for as many keywords as possible.

- Use the potential of your most precious placements (title and subtitle) optimally.

Use the following approaches to figure out the optimal placements for your keywords. Be aware that the algorithm might need several weeks to align search results to new keyword sets. So do not judge your adjustments too early.

- Dump keywords, for which your app ranks worse than #3 although they are in the title. Terms that create less volume but provide a better ranking for your app are more valuable in this precious placement.

- Move a keyword, for which your app ranks #1, from the app title to the subtitle. If the ranking stays the same, move the term to the keyword field and check again. If your app drops on the SERP, undo the latest change. Continue this procedure with all relevant keywords to find their optimal spots. Make sure to not give your most valuable placements to keywords that rank well when put in other placements too.

- If you have two keywords with similar volume, relevance, and difficulty, use the term that is part of more valuable long-tail keywords. In some cases, it is worth putting a keyword into the title, although your app does not rank in the top positions for it. Many good rankings for long-tail keywords will create more visibility than a single term on top of the SERP. To improve the rankings of long-tail keywords that share a mutual term, implement this term into metadata with a higher weight.

Optimizing Keyword Placements on Google Play

Just like on iOS, the results you get out of the initial setup of your Google Play metadata will mostly likely not be satisfying. Therefore you should optimize them on a regular basis.

Here are some suggestions for finding the optimal placements for keywords on Google Play:

- If your app ranks #1 for an important keyword, reduce the number of its appearances in the long description (given it is more than one). Remove it from the title and put it into the short description instead. Check if your app still ranks #1. If not, return to the original wording. If your app keeps its top ranking, replace the open slots in the title with other keywords.

- Dump a keyword, for which your app ranks worse than #5, although it has reached its maximum number of appearances (one in title, one in short description, five in long description). It is better to give the valuable placements in the title and the short description to terms with more potential to gain a top ranking.

- Do not rip your important long-tail keywords apart. Your app will gain visibility for any combination of terms included in your description. Their order does not matter. But perfect matches (combinations in the exact order) outrank other combinations. So the safe way to get a top ranking for a long-tail keyword is to implement it unfractured.

Chapter Summary

The following figure summarizes the process of keyword research.

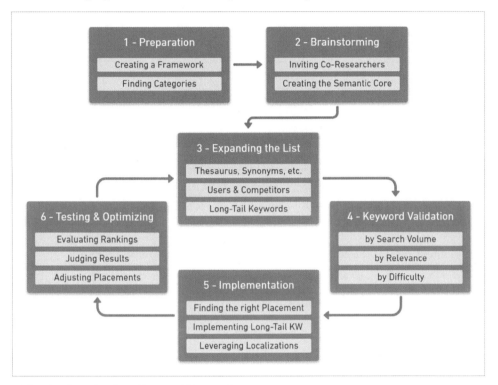

Fig. 15: Step-by-Step Keyword Research
(Source: Author's own illustration)

In addition, here are the key takeaways from this chapter in bullet points:

Keyword Research

• Keywords narrow down the users' intent. Conjunctions or articles are not keywords.

• Focus your research on generic keywords. Stay away from competitors' brand names.

• Use a framework with different segments to channel your research.

• Brainstorm keywords without censoring yourself. Ask family and friends to get a broader variety of results.

- Use word associations, synonyms, and auto-complete suggestions to find more keyword ideas. Also, spy on competitors and scan user reviews.

- Create long-tail keywords by combining single terms.

- Judge keywords by relevance, difficulty, and volume (in this order).

- Use keyword tools to make these validations easier.

Keyword Implementation on iOS

- Keywords in the title outweigh keywords in the subtitle. Both outweigh terms in the keyword field.

- Use keywords only once across your indexed metadata.

- Put single terms, separated by commas, into the keyword field. The algorithm will combine them to give your app visibility for long-tail keywords.

- In each country, the algorithm indexes at least two localizations. Use these localizations to increase the number of keywords your app ranks for.

- The algorithm forms long-tail keywords across different metadata elements, but not across different localizations.

Keyword Implementation on Google Play

- Keywords in the title outweigh keywords in the short description. Both outweigh terms in the long description.

- Use a keyword up to five times in the long description to increase visibility for this term.

- Keep the description rather short to increase keyword density. Cut terms you do not need in terms of relevance or grammar.

- Duplicate keywords and put them into different metadata elements to increase visibility even more.

- The algorithm forms long-tail keywords across different metadata elements, but not across different localizations.

- Use exact long-tail keywords in your long description to ensure your apps ranks for them.

The following table compares how the search algorithms work for iOS and Google Play:

Functionality	iOS	GP
App Title is indexed	yes	yes
Sub Title is indexed	yes	—
Short Description is indexed	—	yes
Long Description is indexed	no	yes
IAP Metadata is indexed	yes	yes
Higher Keyword Quantity increases Visibility	no	yes
Keyword Duplication in different Metadata increases Visibility	no	yes
Long-Tail Keywords are combined across different Metadata	yes	yes
Long-Tail Keywords are combined across different Localizations	no	no

Tab. 5: Functionality of the Search Algorithm on iTunes and Google Play
(Source: Author's own illustration)

PART III

CONVERSION RATE

OPTIMIZATION

CHAPTER 7
HOW TO INCREASE CONVERSION

By increasing your app's visibility, you have created more conversion opportunities. Now you have to realize these opportunities. The second subgoal of ASO is to turn people who see an impression into users who download your app.

All visible metadata elements have an impact on users' decision-making process. But their importance differs. In 2016, a survey by TUNE examined which elements users take into consideration before downloading apps:[54]

Ratings and reviews are the most crucial factor, with 53% of users caring about them. The app description follows, with 52%. Preview videos rank third, with 24% of approval, the app title fourth (22%), and screenshots fifth (19%). App icons rank last with only 18% of users calling them relevant for their decision.

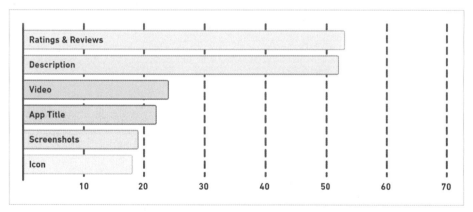

Fig. 16: The Importance of Metadata for Download Decisions
(Source: adapted from Koetsier 2018)[55]

The Three Columns of your Product Page

A product page's ability to increase the conversion rate and create downloads depends on three criteria: Guidance, relevance and beauty. They are the columns that your product page's success is built upon. Only if you optimize all your metadata to match these criteria will you be able to maximize download numbers. If you fail to meet one of them, you will harm the user experience and, in the end, your app's success.

Fig. 17: The Three Columns
(Source: Author's own illustration)

The First Column: Guidance

From the exposure to an impression to the download of the app, users have to make several decisions. They have to determine which app is worth exploring further. They have to decide whether they want to invest time in reading descriptions and swiping through a screenshot gallery. Finally, they have to judge if they consider an app worth downloading or not.

To increase the chance of a download, you must support users in this decision-making process. You do so by providing guidance. There are two kinds of guidance:

Visual Guidance helps users see what you want them to see. By designing your text and artwork properly, you direct their attention, so they recognize the information you want them to receive.

Explanatory Guidance supports users in understanding what they see. It is about explaining but also about entertaining. By telling a congruent story that is understandable as well as exciting, you suck people in and make them stay.

The AIDA Concept

A great framework to create guidance is the AIDA concept. This copywriting technique is very popular in marketing. Its goal is to address potential customers properly at every stage of the decision-making process. From the impression to the download, the concept identifies four of these stages. Their initials form the name AIDA:[56]

- The first stage in this process is to attract **Attention**. Only if people recognize your app can they become users. So when your metadata appears in search results (or in features or charts), it must be eye-catching and stand out against your competitors.

- On the second stage, you must arouse people's **Interest** in learning more about your app. You need to engage them so they stay and invest more time into evaluating your product page.

- The task for stage No. 3 is to awaken the **Desire** to use your app. You need to point out your app's ability to solve users' problems and ideally provide evidence for this claim.

- Finally, you must encourage people to take **Action**, hit the download button, and use your app.

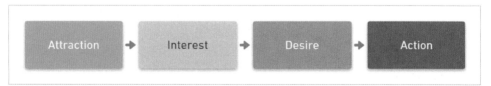

Fig. 18: The AIDA Funnel
(Source: Author's own illustration)

The result of applying AIDA is a comprehensive story that guides users through their experience. As apps provide very different solutions for very different problems, there is no ultimate story that suits all apps. You have to tailor an individual story for your app. However, there are three categories that most stories fit into:

Transaction Stories

A Transaction Story shows the features of an app in the chronological order in which users most likely will experience them. This story focuses on the short-term results of using the app. It is a good approach for apps that provide a clear outcome at the end of each user journey. This outcome can be a purchase, a booking or another transaction.

For a travel app, the Transaction Story could look like this:

• Searching for flights to a specific destination,

• Scrolling through the results page,

• Selecting a flight and checking availability and prices,

• And finally booking and paying the flight.

Transaction Stories also work if no purchase of a good or service is part of the user journey. The requirement is that the journey is linear and delivers a concrete result at the end. In a navigation app, the Transaction Story could be:

• Selecting the destination,

• Determining conditions like preferred roads and stopovers,

• Starting the navigation process,

• Showing the app's navigation commands,

• Arriving at the target.

Transaction Stories are good fits for single-player games with a fixed and finite storyline as well. These include genres like adventure games, single-player RPGs or graphic novels.

Progression Stories

In some apps, the journey is linear, without a clear outcome at the end. But completing the journey over and over again will result in some kind of improvement for users.

For these apps you can create a Progression Story. This story type is about emphasizing the long-term results of using the app. Comparisons of the initial and the future state are a good way to do so.

Think of a fitness app. Users will not see a result after doing one exercise. But if they repeat it over and over again, their bodies will change. The app's story could be:

- Selecting an exercise,
- Reading the instructions,
- Doing the workout,
- Selecting another exercise and repeat.

Progression Stories are very common for games that do not have a predefined end. These include, for example, MMO strategy or role playing games, but also hypercasual single-player games. They are endless, thus there is no clear outcome. But players can constantly progress and become more powerful. In a strategy game for instance, a Progression Story could look like this:

- Collecting resources,
- Building and improving a base,
- Recruiting soldiers,
- Fighting other players,
- Seizing their resources,
- Improving the base, recruiting more soldiers, etc.

Complexity Stories

Some apps contain several functions that people can use in random order. They do not have a chronological dependence. Users can experience these apps in various ways, and their outcome is not a predefined result.

For these apps, it makes sense to present functions according to their complexity. Start by showing the basic, most essential functions. Then progress to more advanced features. Finally, finish with the pro tools that require a deeper understanding of the app.

For example, a photo editing app has different functions to make photos more beautiful. Users can use filters and editing features in random order. Presenting them in the form of a Complexity Story makes sense:

- Adding a simple one-click filter,
- Adjusting brightness and color saturation,
- Retouching small details such as red eyes.

For a calculator app, the story could present features from simple to complex as well:

- Showing basic arithmetic operations like addition and multiplication,
- Calculating percentages and fractions,
- Doing integral calculus and vector analysis.

Picking your Story Type

Some apps might fit into more than one type of story. Puzzle games, for instance, have a transactional character. Players work toward a predefined end (mastering the last level). But they also contain a complexity component, because levels become more and more difficult.

In edge cases like this, you can either pick one of the matching stories or mix them. Try what works best for your app, and use A/B testing (page 232) to find out which approach users like best. The table on the next page shows you which app category matches which story type.

Your Brand is your Story's Hero

No matter which kind of story you pick for your product page, it always should properly introduce your brand. Even if people decide not to download your app, they might become valuable users at a later point. So make sure they remember your app.

Consider your brand the hero of your product page's story. Its name, look, and what it stands for must stick in people's minds. If they remember it, they will be more likely to use your app in the future, and they also might talk about it.

Transaction Story	Progression Story	Complexity Story
Shopping - Physical Goods - Music - e-books - Tickets	Sports & Health - Fitness - Running - Yoga - Meditation	Design - Art - Photo - Video - Music
Travel - Hotels - Flights - Taxis & Private Drivers - Public Transportation - Navigation	Education - Languages - Maths - Programming	Utilities - Translator - Calculator - Clock - Scanner
Games - Single-Player RPGs - Graphical Novels - Adventures - Puzzles	Games - Hypercasual - MMOs	Communication - Chat - Video- & Voice-Chat - Social Networking
Marketplace / Classified Ads - Goods - Services - Real Estate	Hobby - Instruments - Gardening - Pets	News - Weather - Financial - Sports Results
Dating		Streaming - Radio - Music - Video / Movies
		Productivity - Calendar - Task Manager - Diary / Journal - Budget Planner

Tab. 6: App Categories and matching Story Types
(Source: Author's own illustration)

The Second Column: Relevance

The second column your product page stands on is relevance. We already talked about relevance when discussing the criteria for valuable keywords (page 48).

Recall what we learned about the search patterns of users: The intention to solve a problem drives most search queries. To make keywords relevant for users, they must be connected to these problems.

With your metadata elements, it is very similar. If people visit your product page, they assume that your app is capable of solving their problems. Texts and visual creatives must draw a connection between these problems and the app. If they do, they will strengthen users' assumptions by delivering a clear message: This app is relevant to you because it solves your problem.

The WIIFM Concept

To understand the importance of relevance, it is necessary to see things from the users' perspectives.

The WIIFM-concept helps you to do so. It stands for "What's in it for me?" and focuses entirely on users' benefit. How does your app help them? Which benefits does it provide and how will it make their lives better? Try to answer these questions when designing your product page. If you give the right answers, your messages will be much more relevant to your potential audience.[57]

The Third Column: Beauty

Third, your product page (and especially the visual creatives) must be beautiful. Even if your app perfectly matches users' needs, an uncomely appearance can prevent them from downloading.

Users perceive beauty on a subconscious level. So you need to dive into users' minds to get it right. You need to create an experience, that is harmonious and pleases users' eyes. Colors are core to harmony. Thus I dedicated an entire chapter to them (page 247).

Another vital aspect of beauty is accessibility. Although your metadata should be engaging, it must also be easy to read, watch, and understand. If it is too complicated, people will not get your message.

The KISS Concept

Let me introduce another concept that is helpful in this context. The KISS concept focuses on simplicity. It stands for "Keep it Simple Stupid".[58] For you as a marketer, it means to presume that your target audience is diverse: Users have different cultural and educational backgrounds. The core of KISS is to break your message down to the lowest common denominator, so people from all walks of life can understand it.

CHAPTER 8
RATINGS AND REVIEWS

On Google Play and iTunes, users can publish their opinion about an app by giving a star rating. One star is the worst rating. Five stars are the best. Additionally, users can justify their rating with a short review.

Although ratings and reviews are not editable on-page metadata, they are crucial. 77% of users state that they read at least one review before downloading a free app. 80% do so before purchasing a premium app.[59]

For almost 50% of men and more than 70% of women, ratings and reviews are the most critical factor when deciding whether to download an app.[60]

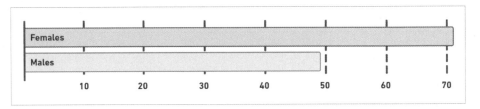

Fig. 19: The Importance of Ratings and Reviews for Download Decisions (Source: adapted from Koetsier 2018)[61]

The importance of ratings reflects in download behavior. Apps that improve their average rating will enjoy higher conversion rates:[62]

- An app that enhances its average rating from one to two stars will increase its conversion rate by 30%.

- From two to three stars, the conversion rate increases by 280%.

- From three to four stars, the conversion rate increases by 89%.

- From four to five stars, the conversion rate increases by 4%.

A study by Paul Medrano supports these findings: He discovered that the conversion rate increases significantly when the average rating improves from 3.9 stars to 4.0 stars.[63]

The differences in conversion rate changes lead to the conclusion that users differentiate only three quality brackets of apps:

- Bad apps with one or two stars.

- Mediocre apps with three stars.

- Good apps with four or five stars.

Another fact backs this conclusion: 46% of users take only apps with at least four stars into consideration when making download decisions.[64]

As a first takeaway, we can formulate the following goal: Aim to have an average rating of at least four stars. Otherwise many users will ignore your app.

The Concept of Social Proof

So without a doubt, the opinions of others matter to people. But why is that? Why do users care about the opinions of strangers? To answer that question we need to make a quick dive into human psychology.

In 1984, Dr. Robert Beno Caldini, an American psychologist and a professor emeritus for marketing and psychology, wrote a book called *Influence: The Psychology of Persuasion*. In it, he proclaimed six principles of persuasion. One of those is the concept of *Social Proof*.

It says "that a person who does not know what the proper behavior for a certain situation is will look to other people to imitate what they are doing and to provide guidance for his actions."[65] According to *Psychology Notes*, Social Proof works best when a large number of people provide it: The more people do something, the more correct the behavior looks to an observer.[66]

Nowadays marketing specialists use this tendency to promote all kinds of goods. By providing Social Proof, they try to convince customers of a product's or service's quality. Tags like "top seller" or "the most popular" indicate that many customers approved a product before. And if many people buy a product, it must be of good quality, right?

It is also very common to use experts to prove that a product is worth buying. Think of phrases like "9 out of 10 dentists recommend this toothbrush." These claims sound impressive although it is almost impossible to validate them.

While in the last example the experts are anonymous (or fictitious), some companies use real experts for advertising. Have you ever heard of the *George Foreman Grill*? More than 100 million of these cooking devices have been sold around the world since 1994. Michael Boehm and Robert Johnson invented the grill. They tried to promote their product on trade shows without any success. Nobody knew Boehm and Johnson, and nobody wanted their grill. But everybody knew the charismatic and successful boxer George Foreman. And when he started advertising for the grill with his famous slogan "It's so good I put my name on it," this was the start of one of the best endorsement deals in sports marketing ever.[67]

There are many other forms of Social Proof that marketers use to promote their products. Here are some of them:

- Stating the total number of customers or sales.
- Listing famous clients ("we work together with A and B").
- Mentioning press coverage ("featured in Magazine C").
- Pointing out awards ("voted the best product of 2017 by Organisation D").

How Ratings and Reviews support the Three Columns

Throughout the following chapters, you will learn different ways to implement Social Proof into your product page's metadata. But for now, let us get back to ratings and reviews.

Guidance in Ratings and Reviews

Ratings and reviews are created by users. Therefore it is up to them whether ratings and reviews provide guidance or not.

The most important element is your app's average rating. It is visible not only on the product page but also in search results, and even in features on Google Play. So the average rating is visible to users very early in their decision-making process.

This visibility in combination with the data about the impact of the average rating (page 84) leads to an interesting finding: An excellent average rating will attract users' attention. It is the gateway to the Mobile Marketing Funnel.

Individual reviews are only visible on the product page. They can raise users' interest in learning more about your app if they prove your app's quality.

On the other hand, a bad average rating and negative reviews can kill users' interest in your app immediately.

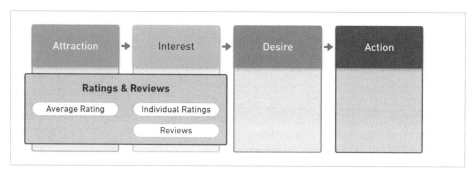

Fig. 20: Ratings and Reviews in the AIDA Funnel
(Source: Author's own illustration)

So to generate positive impacts in the attention and the interest stages of the decision-making process, you must find ways to receive more positive and less negative feedback.

Relevance in Ratings and Reviews

When visiting the product page, users can check individual reviews to learn what others like and dislike about the app. If positive reviews contain relevant keywords, they will help to convince readers of your app's ability to solve their problems.

The lack of impact you have on reviews makes it impossible to provide relevance intentionally though. Again, you are dependent on your users' goodwill.

Beauty in Ratings and Reviews

The same is valid for beauty. Reviews cannot add to beauty, but they can be harmful. If misspellings, grammar errors, and all capitals sections occur in reviews, that is an unpleasant experience for readers. But there is no way to correct these issues for you.

Getting Positive Feedback

We already stated a goal: Having an average rating of at least four stars. That seems like a pretty ambitious task, but it is absolutely possible.

Users are generous when giving their feedback: About 55% of all ratings on Google Play and iTunes are five-star ratings and 15% are four-star reviews.[68] That leaves only 30% with three-stars or less.

But how can you get the positive feedback?

Given the lack of direct influence, you have to focus on indirect measures to increase the number of positive reviews and ratings:

Asking Friends and Family for Reviews

If you are an independent developer or if you work for a young start up, reviews by friends and family can help as a kick-start for your Social Proof. As it is not a big deal to rate an app, do not hesitate to ask your loved ones for this favor.

Be careful with asking the employees of your company to do the same, though. Bell Canada, a Canadian telecommunication company, had to pay a fine of 1.25 million Canadian Dollars in 2015. Their fault was to incentivize their employees to rate their apps on Google Play and the App Store.[69] To avoid a similar lawsuit, better forgo asking employees for reviews.

Asking Users for Reviews

The most common way to get more positive reviews is to ask your users. There is no legal obstacle preventing it.

You can ask in newsletters or at the end of a successful interaction with your support team. Both of these approaches come with limitations, though: You only have the chance to ask if users take action upfront. They have to sign up for the newsletter or contact your team.

An automatic solution in your app allows you to ask a broader portion of your users for reviews. Implement a mechanism into your app to ask them at specific points of their journey. You can use the native solutions provided by Apple and Google, or you can go for a third party tool (check page 275 for suggestions).

Some of these tools include mechanisms that help improve the average rating: Instead of sending users directly to the store for their review, they filter them first. They ask people whether they like the app or not. Those who reply with "yes" are forwarded to the app store so that they can rate and write their review. But the feedback of users who say they do not enjoy the app, goes to the support team instead. This mechanism keeps negative reviews away from the app stores, so it cannot harm the average rating. Additionally, the support team gains insights on how to improve your app and make it a better experience.[70]

No matter which tool you use, when asking your users for ratings you should follow some basic rules:

Do not ask too early

If users launched your app for the first time five minutes ago, they do not know how to use it properly yet. Thus the likelihood that they will give positive feedback is rather small. Give them more time—at least one or two days—to explore your app. People who use your app for a significant time are more engaged and therefore more likely to rate your app positively.

Do not interrupt the Experience

Asking for feedback in the middle of playing the first level of your game will create a terrible experience. It is way better to choose a moment at the end of a specific user journey, in this case after finishing the level. You will not only let users enjoy their experience uninterrupted, you will also reach them in a positive mood afterward, because they just have had a feeling of success by mastering the level. Depending on your app, there are different proper moments for the request. Here are some more examples:

- Shopping: after checking out the cart.
- Traveling: after booking a hotel or flight.
- Educational: after finishing a lesson, a course or an exam.
- Dating: after having a match with another user.
- Sports: at the end of a training session.
- Navigation: when arriving at the target destination.

Do not be overaggressive.

If users do not rate your app after you have asked the first time, leave them alone. Asking again five minutes later will not change their mind. It might even result in an undesired outcome: Users giving you a bad rating because they are annoyed by the aggressive questioning. Better take the "no" for the moment and ask again in a couple of weeks or months.

Do not offer Rewards

It seems like a good idea to reward users with discounts, free in-app items or other benefits for giving you a review. Do not do so. The Google Play guidelines strictly forbid this kind of gratification.[71]

Dealing with Negative Feedback

Of course, it would be great if your app was so beautiful, intuitive, and free of bugs that no user would have a reason to give it a bad rating. But let us stay real: Everybody makes mistakes, every app crashes from time to time, and—most important—not all users have the same taste. Thus you will face negative feedback at some point. How can you handle it?

On iOS, there is only one direct way to manipulate the overall average rating. When uploading a new app version, you can reset the rating and start at zero again. While this is helpful if the previous app version received many negative ratings, you should not do it regularly. Having only a few ratings will look very suspicious to users. On Google Play there is no similar way to reset ratings.

Instead of resetting the rating on a regular basis, try to deal with feedback on an individual level. Replying to reviews is a great way to build rapport with users and create a satisfied customer base.

Answering positive feedback is easy. Show appreciation for users' efforts and say "Thank you."

In contrast, dealing with negative reviews is a slippery slope. But although it holds potential for errors on your side, you should respond to negative feedback for two reasons:

- Only 95% of one- or two-star reviews get a response from the app owner.[72] So you can stand out against competitors in terms of customer service.

- If you address users who gave bad feedback, you have the chance to convince them to improve their rating.

AppTentive has published a great 10-point plan to deal with negative feedback. If you follow it, you will avoid most pitfalls when replying to app reviews. Here is a brief summary (in a slightly different order):[73]

1. Understand that users only review apps they care about. So even negative feedback is a form of engagement, and you can build a relationship upon it.

2. Do not take criticism as a personal attack. Try to see it objectively. Do not argue with users on the basis of hurt feelings.

3. Accept bad reviews as valid criticism. Do not disqualify reviewers. Instead, encourage an open discussion with them.

4. Apologize to users for their bad experience. Sometimes a sincere "sorry" is enough to cool down emotions and pave the road for a fruitful discussion.

5. In case feedback is factually false, do not imply that users have bad intentions. Maybe they need help with your app. Try to explain how to use it properly or point them to the FAQs or the customer service.

6. Invest time in helping users. Just because you cannot replicate their problem, do not assume their criticism is invalid.

7. Give users the feeling that you seriously consider their input. Hold out the prospect of fixing a bug or adding a requested feature with the next update.

8. Prioritize your app development based upon users' feedback, bug reports, and feature requests. And more important: Let them know when you have fixed a bug or added a requested feature. Users get a notification when you reply to their review. This notification might prompt them to review your app again and improve their rating.

9. Take the conversation out of the review section to a more personal channel. Encourage users to contact your team via in-app message, email or phone to discuss issues in detail.

10. Do not feed the trolls. While most users give valuable feedback, some just want to make a fuss. If no constructive conversion is in sight, it is better not to engage further and move on.

Chapter Summary

We have learned that Social Proof is the most important criteria in the decision-making process of users. Let us review what else we can take away from this chapter:

- A good average rating attracts users' attention.

- Positive ratings raise users' interest in learning more about your app.

- Aim for an average rating of 4.0 stars or better.

- The average rating can be reset on iOS, but not on Google Play.

- Ask friends and family for reviews, but not employees.

- Ask users at the right time and in the right way.

- Bad reviews are useful as they point you to weak points in your app.

- Reply to reviews, especially to bad ones.

- Try to get reviewers into a one-on-one conversation so you can understand better how to improve your app.

CHAPTER 9
THE APP DESCRIPTION

Your app description is the most significant piece of written metadata on your product page. It is a manual as well as a marketing copy. No other element allows you to provide more content. On iOS, the description is a text of up to 4,000 characters. On Google Play, it consists of two parts: The long description contains 4,000 characters here too. In addition, you can write a short description of 80 characters.

We have already learned that about half of users consider the app description important for their download decision. More men than women pay attention to it.[74]

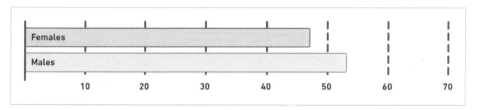

Fig. 21: The Importance of the App Description for Download Decisions (Source: adapted from Koetsier 2018)[75]

Another study underlines this importance: StoreMaven states that optimizing the description can result in an increase of the conversion rate by up to 15%.[76] Thus you should invest a decent amount of time and work to make the best out of yours.

How the Description supports the Three Columns

Both the iOS and the Android description can support the three columns that carry the product page.

Guidance in Descriptions

The app description can contain a lot of information that guides users through their decision-making process. Regarding guidance, it is one of the most powerful elements of your product page.

Unfortunately, the description is not visible for users browsing or searching the stores. People only see it when visiting the product page. Therefore the description cannot attract the attention of users. But it can strengthen the interest of product page visitors and raise their desire to use the app. It also has the ability to call them to action at the end of their decision-making process. The different components of the description impact various stages of the process. I will clarify these components later.

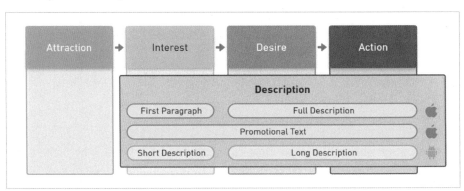

Fig. 22: The App Description in the AIDA Funnel
(Source: Author's own illustration)

Relevance in Descriptions

We know that most users download apps after performing a search with generic keywords which describe their problems. Your app description must address these problems and give readers the feeling that your app can solve them. Only if your texts offer a relevant solution will users consider downloading it.

Beauty in Descriptions

Beauty is an odd criterion when talking about written texts, right? Especially on iTunes, the options to beautify texts are minimal. Even so, it is possible to make your description a better experience for users. Simplicity is key. A massive blue-streak-style wall of text will alienate people. But if you make your description an easy read, it will be more accessible and more people will read it.

The First Paragraph

The first impression counts. If you do not like the first episode of a TV show, you will not watch the rest of the season. And if a book does not hook you in the first chapter, you will lay it down and not touch it again.

It is similar for the app description. The most challenging task about it is to make people actually read it beyond the first paragraph.

When users enter your iOS product page, they do not see the whole description. Instead, they see only the first paragraph. The length of this visible part varies depending on the device and its orientation. Usually, it contains about two or three sentences and around 150 characters on the latest iPhone models.

On Google Play, the first paragraph equals the short description. It is up to 80 characters long.

To read the full description on iOS or the long description on Google Play, users need to tab the *show me more* button. But only 2% of iOS and 5% of Google Play users do so. The majority of product page visitors just see the first paragraph and never read further.

Thus it is crucial to make the first paragraph a captivating read. You need to pin down one or two exciting sentences that awaken users' desire to download the app right away. At least you need to raise their interest in reading further, so they click the *show me more* button.

Clarify what your app is about by naming the industry, category or niche your app belongs to, as well as the products or services you offer. Remember the WIIFM principle: Readers want to know what the app does for them. So state your app's USPs, its outcome and how it benefits users. Is your app the only one in its niche? The most popular? Does it have the best offers or the biggest discounts? Tell people about it. But be truthful. Nothing is more harmful to a business than customers who spread the word about unfulfilled marketing promises.

Make your first paragraph an easy read: Keep phrases short and precise. Use simple wording. Make it understandable for all kinds of people.

Here are some examples for great first paragraphs:

Six Pack in 30 Days – Abs Workout names the category ("abs workout"), states the outcome of the app ("lose fat & get 6 pack abs"), emphasizes its convenience ("at home"), and makes clear that it is suitable for athletes of all levels of experience ("different levels").

> Effective abs workouts with different levels, LOSE
> FAT & GET 6 PACK ABS at home.

Fig. 23: Short Description *Six Pack in 30 Days*
(Source: Google Play)[77]

Fiverr – Freelance Services uses a call to action that states the app's industry ("hire a freelancer") and its outcome ("find professionals"). Furthermore, it outlines the universality of its offers ("for any project") as well as the easy and time-effective use of the app ("in minutes").

> Hire a freelancer in minutes. Find professionals for
> any project.

Fig. 24: Short Description *Fiverr*
(Source: Google Play)[78]

Babbel – Learn Languages focuses on its outcome ("Learn real-life conversations") and its variety of offers by stating the total number of languages included, as well as some examples.

> Spanish, French, German... - 14 languages in all.
> Learn real-life conversations

Fig. 25: Short Description *Babbel*
(Source: Google Play)[79]

Instant Gaming, a shopping app for video games, mentions its category ("PC/MAC games"), and emphasizes its benefits for users regarding price ("up to 70% off") and convenience ("instant delivery, 24/7").

> Your favorites PC/MAC games up to 70% off! Digital
> games, instant delivery, 24/7

Fig. 26: Short Description *Instant Gaming*
(Source: Google Play)[80]

Keywords in the First Paragraph

When drafting the first paragraph, it is crucial to include as many important keywords as possible. Even users who do not hit the *show me more* button will see the first paragraph so that these keywords will have high exposure. Adding the right terms will contribute massively to the relevance of your app description.

Have a second look at the examples we have just discussed. All of them include a lot of very relevant terms that also combine with each other to make even more relevant long-tail keywords:

- workouts, abs, 6 pack, lose fat
- hire, freelancer, professionals, project
- learn, languages, Spanish, French, German
- digital, games, PC, MAC, instant

Adding relevant keywords to your first paragraph is important on iOS to ensure readers that your app is relevant. But it is even more critical on Android, because the short description is indexed. So make sure to put a lot of keywords into the first paragraph. Do not do keyword stuffing, though (for details on keyword stuffing, check the Black Hat chapter on page 267). The text still must be a decent, grammatically correct read.

The Long Description

If you manage to make users unfold your full (or long) description, you have the chance to deliver more information. Now you must lead them from the interest to the desire and finally to the action stage.

The description is the perfect place to tell your story in detail and to substantiate your value proposition. Lay out all the information that did not make it into your first paragraph. Explain the purpose of your app and its features. How are they used? What is their outcome? What goal will people achieve by using them?

The app description is also a great tool to provide relevance. So pick up your keyword list again and use it as the foundation for your description.

You can use different styles for your description. Depending on your app and the type of story you want to tell, one of them might work better than the others. If you are unsure, write different versions for each style and test them. Of course, combining these styles is possible and often absolutely useful.

The Paragraph Style

The Paragraph Style is an excellent way to describe apps that offer a wide variety of services, complex features or in-depth content. If you want to tell a Transaction or Complexity Story, paragraphs are a good match.

Create a short paragraph of one to three sentences for each feature. Separate them from each other with blank lines or paragraph headlines (or both). This visual distinction helps to guide users visually.

Paragraphs can provide additional relevance too. If you use feature keywords as headlines for the paragraphs, these terms will stand out and catch readers' eyes. Doing so will help users to determine your app's ability to solve their problems faster. Furthermore, it gives them the chance to skip a paragraph about a feature which is not interesting to them.

Let us have a look at a Paragraph Style description, taken from the Google Play product page of *Remente – Self Improvement*.

In this description, the features' names are used as headlines for the paragraphs. They guide users to the sections they are interested in. Each paragraph contains at least two elements: A goal ("reach goals and form habits", "reduce stress and anxiety", "understand consequences") and the way to achieve this goal by using the described feature ("be reminded...", "determine what to focus on", "track your moods"). Most of these terms are relevant long-tail keywords.

> Goal setting guide
> Becoming better and achieving personal growth and development can only be achieved by creating good goals and habits. Remente acts as your coach and offer guides and tips for setting and achieving goals that form sustainable habits which result in healthy behavior.
>
> The Day Planner
> To reach goals and form habits you need to plan, and be reminded of, when it's time when to take action. The day planner is a smart and dynamic to-do list which plans your days for you based on your goals.
>
> Life assessment
> Tracking how your life is balancing is important for your mental wellbeing and to reduce your stress and anxiety levels. The life assessment tool helps you determine where you should focus your personal development efforts to become mindful and healthy.

Fig. 27: App Description *Remente*
(Source: Google Play)[81]

The Bullet-Point Style

The Bullet-Point Style is all about simplicity. It provides a decent level of guidance but reduces the amount of text to read. By doing so, it increases the chance that readers get through the whole description. Bullet points are an excellent fit for apps with simple features that are explainable with few words. This style matches both Transaction and Progression Stories.

If you want to apply it to your description, try to summarize each feature in only one short bullet point. Build each phrase around one relevant keyword. Terms from the features, actions or goals section of your keyword sheet are good candidates for this purpose. Make the bullet points short, simple, and easy to understand.

Uber tells a Transactional Story in their description. Their brief bullet points reflect the user journey in the chronological order in which users will perform them: choosing the destination, ordering, tracking, paying, and finally rating.

> Requesting your Uber is easy—here's how it works:
> - Just open the app and tell us where you're going.
> - The app uses your location so your driver knows where to pick you up.
> - You'll see your driver's picture, vehicle details, and can track their arrival on the map.
> - Payment can be made by credit card, cash in select cities, Android Pay, PayPal, and more.
> - After the ride, you can rate your driver and provide feedback to help us improve the Uber experience. You'll also get a receipt by email.

Fig. 28: App Description *Uber*
(Source: Google Play)[82]

The Running Text Style

For some apps, it does not make sense to split the feature description into bullet points or paragraphs. Read this abstract from the description of *Grow Empire: Rome*, a strategy game on Google Play:

> Turn a small republic in the heart of the Italian peninsula into the greatest civilization the world has ever seen. Lead a bunch of weak peasants into the fierceness of battle to turn them into invincible warriors!
> Upgrade your stronghold to defend yourself from the most fearful barbarian clans and armies from Italy, Gallium, Carthage and Iberian peninsula. Conquer them to expand your domains and see your national wealth grow.

Fig. 29: App Description *Grow Empire*
(Source: Google Play)[83]

The description illustrates the different aspects of the game in a Progression Story. Players build their realms from nothing. They train an army and use it to defend their land against enemies. Finally, they counterattack to grow their empire and their power. This cause of events (training to defending to attacking) will happen over and over again. There is no predefined end to this story.

But why is running text a better choice than bullet points in this case? A game is a piece of fiction, and fiction sucks the reader in by creating emotions. The authors of *Grow Empire*'s description manage to do this by addressing readers with *Calls to Action (CTAs)*. These CTAs include emotionally charged words like "fierceness" or "invincible". The result is a very intriguing experience for readers. Breaking off the text into bullet points would also break off this emotional experience. No bullet point ever transported an emotion, right? Thus running text is a better choice in this case.

The Running Text Style can work for Progression Stories as well as for Complexity Stories. Transaction Stories rarely have strong emotional components, so running texts do not provide benefits for them.

The "Call to Action" Style

Let us stay a moment with the CTAs. They are a great way to make a technical text more engaging and exciting by addressing readers directly. In the last example, the CTAs prompted users to take the position of a Roman emperor.

In the next example, we will compare two sections taken from the descriptions of similar tracking apps for outdoor athletes. While reading, ask yourself: Which one do you like better? Which one is more interesting or more engaging to read?

> TURN-BY-TURN NAVIGATION
> Spoken instructions and pleasantly large navigation arrows on your display. By means of spoken instructions, the phone can remain in your pocket which is energy-saving. Spontaneous deviation from a planned route is no problem - Naviki automatically calculates a new route to your destination.

Fig. 30: App Description *Naviki*
(Source: Google Play)[84]

> **Turn-by-Turn Voice Navigation**
> Never take your eyes off the road with turn-by-turn
> voice navigation: your precise, down-to-the-inch
> verbal navigator that doesn't distract you from
> your surroundings. Keep your eyes firmly on the
> adventure in front of you and navigate with ease,
> even on small trails or in the woods.

Fig. 31: App Description *Komoot*
(Source: Google Play)[85]

The first version lists the benefits of the app *Naviki* in a technical way: The navigation arrows are clearly visible. The app is energy-saving. Calculating a new route is possible. Although the text gives plenty of information for potential users, it is a boring read.

The description by *Komoot* communicates users' benefits in a more emotional way by using CTAs: Keep your eyes on the road. No distraction from your experience. Focus on your adventure.

This style forces readers to imagine themselves "in action" while using the app. By fabricating these pictures in peoples' heads, the description creates a much more engaging experience.

CTAs work in running texts as well as in bullet points or paragraphs.

The "You and Me" Style

With CTAs you address users directly, but this may come across as a little bit bossy: Do this, do that, download now!

An equally intense but less bossy approach to engage users is the "You and Me" Style. It focuses on the WIIFM principle and consists of two elements: Telling users what to do, but also stating what you (or your app) will do for them in return. Every user action is connected directly to a reward.

This approach makes the "You and Me" Style a nice interplay of taking and giving. It creates a symbiotic relationship between users and the app.

A great example is the description of *Runtastic Running App & Fitness Tracker* on Google Play.

Like the sample from *Remente*, the description of *Runtastic* devotes one paragraph to each feature. Each paragraph names the app features, explains their purpose, tells users what they have to do and lines out the outcomes. The difference is the absence of blank lines.

> * Monitor your running statistics to **analyze your training patterns**.
> * Set your **Yearly Running Goal** & we'll help you to reach it with your run tracker.

Fig. 32: App Description *Runtastic*
(Source: Google Play)[86]

Besides paragraphs, you can also combine bullet points with the "You and Me" Style. In running text, it is harder to get the interplay of taking and giving across. The reason is the lack of visual separations. Still, it is not impossible.

The "Question and Answer" Style

Another interesting way to structure your description is the "Question and Answer" Style (Q&A). Q&As are dialogues between a fictive user and you, the app owner. The user asks questions about the app and gets the proper information in response. As Q&As are common for many online services, people are familiar with this style.

The "Question and Answer" Style is a proper approach for apps that need only little explanation and are not based upon an intriguing emotional story. For example, all shopping apps work more or less the same: Select an item, put it into the cart, check out, and complete the payment process. These apps usually do not have innovative features that require detailed explanations. Thus a Q&A giving the essential information (product line, availability, delivery, payment terms) does the job.

Applying the "Question and Answer" Style to your product page is easy: Pin down relevant questions and answer them briefly. Follow the KISS principle. Questions and answers must be clear and to the point.

The description of *Walmart Groceries* includes a Q&A section that gives the most important information about their services very briefly: the offered services, the pricing, and the availability. It also outlines the user journey.

However, the answers are a little too general in my opinion. “Most deliveries” or “a little extra” are vague wordings that you should avoid.

There is another point of critique: The given information is not app-specific. It could as well be the description of a website or an online store. I recommend including more app-specific information in your Q&A, especially about its functions.

What's available?
Fresh produce, baked goods, meat, pantry items and more.

What's the cost?
Most in-store pickups are free. Delivery is a little extra.

Where's it available?
Use your location or enter your ZIP Code to check availability.

How does it work?
Simply register, select a convenient pickup or delivery time, and build your basket. If you pickup your groceries, we'll load them into your car when you arrive for free.

Fig. 33: App Description *Walmart Groceries*
(Source: iTunes)[87]

Adding Information beyond Features

As said at the beginning of this chapter, your app description should be a mix between a technical manual and a marketing proposal. In this context, the purpose, features, and outcomes of your app are the most critical pieces of information to share. But beyond these details, there are other details that might help users in their decision-making.

Social Proof

In the chapter about ratings and reviews, you learned that users' feedback helps to convince other potential users to download your app. Thus you should leverage Social Proof wherever you can. Your app description is a great opportunity to do so.

State your success in the app stores: If your app ever made it to the top of the category charts or was selected for a feature, let people know about it. If you have an excellent average rating, emphasize it in your description. Be aware that you may state your average rating, but you cannot quote individual user reviews.

At least for Android apps, this is not allowed according to the Google Play guidelines;[88] there is no rule prohibiting it on iOS apps though.

Do not limit Social Proof to the feedback of app users. Mention journalists' opinions as well. Quote positive press coverage from newspapers, magazines, websites or blogs. Name awards your app won.

In case you have no great feedback and no success to share, you have other options to create Social Proof: State how many users downloaded your app so far. You can also bring up how many problems your app has solved for users, for instance:

- The number of photos that people edited with your app.
- The number of matches users had on your dating platform.
- The number of levels players completed in your game.

As stated before, Social Proof can help boost users' interest in an app very early in their decision-making process. For this reason, it makes sense to implement it into the first paragraph of your description.

But Social Proof can also be the last push, that takes users from the desire to the action stage, so you can put it at the description's end as well. Especially in combination with a CTA, it can support the last step on users' way to the download. Here are some examples of great CTAs that emphasize Social Proof:

- Join our community of 1,000,000 happy users.
- Try out our award-winning app.
- Download the best-rated dating app on Google Play now.

The description of the strategy game *Clash of Lords 2: Guild Castle* mentions the app's average rating and its chart rankings:

> A top 10 strategy game all around the world!
> 4.5 stars! A top-rated game!

Fig. 34: App Description *Clash of Lords 2* (Source: iTunes)[89]

The writers of *OpenTable*, an app for making restaurant reservations, use Social Proof extensively. They dedicate a whole paragraph to their media coverage:

> · OpenTable Is Secretly the Best Thing on the Internet (Gizmodo)
> · World's Greatest Apps (Business Insider)
> · 100 Best iPhone Apps of All Time All Time (Mashable)
> · 12 Travel Apps Worth Keeping (The New York Times)
> · Best Restaurant Dining Apps (People Magazine)

Fig. 35: App Description *OpenTable*
(Source: iTunes)[90]

Technical Requirements

For transparency, you should tell users the technical requirements for using your app. Nothing is more frustrating than downloading an app and then experiencing that it does not work.

Technical requirements include for instance:

- The devices and OS versions, supported by the app.

- The permissions it needs to work correctly, like access to location services.

- Whether it works in flight mode or requires an active Internet connection. This question is very important for games.

Optionally, you can mention which localizations are available in the app. Users tend to expect that an app supports a specific language if the app description is available in that language. For example, if an app description is available in French, users expect that the app is available in French as well. But this might not be the case, because translating an app costs far more time and money than localizing only its product page. This experience can be disappointing for people and—in worst case—result in a bad review. To avoid this negative experience, clarify which languages your app supports.

Last but not least, many descriptions for freemium apps list available premium features. This preview of the paid version's benefits makes sense for functions with great additional value that are locked for free users.

However, you should not mention in-app purchases for a game, if they only speed up or simplify features that are also available for non-payers. Many players consider these IAPs unfair and call games, which contain them "pay to win." Avoid this label as it will alienate potential players.

Technical information is dull to read and not a tool for engaging undecided readers. It is only interesting for users who have already developed a desire for your app and are seriously considering downloading it. Thus it should stand after the feature section and the Social Proof because only users who have that desire will make it that far.

Contact Details

If you want to engage users on a long-term basis, you need to give them the chance to communicate with you.

Social media is the key to do so. But users who do not know about your social media cannot connect with you. So use your app description as a business card.

Let people know how to find you. Encourage them to subscribe to your YouTube channel, follow you on Twitter and Instagram, and to connect on Snapchat, Pinterest, and Facebook. If you own more content sources such as a website or profiles on Medium or Steem, mention them too.

Furthermore, add the contact details of your support team for users with a problem or a question. Give them the email addresses or phone numbers to reach someone who can help.

Finally, use the description to promote additional products, services, and sources. Point users to other apps in your portfolio. You need just one sentence like "also try these apps" or "play our other games" and a list of your app titles to do so. Users who like your app might be willing to test them too. So do not waste this chance for cross-promoting your portfolio.

Make sure not to promote Android apps in iTunes descriptions and vice versa—neither Apple nor Google like to see their competitor's brand name on their platform.

Contact details should stand at the very end of your description. Use brief bullet points.

The app description for *Duolingo*, a service to learn languages, is a good example for encouraging users to connect on social media. It also cross-promotes their merchandise shop. Find the excerpt from Google Play on the next page.

Buy Duolingo gear at https://gear.duolingo.com

Facebook: https://www.facebook.com/duolingo

Twitter: https://twitter.com/duolingo

Google+: https://plus.google.com/+duolingo

Use Duolingo on the Web at
https://www.duolingo.com

Fig. 36: App Description *Duolingo*
(Source: Google Play)[91]

The Right Order

Make sure to order the different sections of your description properly. The first paragraph comes first, obviously. The feature section is next. Then Social Proof, technical requirements, and finally contact details.

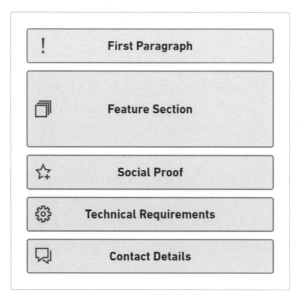

Fig. 37: Components of the App Description
(Source: Author's own illustration)

In case you need to shorten your description because it exceeds the character limit, cut the technical requirements first. If it is still too long, try to erase minor features from the feature section. Go after the Social Proof only if the text is still too long afterward.

Beautifying the Description

After writing your description to provide guidance and relevance to readers, the next step is to beautify it. As said in the introduction to this chapter, beauty in texts is primarily about legibility. It is about giving it a format that does not strain the reader's eye. And it is also about setting eye-catchers to provide additional guidance and relevance.

The measures for this purpose are limited, in particular on iOS. However, no matter which store you write for, you can make your description a more accessible read with the proper format:

- Use line breaks to create smaller portions of text, even if you follow the running text style. A text wall of up to 4,000 characters without any empty line looks terrible. To create line breaks on Google Play you need to apply HTML tags to your text. You will find the proper tags in the table below on the next page.

- Put blank lines between paragraphs as well, to help readers to distinguish information.

- Create headlines for paragraphs, so users see at first glance what the following section is about.

- Use all capitals to make relevant keywords stand out and catch readers' eyes. You can do so for headlines or single terms in longer text sections.

Rich Formatting

On Android, you have more options to make your description stand out visually: Google Play allows you to use HTML tags to apply rich formatting to your text. You can create headers of different font sizes as well as bold and italic fonts. You can underline and even color text. HTML tags consist of two parts: one for the beginning and one for the end of the new text format. Be aware that all HTML tags count against the 4,000 character limit of your description.[92]

Format	HTML Syntax	Result
Bold Fonts	\Your Text\	**Your Text**
Italic Fonts	\<i>Your Text\</i>	*Your Text*
Underlined Fonts	\<u>Your Text\</u>	<u>Your Text</u>
Line Breaks	1st Line\ 2nd line	1st Line 2nd Line
Headlines	\<h1>Your Headline\</h1>	**Your Headline**
Colored Text	\<font color="red">Your Text\</font>	Your Text

Tab. 7: Supported HTML Tags on Google Play
(Source: adapted from Zolotareva 2017)[93]

Do not use rich formatting too extensively. Texts that are all bold, have every second word underlined, and blink in 20 different colors are a pain to the eye. Even worse, they destroy the purpose of rich formatting. If users do not know where to look first because of all the colors and highlights, they will not take notice of the important parts. Use rich formatting selectively to emphasize only words or phrases that shall catch readers' eyes because of their relevance.

To avoid accidental formatting (that results in a lousy user experience too), double-check to close all HTML tags. If you do not, you will create something gruesome like the German description of *Shoot Goal*. Its author forgot to close a tag which resulted in a text that is about 70% bold. Here is a screenshot:

Mit dem **neuen PvP-Fußballmodus kannst du im Online-Fußballspielmodus Competitive Multiplayer Soccer gegen Gegner aus der ganzen Welt antreten, in denen du die Spiele von Fouls und Strafen gegen Leute aus der ganzen Welt, zeigt, dass du der beste Spieler bist und alle deine Rivalen durch den Gewinn aller Spiele besiegt und zeigt, dass du im Multiplayer-Online-Fußball der König des PvP bist.**

★ FUSSBALL-PARTY : Erziele Tore, damit dein Team der Gewinner der Weltmeisterschaft 2018 wird.
★ STRAFE : schwierige Situation zwischen dem Spieler und dem Torwart. Sie brauchen Konzentration, um ein Tor zu erzielen.
★ Schuss von Fehlern : Eine Barriere von Spielern verhindert, dass der Schuss einfach ist. Zeichnen Sie eine Kurve, um einen perfekten Fehler mit Effekt zu schießen.

Fig. 38: App Description *Shoot Goal*
(Source: Google Play)[94]

Last but not least, be aware that hyperlinks in Google Play are always underlined and cannot be colored. So adding rich formatting to them does not work.

Building Links for all Platforms

Let us talk a little more about hyperlinks. To send users to your social media, you must build them into your description. Although the purpose of a hyperlink is to send people directly to the linked website, iTunes does not support this function. Users cannot even copy links out of the app description. Instead, they have to type the URL into their browser manually. Unfortunately, there is no way around this process.

Google Play is more user-friendly in terms of hyperlinks. Any URL in your description is clickable and leads to the linked website.

Let us pretend you want to lead users to your website, which is

https://www.YourWebsite.com

If you insert this URL into your app description, readers who click it will be redirected to your site. That is also true if you leave out the https or the www. All of the following ways to write your URL will work for this purpose, given users click them inside the Google Play App:

https://www.YourWebsite.com

www.YourWebsite.com

YourWebsite.com

But when users visit your product page via the Google Play website, these URLs are not clickable. To make a link work for web users, it needs to be embedded into HTML code that consists of three parts:

The first part defines where the link begins and to which website it redirects. It looks like this:

```
<a href="https://www.YourWebsite.com">
```

Note that the angle brackets are part of the code. The space between the quotation marks is where you must put your URL.

The second part of the code defines the term (or phrase), which users actually see and can click. It can be the name of your website, the full URL or any other word. Let us take a short version of your URL for this example:

YourWebsite.com

The third part of the code indicates the end of the link and is identical for every link and every website:

</a>

When combining the three elements, the complete HTML code for your hyperlink looks like this:

<a href="https://www.YourWebsite.com">YourWebsite.com</a>

The visitors of your product page will only see this part though:

YourWebsite.com

Unfortunately, you face another problem now: HTML links work on the web, but not in the Google Play App. So this link will only be clickable on the Google Play website.

There is a workaround to solve this problem, though: Combine both approaches. Replace the middle part of the HTML link with a generic CTA like "Visit now", "Click here" or "Our Website", followed by a colon. Now add your URL again right behind the HTML code. The complete line should look like this:

<a href="https://www.YourWebsite.com">Visit us:</a>https://www.YourWebsite.com

The result looks the same for all users, whether they use the Google Play App or website:

Visit us: https://www.YourWebsite.com

For web users, the first part ("Visit us:") is a clickable link, but not the URL they see. For app users it is vice versa: The URL will work properly as a link. This workaround consumes a lot of the 4,000 characters you can use for your description. However, it is the best approach to deal with hyperlinks on your Google Play product page.

Adding Special Characters

A good way to emphasize single phrases or words on iOS are special characters. Suitable characters for this purpose are, for instance, the asterisk (*) and the plus symbol (+). Both are good replacements for the standard dash in bullet point lists. Have a look at the description for *Move Well* for example. Its writers use the asterisk instead of a bullet point:

> ====
> MAIN FEATURES
> * Choose specific exercises, or pick a full timed routine. Full routines last between 10-14 minutes.
> * MoveWell leads you through simple exercises that help to release tight muscles, and improve flexibility, stability, and muscle strength.

Fig. 39: App Description *Move Well*
(Source: iTunes)[95]

In their description, another character is used to separate different sections of the text: The equal sign (=). By placing multiple equal signs next to each other, the author cleverly created horizontal lines. That is a great idea to give an app description a better structure. The tilde (~) and the dash (-) are good alternatives for the same purpose.

You see, even with the rather unspectacular special characters you can create some visual improvements for your texts on iOS.

Adding Emojis

The funny cartoon characters and symbols called *emojis* are omnipresent in the digital world. Sometimes they even invade the analog sphere. For app descriptions, they offer great beautification potential:

• They are good eye-catchers to get users' attention.

• They can transport emotions.

• They can help to explain what is not obvious at first glance.

On Google Play, you may use the cute little faces, people and symbols to jazz up your texts. This goes for the long description, the short description, and the app title. The motives for implementing emojis are varied.

The description of *Home Street*, a life simulation game, contains paragraph headlines with emojis. Each emoji perfectly matches the game aspect the paragraph describes, for instance:

- a house for the building feature
- a single character for the character creation
- a couple holding hands for the social components

The emojis emphasize terms which describe essential functions. They guide readers' eyes and add relevance because they force them to notice relevant keywords.

> 🏡 CREATE YOUR DREAM HOME
> ✓ Design a dream home and extend or remodel your house to create the perfect pad
> ✓ Build a home and decorate it with a home layout that will reflect your personal style best
> ✓ Decorate your own house and design it with great amenities like a relaxing hot tub, big-screen TV, and much more! The choices are yours!
> ✓ Unleash your home design passion and house flip in this house game!
>
> DESIGN YOUR OWN CHARACTER

Fig. 40: App Description *Home Street*
(Source: Google Play)[96]

In *Bikemap*, a navigation tool for cyclists, bike emojis replace the common bullet points. They match the app category and improve the visual appearance of the description. They do not have an impact on relevance or guidance, though.

> 🚲 Explore more than 3.8M bike routes in 100+ countries
> 🚲 Discover amazing national & international cycling regions
> 🚲 Get personalized cycling route

Fig. 41: App Description *Bikemap*
(Source: Google Play)[97]

Not every App is a good Fit for Emojis

You realize that decorating your texts with emojis can work for apps, even if they target adults. It strongly depends on the category and the context of the app, though. The apps we discussed above are leisure time apps. They target fun activities. In this context, emojis work great.

For *Star horoscope - daily zodiac and palmistry free*, the use of emojis is almost a must: The different sign symbols match the app's context perfectly.

Fig. 42: App Description *Star Horoscope*
(Source: Google Play)[98]

But using emojis where it is inappropriate can hurt your conversion rate. That is, in particular, true for apps that are used in a business environment. For these apps, the funny and playful spirit of emojis does not match the users' expectations. Ask yourself: Would you put your trust into a banking app whose description is packed with smileys and banknote emojis? I would not.

Emojis must match the character of your app as well as your target audience and their expectations. Decide carefully whether this is true for your app and users before adding emojis to the description.

Last but not least, you need to test if the emoji of your choice actually works with Google Play. Not all emojis that you know from messengers like *Whatsapp* do. Others will work, but they look different from the appearance you know.

Beautification Techniques on iOS vs. Google Play

To conclude the beautification section, have a look at the following table. It summarizes which styling techniques are available on iOS and Google Play.

Technique	Google Play	iOS
Bold, italic, underlined, and colored Text	yes	no
Headers with bigger Font Size	yes	no
Line Breaks	yes	yes
Hyperlinks	yes	no
Special Characters (Tilde, Asterisk, etc.)	yes	yes
Emojis	yes	no

Tab. 8: Beautification Techniques on iOS and Google Play
(Source: Author's own illustration)

The Description's Branding Power

So far we have not talked about one vital part of telling a story: introducing your brand.

As your description contains up to 4,000 characters, you should not be thrifty with naming your brand in it. Make sure people know your brand name after reading the last phrase. Mentioning your brand name will not be judged as keyword stuffing. So do not hesitate to exceed the five-times limit that applies for generic keywords. Your brand name should show up:

- at least once in the first paragraph,
- at least three to five times in the features section,
- and once in every line or phrase of the Social Proof section (URLs, Twitter handles, and channel names qualify as an appearance if they contain the brand name).

Except for the short description on Google Play, which is limited in terms of characters, always write your full brand name.

In the app description, you obviously can implement your brand only as text. You cannot use your logo, and you cannot use your corporate font type either. But to ensure your app name stands out in your description, you can use one of the beautification measures. Use all-caps on iOS and bold or italic fonts on Google Play. In case your logo contains a specific corporate color, use HTML tags to apply this color to your brand name.

Description Analysis

The short examples we have seen so far usually shed light on only single aspects or styles. But when creating your description, you will have to combine many different aspects. You need to decide about the type of story you use, the text style, the features you describe, the keywords, and formatting.

Let us have a look at two complete app descriptions to get a better feeling for good and bad practices.

Example A: Affinity

The first paragraph (or more precisely the first and second paragraphs) of the description of the photo editing app *Affinity* is a properly written marketing proposal. It points out the app's benefits, it includes one piece of Social Proof ("our award-winning desktop version"), and it challenges users ("you will find hard to believe"), which is an excellent way of raising their interest in the app.

The rest of the description contains brief bullet points. By grouping them with summarizing headlines, the text gets a good structure. This structure helps guide users to the information they seek.

The bullets section holds an incredible amount of information on every single feature of the app. It creates the impression of an ultimate app that fulfills every wish of a passionate photographer.

And *Affinity* clearly addresses this niche audience of people who are or want to become experts in photo editing. The technical overload is the proper approach to awake their desire to use the app. But for a random reader, the level of detail is overwhelming and might be alienating. Despite these details, the text is surprisingly engaging because of the selectively used CTAs.

The description is far from being perfect, though. There are several valid points of criticism.

** Affinity Photo for iPad supports iPad Pro, iPad Air 2 and iPad (early 2017). Please note that older iPads are not supported. **

Affinity Photo is the first fully featured, truly professional photo editing tool for iPad - built from exactly the same back-end as our award-winning desktop version and fully optimised to harness the power of iPad's hardware and touch capabilities.

Photo for iPad offers an incredibly fast, powerful and immersive experience whether you are at home, in the studio, or on the move. With meticulous attention to detail each tool, panel and control has been completely reimagined for touch. All rendering, adjustments, brushes and filters have been fully hardware accelerated using Metal. The result is an all-new way to interact with your images, with performance you will find hard to believe.

Unsurpassed productivity
• Full support for unlimited layers, layer groups, adjustment layers, filter layers and masks
• Resize layers without any loss of quality. Lock, hide, duplicate and merge layers easily
• Edit live filters, adjustments, effects, blend modes and masks non-destructively
• Undo history can be saved with the document so you can always undo your changes
• Task-focused workspaces for developing, post-processing, tone mapping and liquify

Professional image processing
• Open RAW and other images in a dedicated pre-processing workspace
• Adjust exposure, blackpoint, clarity, vibrance, white balance, shadows, highlights and much more
• Recover detail thought to be lost by editing in an unbounded linear color space
• Advanced lens corrections including chromatic aberration, defringe, vignette and best-in-class noise reduction
• View histograms, blown highlights, shadows and tones as well as EXIF information
• Focus Merge, HDR Merge and Tone mapping for advanced image processing
• 360° image support including full projected image editing
• Panorama stitching including full perspective corrections and lighting adjustments
• Full support for image channels
• Massive collection of effects available, including blurs, distortions, tilt-shift, shadows, glows, lighting and many more

Quality retouching and correction tools
• Intuitive selection brush and refinement makes selections simple, even down to strands of hair
• Instantly remove unwanted objects with an incredibly advanced Inpainting brush
• Dodge, burn, clone, patch, blemish and red eye tools
• Smooth and retouch skin with built-in frequency separation
• Apply high quality single-plane and dual-plane perspective correction as well as fully customisable mesh warps - all in real time
• Dedicated Liquify persona gives freehand control over warps, twirls, pinch, punch and turbulence

Advanced brush engine
• Huge library of painting, drawing, textures and professional DAUB® Brushes included
• Create custom brushes and nozzles with full control over advanced dynamics
• Extensive collection of brush tools including Paint, Mixer, Pixel, Colour Replacement, Blur, Smudge, Sharpen and Undo brushes

Engineered for Professionals
• Open, edit and save Photoshop® PSD files
• RGB, CMYK, HDR, Greyscale and LAB colour spaces
• End-to-end CMYK workflow with ICC colour management and OCIO support
• Full 16 and 32-bit per channel editing
• Work with all standard formats like PNG, TIFF, JPG, GIF, SVG, EPS, EXR, HDR, PSD and PDF
• Cross-platform compatibility with iOS, macOS and Windows® with 100% file compatibility

Optimised for iPad
• Metal accelerated to achieve blazing-fast performance, even when editing large images
• Sensitive to pressure, tilt and angle, Affinity Photo harnesses the full power and precision of Apple Pencil
• Full iCloud drive integration allows for seamless file management, storage and sharing

Fig. 43: App Description *Affinity*
(Source: iTunes)[99]

It is evident that a Complexity Story underlies *Affinity*'s description. However, the order of features is not ideal. The evolution from basic features to expert functions is missing. Instead, the order seems to be random.

Another weakness is the lack of Social Proof although an app as fulsome as *Affinity* should have some awards, media covering or reviews to share. The text also provides no contact details to give users the chance to communicate with the team behind the app.

Furthermore, the very first sentence of the description states a technical requirement. It is fine to give this information to users, but the prominent first paragraph is the wrong place to do so.

All in all, the description does address its target audience properly. But it has weaknesses in terms of structure and lacks information that goes beyond explaining features.

Example B: Forex Calendar, Market & News

Forex Calendar, Market & News is an app for traders of financial assets on Google Play.

Its description's first paragraph includes a lot of relevant keywords. They are tailored together to tell users about the needs the app addresses ("track", "analyze", "trade", "stay up to date"). The paragraph also contains a lot of Social Proof ("hundreds of thousands of users", "leading community", "over one million accounts"). It creates the impression that the app is indispensable for traders ("our app is a must") and leaves no wish unfulfilled ("everything you need").

The list of bullet points, following the first paragraph, summarizes feature-related information. The list is very clean but uses very technical vocabulary: No CTA, no judgmental adjectives (the last point is an exception), and no marketing speech. Just like the *Affinity* description, this part addresses people who know what they are looking for.

There is potential for improvement regarding the wording. I dislike that seven out of the ten bullet points include the word "live" (and six of them start with it). I would rephrase some of them to diversify the appearance of the list, but also to get more relevant keywords in.

Both the first paragraph and the bullet point list address users in the interest stage of the AIDA process. They aim to raise the wish to learn more about the app.

The purpose of the next section of paragraphs is to take people from to the interest to the desire stage (despite the fact that each point starts with a bullet, I consider this part written in paragraph style, because more than one sentence is used per feature). Each paragraph explains one function in detail. Although they include many technical details, the wording is more engaging. It contains CTAs as well as question-and-answer interactions. For that reason, this section is a varied read.

In the last part of the description, the authors share some reviews with readers. Although stating Social Proof is great, this approach is dangerous. The text does not clarify whether app users, the media or other sources provided the reviews. As we learned, Google Play forbids the first option. It would be better (and safer) to name the source of the reviews or use another form of Social Proof.

Finally, the description opens the most basic channel for communication by giving readers the company's email address. Some more options via social media would be great.

A big minus is the lack of visual highlights. Emojis would not be a good fit for a trading app, because they are too playful. But rich formatting to emphasize keywords such as "over 60 different currency pairs", "technical analysis" or "streaming feed of economic news" would upgrade the description in terms of beauty and relevance.

Another problem is the story structure. In the case of *Forex Calendar*, it is a Complexity Story. But its order is not proper. Basic features like the calculators should come first, pro tools like the Forex Charts later.

Let us summarize: As the *Affinity* description, the description of *Forex Calendar* presents an enormous amount of feature details to address a niche audience. But it lacks a proper structure. It also misses many chances to provide additional guidance and relevance.

Forex Calendar, Market & News

Forex Portfolio, Charts, Economic Calendar, Outlook, Live Forex Rates, News

If you're a forex trader, our app is a must! Everything you need to track, analyze, and stay up to date with your forex portfolio and the forex markets on the go. Join the hundreds of thousands of other traders already using our app.
Brought to you by Myfxbook - the leading social forex community with over one million trading accounts connected!

What makes us the best forex app you'll ever use?
- A complete view of your forex portfolio including watched accounts.
- A live forex calendar with complete event data, notifications, custom alerts and widget.
- Live streaming rates for over 60 forex currency pairs and commodities.
- Live Forex charts with technical analysis and indicators.
- Live forex patterns analysis.
- Live forex news.
- Live price notifications.
- Live community outlook with custom notifications.
- Calculators to help you plan your trades.
- Simple, intuitive and lightning fast user interface.

An overview of the different sections:
- Portfolio: the portfolio section will show you your Myfxbook portfolio including a growth chart, quick stats and the current status of the account (trades, orders and history). Don't have a portfolio yet? Then go to our website and register a free account.

- Economic Calendar: be in sync with the markets up to the minute with our real-time economic calendar covering over 30 different currencies with easily readable data. Each event can be drilled down for an explanation and historic levels.

- Markets: you can view over 60 different currency pairs in truly real time, tick by tick (EURUSD, GBPUSD, USDCAD, USDJPY, AUDUSD and more), including the changes in 9 different time-frames in just one glance. Want to be alerted of a specific price? No problem - just set up an alert and get notified in real time. The markets section shows you forex patterns in real-time in each and every timeframe in one simple screen.

- Forex Charts: enabling you to use technical analysis on the go with our high performance charts. Bundled with 5 drawing types (line, speed line, Fibonacci Retracement, Fibonacci fan, Fibonacci arc) and 9 indicators (SMA, EMA, Bollinger Bands, RSI, Stochastic, MACD, envelopes, ATR and ADI). Instantly share your chart with your fellow traders.

- Forex News: the news section will show you a streaming feed of economic news items in real-time from major news providers - you can even filter news of specific instruments (for example EUR, USD or Gold).

- Community Outlook: a real-time outlook for different currency pairs as can be seen in the Myfxbook website. Each pair will include the full data such as the amount of open positions, total volume and more. Set up unlimited notifications for different levels (for example if long sentiment is over 50%).

- Calculators: when planning your next trade, use the calculators to calculate an entry price, position size, margin or risk value for a better money management.

Some of our reviews:
- "Awesome Must have for any forex trader"
- "5 star Best application to help me monitor the market"
- "Brilliant! Can check my portfolio anywhere, anytime."

Please rate us and provide feedback so we can enhance the Myfxbook app even further - contact us at android@myfxbook.com.

Fig. 44: App Description *Forex Calendar* (Source: Google Play)[100]

Step-by-Step: Writing an App Description

You have all the theoretical knowledge to write a great app description now. It is time to get into the practical work.

We know that the description serves different purposes on iOS and Google Play. It has an impact on Conversion Rate Optimization for both platforms. But on Google Play, it is also crucial for creating visibility.

So if your app is available on both iOS and Google Play, I suggest starting with the Google Play description. Later adjust it for iTunes.

Step 0: Keyword Research

To unleash its full potential, the Google Play description needs to be based on your most relevant keywords. Thus, the keyword research process is the basic requirement for a good description. You have already learned about this process in the second part of this book. So I assume you have a nice list of relevant keywords available by now.

Step 1: Creating a Structure

Before you start writing, collect all the information you want to put into your description. Make sure it includes:

- the features you want to introduce,
- the USPs of your app,
- the outcome for users,
- testimonials, media quotes, the average app rating, and other forms of Social Proof,
- contact and social media details,
- and the technical requirements for using your app.

Decide which kind of story you want to tell and which styles you want to use to do so.

Now create an outline. Determine the content order, and make sure it fits your story type. Remember, the first paragraph matters most and thus should contain your most persuasive arguments.

Set a target character count for each section of your app description. Make sure not to cross the 4,000 character limit. It might be a good idea to keep it shorter if you want to apply HTML tags for rich formatting or hyperlinks later. Aim for 3,800 to 3,900 characters in this case.

Step 2: Writing the First Draft

Write your app description, based upon your outline. Place your keywords in your text up to five times each. But make sure you do not put the same term into five consecutive sentences. Spread it across your description. Remember to insert long-tail keywords as a perfect match whenever possible. If your app is only available for iOS, the five-times rule obviously does not apply. However, implement important keywords multiple times, so readers will perceive your description as relevant.

Try to match the character counts you defined before. If it turns out you need more (or fewer) characters for a specific part of the description, adjust your outline.

Step 3: Proofreading and Editing

After finishing your first draft, proofread it. Use online tools to double-check spelling, grammar, and style (see the Tools & Sources section on page 275 for recommendations). Test all hyperlinks to ensure they redirect to the correct website or social media profile.

Give your description to friends. Let them search for errors and ask for their feedback. Do they understand what your app is about by reading it? Do they get its USPs? Can they tell which problems and audiences it addresses? If not, you might need to rework your description.

Also, check the keyword density. You can find out how often a keyword appears in your text by using the search function of your text processing program. To increase the keyword density, consider deleting unnecessary words like adjectives or adverbs.

Step 4: Beautifying the Text

When you are happy with your text, the next step is to beautify it.

Give it a proper structure that makes it easy to read. Use rich formatting to emphasize relevant sections. Highlight important keywords with bold, underlined or colored fonts. Apply special characters and emojis.

Step 5: Adjusting the Google Play Description for iTunes

To adapt your Google Play Description for iOS, you need to make three different kinds of adjustments:

First, merge your short and your long descriptions. To meet the 4,000 character limit, you might need to cut passages in this process. Take special care with the first paragraph. Remember, it contains 150 to 240 characters on iOS, while on Google Play it is only 80 characters long. That means you can extend your central value proposition. Pick some vital information such as Social Proof from the original long description and move it to the first paragraph.

The second adjustment concerns keywords. It is likely that your keyword research delivered different results for iOS and Android. So your Google Play description might contain keywords that are not valuable on iOS regarding relevance, volume or competition. Although the iOS description does not affect the search results, you should exchange them. Remember, keywords with good volumes and high relevance will strengthen readers' perception that the app will solve their problems.

Third, you need to take care of your beautification measures. Many effective techniques that work on Google Play do not apply for iTunes. Thus you must adjust them. Check the table on page 116 for details. Here are the adjustments, you need to make:

- Remove all HTML tags, including those for hyperlinks.
- Replace rich formatting (bold, italic, and underlined text) with all capitals where appropriate.
- Use special characters such as the asterisk to emphasize headers.
- If you use emojis as bullet points in Google Play descriptions, substitute them with dashes or special characters.

Step 6: Localizing

Translating relevant keywords is not hard. With a program like *Google Translate* and a keyword tool to judge the translations, you can easily create good keyword sets for different languages (see page 272). But implementing them into a text that shall contribute to guidance, relevance, and beauty is difficult, at least if you are not a native speaker yourself. It is even harder for languages that do not use the Latin alphabet.

Try to find help in your social circle. Ask family, friends or colleagues who speak your target languages. If you do not know anyone, you can try freelancing services. Be aware that the quality of the work might differ significantly, so do not be too thrifty when looking for help.

Step 7: Uploading

The last step is uploading your new description to the app stores. You are almost done; there are just a couple of things left that you should consider:

Make sure not to confuse localizations. This fault would cause a rejection on iTunes and could cost you at least one to two days before your updated product page can go live.

As soon as the description is live on iOS, check how the first paragraph looks on the latest iPhone models. Is it completely visible without clicking the *show me more* button? If not, adjust it for the next update.

On Google Play, your new description will be live within minutes of uploading it. Check it for errors: Is rich formatting applied correctly? Do emojis look like you expected? If you want to avoid mistakes, use a preview website to double-check your description's appearance before setting it live (see page 275 in the Tools & Sources chapter).

Chapter Summary

All right, you have made it through the description chapter. Good work. You have learned a lot about the information you should put into your app description, how to structure it, and how to improve its visual appearance. Here is a short list with the essential findings and best practices:

- The app description is important for raising interest and desire, and it can also call users to action.
- Give your central value proposition in the first paragraph.
- Implement the most valuable keywords into the opening lines.
- Use the Paragraph Style to explain complicated features in detail.
- Use bullet points for less complex information.
- Use running texts to tell emotional stories.
- Engage readers with CTAs.
- Create symbiotic connections with the "You and Me" Style.
- Use a brief Q&A if your app's functions are self-explanatory.
- Provide Social Proof.
- If technical requirements apply for your app, state them.
- Let people know how to connect to you.
- Use word wraps, empty lines, headlines, and special characters to give your description a proper structure.
- Emphasize relevant keywords on Google Play with rich-formatting and emojis. On iOS, use all capitals.
- Check for typos, grammar errors, and keyword density.

CHAPTER 10
SCREENSHOTS

Screenshots are the most prominent visual creatives of your product page. Almost 20% of men and about 13% of women consider screenshots the crucial factor for their download decisions. Especially younger users pay much attention to them.[101]

Fig. 45: The Importance of Screenshots for Download Decisions (Source: adapted from Koetsier 2018)[102]

On iTunes, you can upload up to ten screenshots. Up to three of them appear as a gallery in search results. If a preview video is available on a product page, it shows up in the gallery with only two screenshots. On Google Play three of the eight screenshots appear on SERPs, but only for brand searches.

StoreMaven found that only 33% of iOS users and 15% of Android users inspect all screenshots. Most people will just see the gallery. That makes the first two screenshots extraordinarily important. By optimizing them, you can increase your conversion rate by up to 25%.[103]

This data proves that you should put some effort into creating stunning screenshots. On the following pages, we will discuss in detail which options you have to do so.

How Screenshots support the Three Columns

Before we go into design details, let us discuss briefly how screenshots impact viewers' experiences.

Guidance in Videos

Proper screenshots contribute to all phases of the decision-making process. They can drive users all the way down the AIDA funnel.

As screenshots show up on SERPs, they can draw users' attention to your app. But besides that, they visualize your app's story. That is valuable in particular to address people who do not want to read the description. You can use screenshots to increase users' interest in your app and raise their desire to test it. And you can call people to action and download your app by using text elements in your screenshots.

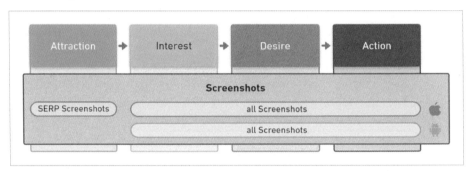

Fig. 46: Screenshots in the AIDA Funnel
(Source: Author's own illustration)

Relevance in Videos

By showing users content that is connected to their problem, you can create a high level of relevance with your screenshots. Creating this relevance is particularly important for decisive users who see your app on the SERP. If screenshots indicate relevance, you will convince much more people to download your app.

Beauty in Videos

The appearance of most in-app footage is rather boring. Games with stunning graphics, cute characters, and colorful levels are an exception. But even if your app is not a gorgeous game, you can improve your screenshots' beauty and make them real eye-catchers.

Feature Screenshots

The original idea behind screenshots was to present a non-manipulated demo of an app's look. Apple's guidelines emphasize this idea.[105] Many developers follow this WYSIWYG approach by uploading raw, unedited in-app footage to their product pages. Check out the example of *Time Tune*, a scheduling tool on Google Play.

Without question, using in-app footage is the most honest way to present an app. But it often lacks a congruent story to guide users, a relevant connection to users' problems or a nice appearance. For this reason, marketers have developed many techniques to upgrade their screenshots. Let us have a look at them.

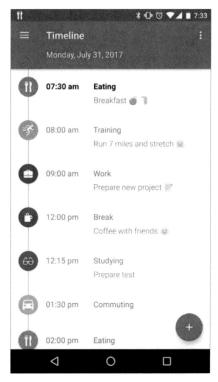

Fig. 47: Screenshot *Time Tune* (Source: Google Play)[104]

Device Frames

One of the most common techniques is to embed in-app footage into device frames. Across the app stores, you will find many screenshots showing one device in portrait orientation with unedited in-app footage. You can see one of them, taken from the product page of *CacheToolBox*, on the next page.

Some designers add an animated or a photographed hand holding the device. This approach encourages users to picture themselves using the app. Check the example from the app *MyTaxi*.

Other screenshots show animated mock-ups instead of realistic device frames. These reduce the risk of distracting people from the in-app footage or the background art. *Pill Alert* shows their app in very plain sketches of an iPhone.

Embedding a screenshot into a device frame (with or without a hand holding it) is only a small upgrade in terms of guidance. But this technique has another advantage: By scaling down the device with the in-app footage, you can create free space around it. If you use this space for additional content such as captions, you can create a bigger level of guidance, relevance, and beauty. But more on captions later.

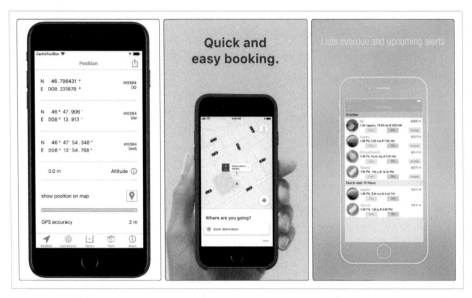

Fig. 48: Screenshots *CacheToolBox*, *MyTaxi*, *PillAlert*
(Source: iTunes)[106,107,108]

Multiple Devices

For some apps, showing multiple devices in one screenshot is a great way to increase its guidance.

That is true in particular for apps with major social features. These includes chat, mailing, and dating apps, but also multi-player games. Have a look at the following example, taken from the iOS product page of the dating app *Bumble*. Putting two devices with different user profiles next to each other explains simply but effectively what the app does: It connects users to other people.

Multiple device screenshots are also great to emphasize cross-platform functionalities. *Todoist* offers app versions for tablets and smart watches. Users who see their screenshot understand this fact without reading a word.

If you want to promote the variety of your content, you can use the multiple device approach too. *Wetter.com* does so by presenting two devices in the same screenshot. Both show different aspects of the app's weather forecast feature: the daily forecast and the hourly prediction.

In the last example, the two devices do not provide much guidance, but they add to beauty. Two very similar looking screenshots with one device each would be boring. But the two device screenshot makes the set as a whole more diverse and thus more interesting to look at.

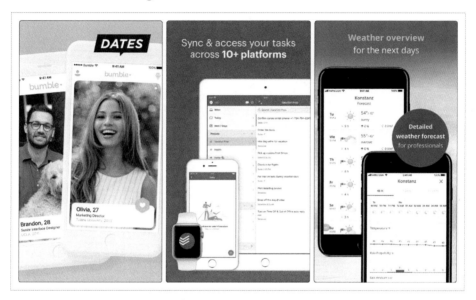

Fig. 49: Screenshots *Bumble, Todoist, Wetter.com*
(Source: iTunes)[109,110,111]

Partial Devices

Device frames also help to guide users visually. Let us pretend that you want people to recognize a navigation element in the bottom part of your in-app footage. To achieve this goal, you need to minimize the risk of distractions. Simply cut off the upper portion and enlarge the remaining partial device. That is precisely how the designers of the *Hootsuite* screenshot did it (see next page).

Of course, you can also make a vertical or diagonal cut if it fits your goal better. Check the screenshot by *SumUp*, for example.

Like using multiple devices, partial devices make a screenshot set diverse. So they add to both guidance and beauty.

Device Size

For all screenshots including devices, you must be careful about size. Make sure that devices and the in-app footage are big enough that viewers can see and read all the content. If you do it wrong, you will create a screenshot like the one by *Salesforce Authenticator*. The device takes less than one third of the picture size, and in-app content is barely eligible. Do not make this mistake. Adjust device sizes and make all content readable.

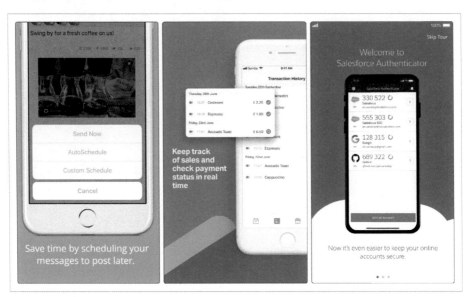

Fig. 50: Screenshots *Hootsuite, SumUp, Salesforce Authenticator* (Source: iTunes)[112,113,114]

Augmentation

Sometimes cutting off a portion of a device and enlarging the rest is not enough to ensure visual guidance. That is especially true when you want to point users to small elements such as buttons or icons.

A great technique called *Augmentation* solves this problem. Augmentation is about adding new layers to your in-app footage. By popping off the element you want to emphasize, you create a new foreground layer and push it into viewers' focus.

Have a closer look at the screenshot by *Joom* below. You will notice the magnifier at the bottom. It enlarges the price tag of one product to make people aware of the massive discount. Forcing users' eyes to this part of the picture is crucial because it supports the message "Unbeatable Prices". The visual guidance by the magnifier makes sure viewers can see this connection.

A magnifier is not necessary when using the Augmentation technique, though. You can also cut out the elements you want to push to viewers' attention and lift them from the rest of the picture. *VivaVideo* presents, for instance, their social sharing features by emphasizing the navigation bar.

The Augmentation technique looks even better if you rotate the device a few degrees. Check how the designers of the *Gmail* screenshot did it. They cleverly played with perspective and created a great three-dimensional illusion. Furthermore, they added not just one, but two extra foreground layers. First, they highlighted the three category buttons by lifting them from the device. Second, they popped off the *new* icons a little bit further.

If you manage to produce screenshots as terrific as this, you will not only provide visual guidance, you will also create a lot of extra beauty.

Fig. 51: Screenshots *Joom, Viva Video, Gmail*
(Source: iTunes)[115,116,117]

Creating a tutorial

While Augmentation is fine for guiding users' eyes, it cannot provide explanatory guidance. To help users to understand your in-app footage, you require other techniques.

A simple way is to create a tutorial style screenshot. Add animated hands or fingers that indicate how to use the app. The app owners of *WordWhizzle* did so to demonstrate how to play the game.

If you are willing to invest more effort, present real people using your app. For example, a screenshot by *Google Translate* shows a user pointing his device at a street sign. The in-app footage displays the translated sign to illustrate the outcome of this action.

A person is not needed to create a tutorial, though. The screenshot by *Air Key* manages to do it with in-app footage embedded in a device frame and a background picture of a door. The app can open or lock this door. A WiFi symbol clarifies this function.

Fig. 52: Screenshots *WordWhizzle, Google Translate, AirKey*
(Source: Google Play, iTunes)[118,119,120]

The use of some apps is not limited to tapping and swiping on the phone. If people use your app in a unique way, show it. The makers of *Heads up* present a girl playing the game with her phone, without even showing how the app looks like.

The designers of *Fender Play* use a similar approach. They display a student learning to play the guitar with their app. Although a device with in-app footage is in the picture, it is too small to recognize anything on its screen. Obviously, the screenshot's purpose is not to show what the app looks like, but how people use it in real life.

One screenshot of *Pillow: Smart sleep tracking* takes this idea one step further. It lacks not only in-app footage; it does not even display a device. It only shows happy people in a bed and nothing more.

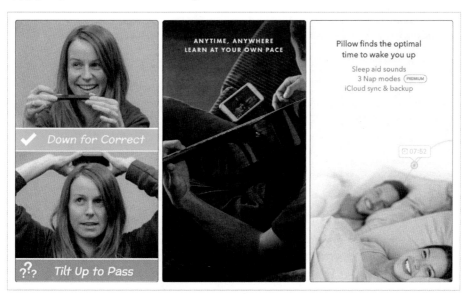

Fig. 53: Screenshots *Heads Up, Fender Play, Pillow*
(Source: iTunes)[121,122,123]

Telling a Story with Screenshots

Until now we have investigated single screenshots. To make the most out of your product page, we need to look at the bigger picture now. Let us analyze how screenshots work together as a set.

Have a second look at the *Pillow* screenshot. When users see it disconnected from the other metadata, it will probably not make much sense to them. Without a device and in-app footage, the image is neither relevant to user problems nor does it help to explain the app. Most viewers will not even relate it to an app. But when put in context with the other screenshots, it does make sense. It fits into the story which connects them. While the other screenshots explain the app's function, our example shot promotes its outcome: People sleep well and feel better. The context of the story is the key to understanding this screenshot.

What is true for *Pillow* is also valid for other apps. Creating explanatory guidance is easier if all screenshots fit into a story, which connects them and creates a coherent experience.

A good example of a well-crafted story is the screenshot set by *Uber*. The app helps users to find private drivers. From the table on page 81 you can see that a Transaction Story is the best choice for this purpose.

Accordingly, the screenshot set presents the app's features in the order that matches the user journey. It starts with selecting a destination and learning about the prices. Then it proceeds to introducing the driver and finally shows the payment process. The screenshots illustrate all the steps, from the user need to the final result of using the app.

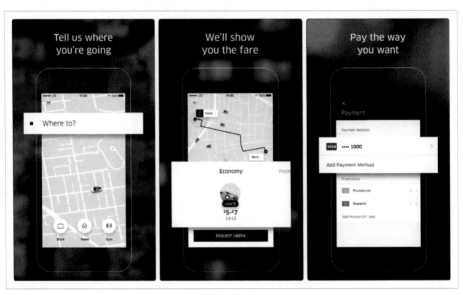

Fig. 54: Screenshots *Uber*
(Source: iTunes)[124]

By the way, have you noticed how the Augmentation technique supports this story? All elements crucial to the explained features are popped off the screenshots. Keep that in mind: Augmentation helps to clarify how a single screenshot fits into the overall story.

For games, story-telling is extraordinarily important. Remember when we discussed the game *Grow: Empire Rome* (page 100)? I pointed out how their app description tells an emotionally loaded Progression Story. It makes sense to create the same type of story for screenshots. Visualize players' progress to do so. Here is an example, taken from *Tribal Wars*, a massive multi-player strategy game. First, the screenshots present the start: the founding of a tribe. They then show the recruitment of an army and finally users' desired result: conquering enemy bases and defeating their troops. An even better way to emphasize the progression in a game is to show content from different stages. For example, you could show a low-level settlement in comparison to an endgame fortress.

Fig. 55: Screenshots *Tribal Wars*
(Source: iTunes)[125]

Adding Captions

So far we have discussed a couple of techniques to provide guidance. We have not talked about one of the most common ways to do so: adding captions. For a screenshot, text elements are often necessary to ensure users understand its content.

Have another look at the *Uber* creatives (page 136). The captions in each screenshot explain the highlighted function. They make sure that users understand what they see.

Captions can also create relevance. Sometimes the connection between the user problem and in-app footage is not obvious. With a few simple words, you can create this connection. Users who search for a keyword and then see it in a screenshot will instantly feel assured of an app's relevance to their problem.

On iOS, two to three screenshots show up in search results. Their captions can address users very early in their decision-making process. Thus you should implement your most relevant keywords into the gallery shots. Usually, long-tail keywords are better picks than single terms, because they are more relevant.

Remember, your app must rank well for a keyword for this term to drive users to your product page. Thus it makes no sense to include keywords for which your app ranks poorly in your captions.

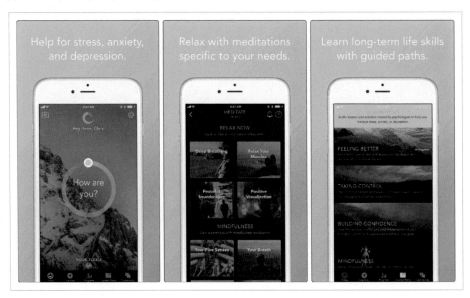

Fig. 56: Screenshots *Pacifica*
(Source: iTunes)[126]

Let us have a look at the screenshots of *Pacifica for Stress & Anxiety*. Their captions emphasize the app's Progression Story. They point to the initial user problems, explain the solutions, and promote the result of using the app.

Caption Length

A critical aspect of captions is their length. According to the KISS concept, captions must be short and understandable (see page 83). Avoid long, bulky phrases, and use only one to four relevant terms. It might be difficult to explain a screenshot with so few words. Still, stick to short captions. Besides simplicity, caption size is crucial. Space in screenshots is limited, and long phrases would force you to reduce the font size. That would make it harder for users to read your captions. Remember that in iTunes SERPs, people see up to three screenshots at a reduced scale. Make your captions readable at this size.

Fig. 57: SERP Screenshots *uSwitch*
(Source: iTunes)

The designers of *uSwitch: Switching Made Simple*[127] included a lot of keywords into their first two screenshots: "Energy bills", "save", "SIM", "broadband package", "deals", "credit card". They promote the app's outcomes and its USPs.

But the font size of their captions is too small. To fit all the words into the screenshots, the designers had to scale them down massively. As a result, the captions cannot unfold their full relevance, because they are not legible. With fewer words, they could have been enlarged to create a better experience.

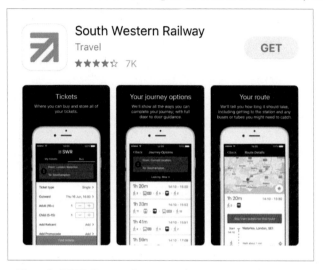

Fig. 58: SERP Screenshots *South Western Railway* (Source: iTunes)

Fig. 59: SERP Screenshots *Budget Planner* (Source: iTunes)

The screenshots of *South Western Railway*[128] are even worse. The makers put up to 25 words into them, and most do not even qualify as keywords. On the SERP they are absolutely unreadable because of their size.

An excellent example for meaningful yet short captions is *Budget Planner – Control your Finance*[129]. With only three to four words each, the screenshots present the app's main functions accurately. And all wordings are perfectly legible on the SERP.

Self-explanatory Pictograms

As mentioned before, it might not be easy to explain screenshots with few words. If you struggle, think about inserting self-explanatory symbols. Simple pictograms can replace words without reducing guidance or relevance.

Look at the example from *Takeaway.com*, a food delivery platform. The symbols complement the captions superbly. Some of them would do the job even without the text components.

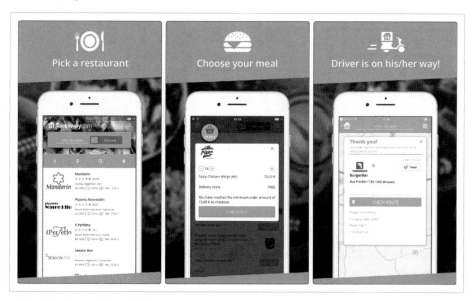

Fig. 60: Screenshots *TakeAway.com*
(Source: iTunes)[130]

Readability

Besides the font size, you must take care of contrast. Make sure that the colors of the captions and the backgrounds create good contrast. Otherwise, users will have a hard time reading them.

Here is a bad example: The white text in the screenshot of *Butt & Leg 101 Fitness* is almost invisible. The background is too bright to create a good contrast.

For *Audio Book – Free Audio Books Player*, the situation is similar. The white fonts on the yellow-green background are a pain in the eye and hard to read.

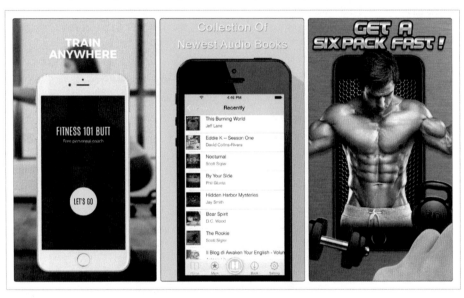

Fig. 61: Screenshots *Fitness 101, AudioBook, Ab Exercise Trainer HD* (Source: iTunes)[131,132,133]

You might have committed yourself to a color (for instance because of your company's corporate identity) that does not create great contrast. In this case, here are two solutions to improve readability:

Outline captions. In the screenshots of *Ab Exercise Trainer HD*, the captions have a similar color to the background. Nevertheless, they are perfectly readable because they have a black outline.

Alternatively, you can add a unicolor layer under the text to achieve the same goal. This technique is particularly useful if your background is a photo with an uneasy motif. Check the iPad screenshots of *Raw Food Diet Free* as an example of this layer technique.

Fig. 62: Screenshot *Raw Food Diet Free*
(Source: iTunes)[134]

Adding Background Art

Until now, we have focused on options to manipulate the foreground of screenshots. Our goal was to improve guidance and relevance. When appropriately designed, screenshots' backgrounds can do the same. And of course, they can make screenshots more beautiful.

Unicolor Backgrounds

Many designers use unicolor backgrounds, sometimes with a color gradient, for their screenshots. While some take plain white or light gray, others prefer more attention-grabbing colors.

Shpock, an app for classified ads, uses green as their background color. It is the same color that they use for their app icon. If your company has a specific corporate color, that is a reasonable approach. Using a corporate color for screenshot backgrounds can help to build brand awareness among potential users.

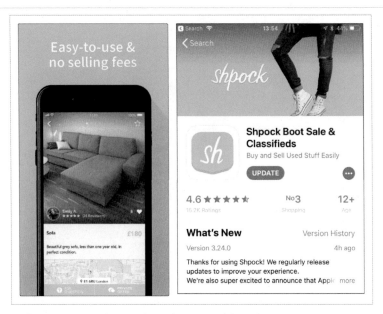

Fig. 63: Screenshot and Product Page *Shpock*
(Source: iTunes)[135]

The developers of *Unit Converter* use a different background color for each screenshot. Their colorful screenshot set stands out against competitors who follow the unicolor approach. In this case, the background colors also roughly match the navigation menu's colors in the in-app footage. In combination with the app icon, the screenshots form a congruent color scheme.

Fig. 64: Screenshots and Icon *Unit Converter*
(Source: Google Play)[136]

Background Photos

Instead of a unicolor or color-gradient background, you can also use a photo. A photo increases a screenshot's beauty massively. But the right motif also contributes to relevance.

Photo backgrounds are popular in particular for food and travel apps. Check the screenshots by *World Explorer – Travel guide*. Nice weather, beautiful land-scapes, and sightseeing places—that is what travelers desire. Don't you feel like getting onto the plane and heading toward the Caribbean when watching it?

The sunset picture in *World Explorer*'s screenshot is sharp and high-resolution. It is also a common technique to blur background photos. Blurred backgrounds do not distract the viewer from the motifs in the foreground. Here is a smart yet simple example: The makers of *10 Day UK Weather forecast* use a blurred version of the in-app footage for the background.

The screenshot of *Google Earth* is similar. It shows the same motif as in the in-app footage but from another angle.

Fig. 65: Screenshots *World Explorer, 10 Day Weather forecast, Google Earth* (Source: iTunes)[137,138,139]

The Connected Style

We learned that a great story spans across your entire screenshot set. So it is reasonable to set background arts in context to each other as well.

The Connected Style is a great way to do so. This technique is about creating background arts that merge into each other. When screenshots are viewed next to each other, their backgrounds appear to be one big picture.

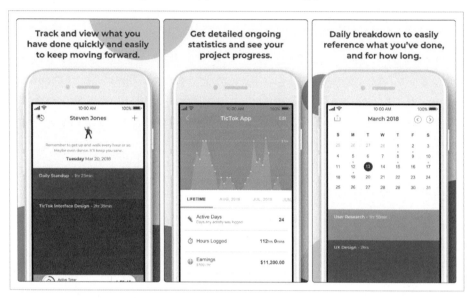

Fig. 66: Screenshots *TicTok*
(Source: iTunes)[140]

Look at the screenshots of the productivity app *TicTok*. A simple pattern with colorful bubbles creates the connected background. Although the design is simple, it is much more beautiful than a unicolor background would be.

The artwork of the photo editing app *Airbrush* is a bit more complex. The colorful backgrounds match the app's purpose well. To support the experience, the designers use animated instead of realistic device frames. Their transparency allows viewers to see more of the background art.

You can also combine the Connected Style with background photos. High resolution, as well as blurred versions, work well in this context. The product page of *Out of milk* shows a picture of cookies to connect its screenshots.

Fig. 67: Screenshots *AirBrush*
(Source: Google Play)[141]

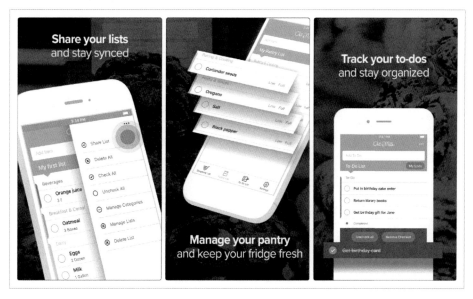

Fig. 68: Screenshots *Out of Milk*
(Source: iTunes)[142]

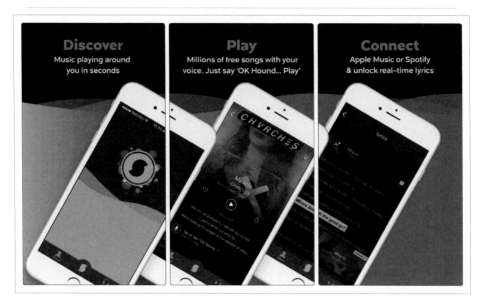

Fig. 69: Screenshots *Soundhound*
(Source: iTunes)[143]

The Connected Style is not limited to the background. You can also use it for foreground elements or for both the foreground and the background. The app *Soundhound* helps users to identify song titles and artists. Across their screenshots, they fragment the devices to create a connected foreground.

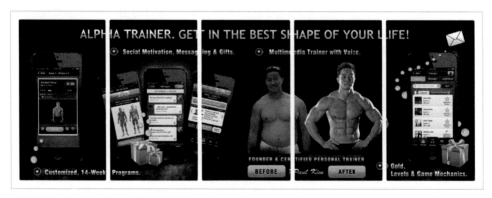

Fig. 70: Screenshots *Alpha Trainer*
(Source: iTunes)[144]

The owners of the fitness app *Alpha Trainer* pushed the Connected Style to the limits. They not only fragmented the background picture and devices across the screenshots, they did the same with the captions. The set as a whole is a great visual experience that stands out against competitors. However, when viewed alone, the screenshots make little sense. They might even confuse users because they do not contain enough content to deliver a reasonable message.

To minimize this risk, better go for a middle way: Design screenshots that make sense when viewed alone but also connect to each other in the gallery.

The designers of *Lose It! – Calorie Counter* did it right. They fragmented the background art as well as the devices with the in-app footage across their screenshots. But every single creative contains enough content to deliver a clear message.

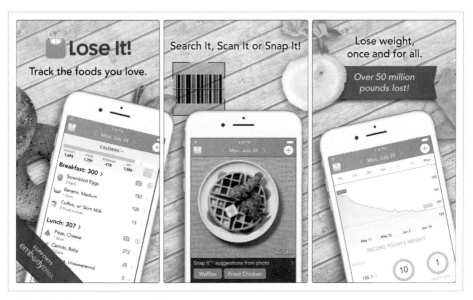

Fig. 71: Screenshots *Lose It!*
(Source: iTunes)[145]

Screenshots' Branding Power

To introduce your brand in your screenshots, you can use different measures. You already know one: using your corporate colors in backgrounds or caption fonts. This approach only works for companies that are already well-known in their niche, though. As a newcomer, you need a more aggressive way to push your brand into the memory of potential customers.

Presenting your Logo

The straightforward way is to implement your brand's (or company's) logo into screenshots. Many game publishers follow this approach. Xyrality, a German games company, is one of them. All screenshots for their strategy games *Celtic Tribes* and *Lords & Knights* show the game logos. Users face them no matter which creative they see. If you choose this way, make sure to not cover any crucial element of the in-app footage, though. Also, your logo must be big enough to be legible. For the screenshots of *Lords & Knights*, this is not given. It is too small and barely legible.

Fig. 72: Screenshots *Celtic Tribes, Lords & Knights, Amazon* (Source: iTunes)[146,147,148]

For some screenshots, it is not necessary to add logos, because the in-app footage already contains them. The *Amazon* app is one of them. Their logo is part of the upper navigation menu. Thus it is visible in most of their screenshots. If you have a memorable logo, consider implementing it into your app design. This technique has a significant advantage: Your in-app footage will do the branding work for you, no matter how you design the screenshots.

Mascots and Testimonials

Another way to increase users' awareness of your brand is a character that is associated with your app. Many developers use their game's main character for this purpose. Check the game *Doodle Jump* for example. Its hero, the Doodler, is present in every single screenshot.

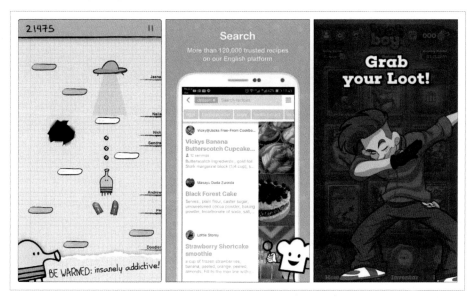

Fig. 73: Screenshots *Doodle Jump, Cookpad, Lootboy*
(Source: iTunes, Google Play)[149,150,151]

But non-gaming apps use cartoon characters too. *Cookpad* is one of them. In their screenshots, you see a little chef-hat that presents the content with various gestures. Another example for this approach is the app *LootBoy – Grab your loot*. Their character is present in all screenshots and the app icon as well.

An even better testimonial than a cartoon character is a real celebrity. As mentioned in the chapter about ratings and reviews (page 85), famous experts are a great form of Social Proof. Testimonials work for all kind of apps: The football legends Gareth Bale and Sergio Ramos represent the game *Real Madrid Fantasy Manager*, Blogger Kevin Curry supports *FitMenCook*, and the training app *Sweat: Kayla Itsines* is endorsed by the fitness model, who lends her name to it.

Fig. 74: Screenshots *Real Madrid Fantasy Manager, FitMenCook, Sweat* (Source: iTunes)[152,153,154]

For a new app without a track record of success, it is unlikely to find a celebrity who agrees to promote it. However, keep this idea in mind for later. As soon as your app makes some noise in your niche market, chances to find a testimonial expert will rise.

Remember the KISS Principle

Adding logos or characters can overload a screenshot and make it confusing for viewers. All the techniques we have discussed carry this risk. Have another look at the *LootBoy* screenshots on the previous page. Their character is very dominant—too dominant in my opinion. It is hard to distinguish between in-app footage and added artwork. Thus viewers do not get a real preview of the app's look. It is also not obvious what the app does. Ask yourself: Can you—without any knowledge of the German language—say what it is about? For me, it was not evident at first glance, although I am a native speaker.

When too many elements distract users, they might not get your actual message. Do not make this mistake. Branding is important and necessary. But it should not take users' entire attention away from the in-app footage.

Branding Screenshots

To avoid overloading feature screenshots with logos or characters, you can bundle your branding efforts in just one dedicated screenshot. A branding screenshot for this purpose should not contain in-app footage. Instead, present only branding assets like the app logo and title.

These elements must be perfectly recognizable on the product page and on SERPs. For this purpose, the branding screenshot has to be the first in your gallery's order. Reserve at least one third of its space for logo and app title. Also, make sure that branding assets and backgrounds provide proper contrast.

Use the remaining space for other elements that are associated with your brand. Use recognizable characters like the three warriors in the branding screenshot of the game *Battle Hordes*. In combination with the background art, they show the app's exciting and challenging mood greatly.

Fig. 75: Screenshots *Battle Hordes, Sports Direct, Dezide+*
(Source: iTunes, Google Play)[155,156,157]

If you do not have a recognizable character, you can also go for additional text elements. The designers of *Sports Direct* implemented a CTA to state their central value proposition: "Access over 800 brands from the palm of your hand." Although the general approach is right, this is not the best example. Both the logo and the claim are too small to be legible on the SERP. The designers could have avoided this mistake, because there is plenty of space left, which should have been used to scale up both the logo and the CTA.

I suggest giving your app name more space than *Sports Direct* does. Use only one extra phrase, either the marketing CTA or Social Proof. Make sure that all elements are big enough to be readable.

The app owners of *Productivity Helper Dezide+* did it better. Both their logo and their marketing claim are written in big fonts and are readable on the SERP.

Promotion Screenshots

There is another kind of screenshot that works without in-app footage: the promotion screenshot. Its purpose is to communicate general marketing messages. These include, for example, temporary promotions such as special offers and discounts. Below you can see a promotion screenshot by the app *Mollie Makes*. In their screenshot, they announce a limited time trial subscription for their magazine.

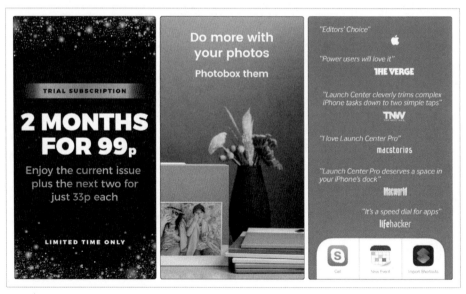

Fig. 76: Screenshots *Mollie Makes, Photobox, Launch Center Pro* (Source: iTunes)[158,159,160]

Promotion screenshots are also an excellent way to spread your value proposition more prominently. *Photobox* dedicates one screenshot to their marketing slogan "Do more with your photos."

Finally, you can transport all kind of Social Proof via promotion screenshots. *Launch Center Pro* does so by presenting press coverage. Besides awards, you can also name awards you won or mention your app's average rating.

Screenshot Analysis

After discussing many single techniques to manipulate screenshots, let us see how they work together. We will analyze two screenshot sets from the finance and gaming categories.

Example A: Fudget

Fudget: Budget Planner Tracker is an iOS app for managing personal finances. Their product page contains five screenshots.

The first two form a connected picture. They present a device with in-app footage and a lot of Social Proof. Besides the number of users and the average rating, they show a list of media outlets that featured the app in the past. The captions' core messages are set in orange, making them stand out and helping users notice them right away. As the text elements have no relevance to the in-app footage, the first two screenshots have a promotional character.

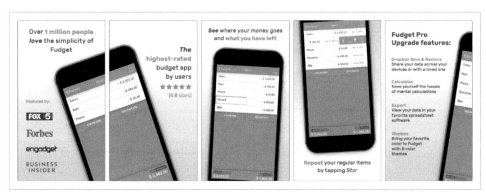

Fig. 77: Screenshots *Fudget: Budget Planner Tracker*
(Source: iTunes)[161]

The screenshots No. 3, 4, and 5 are feature screenshots. They present different aspects of the app. The in-app footage is very similar to the footage shown in the promotions screenshots. Actually, it is almost the same. Still, the set does not look boring. The reason is the use of different device orientations.

The third screenshot focuses broadly on the outcome of the app, while the fourth emphasizes a convenience feature. Note how the color gradient is reversed for the latter. This change ensures that the caption stands on a white background to produce a good contrast.

The fifth screenshot points out the advantages of the app's pro version. It includes tons of text elements that promote several paid features. For this purpose, the designers cut off the device, so only about 25% of it is visible. For the first or second screenshot, this design would not work because the captions are too small to be readable on the SERP. But as the fifth screenshot appears only on the product page, users always see a scaled up version of it. Thus the amount of text is acceptable in this case. Besides, people who view it already have a decent level of interest in the app. For those reasons, providing massively concentrated information in the last screenshot makes sense.

Across all screenshots, the color scheme is consistent. The color gradient of the background looks good in combination with the dark orange in-app footage. Furthermore, it has a good contrast to the caption colors. The highlights in the captions have the same orange tone as the in-app footage. They fit great into the screenshots' color scheme. The only drawback is the reversed color gradient in screenshot No. 4. As I said, it is necessary for the contrast, but it breaks the overall background design of the set.

The *Fudget* app looks rather dull and has few interesting functions to present. But their product page is an excellent example of how to create a diversified screenshot set. Various device orientations and the caption color highlights create a decent visual experience. Furthermore, the consistent color scheme has the potential to develop branding effects.

The connected promotion screenshots are a good pick. On SERPs, the design in combination with the Social Proof is capable of attracting users.

The order of the other screenshots is fine, too. By presenting the basic functions first and the pro features at the end, the set tells a reasonable Complexity Story.

Example B: Battleships – Blood & Sea

The second set we want to analyze belongs to the strategy game *Battleships – Blood & Sea*. Their screenshots are interesting for a couple of reasons.

Fig. 78: Screenshots *Battleships – Blood & Sea*
(Source: Google Play)[162]

First, all of them are consistently branded with the game's logo in the upper right corner. It is not 100% readable, though. Especially the "Blood & Sea" part is tiny. But the logo is unique enough to be recognizable to potential players.

Second, the screenshots are in portrait mode, but the in-app footage is in landscape orientation. The problem with this approach is obvious: The designers had to scale down the in-app footage to make it fit. On the SERP, it is almost impossible to recognize it. Even when zoomed in, it is hard to get all the details.

Third, the in-app footage is not the foreground layer of the screenshots. Decorative elements like the battleships and the airplane overlie it. The same is true for the branding elements such as the logo and the character portraits. Only the background art lies behind the in-app footage. Why is that? Well, the in-app graphics are of rather low quality. They are not really ugly, but they are not beautiful either. In contrast, the high-detail warships look impressive. They are presented in action, with explosions and waves breaking against the hulls. This scenery makes the screenshots much more exciting and beautiful for viewers. I guess you could say that it distracts viewers from the low-quality in-app footage on purpose.

Fourth, the captions are gigantic. In contrast to the in-app footage, they are perfectly readable wherever the screenshots appear. Also, their metallic look matches the warship theme. The orange glow and the flying sparks complete the action-packed scenery.

The order of the screenshots is irritating, though. For a strategy game, a Progression Story would make sense, and the motifs fit this story type. Unfortunately, the order of screenshots does not match it. A proper arrangement would be:

1. Start Your Conquest

2. Steel Real Warships

3. Develop Your Warship Empire

4. 9 vs 9 Ocean Conquest

5. Experience Classic Battles

Let us conclude. The screenshots of *Battleships* manage to create a great mood matching the app's theme. They distract from the in-app footage, which is not capable of exciting users. This approach comes with the risk of disappointing users who play the game.

Nevertheless, the screenshots are well-designed and provide a good experience. If they were ordered properly, this experience would be even better, though.

Step-by-Step: Designing Screenshots

Alright, so you know the different techniques to improve screenshots. Now it is time to create your own set. As screenshots must meet requirements in terms of size and orientation, let us have a quick look at them.

Screenshot Sizes

On iTunes, you must upload screenshots for the iPhone 8 Plus in 1080x1920 (or 1920x1080) pixels; otherwise you cannot publish your app. In addition, you can provide up to eight device-specific sets for various iPhone and iPad models. These sets will be shown only to people who use the matching device. On the next page, you can find a table with the different sets and sizes.

Device	Screensize	Portrait Dimension (px)	Landscape Dimensions (px)
iPhone 6+/7+/8+	5.5 inch	1080 x 1920	1920 x 1080
iPhone 6 / 7 / 8	4.7 inch	750 x 1334	1334 x 750
iPhone 5	4.0 inch	640 x 1136	1136 x 640
iPhone 4	3.5 inch	640 x 960	960 x 640
iPhone X / Xs	5.8 inch	1125 x 2436	2436 x 1125
iPhone Xs Max / XR	6.5 inch	1242 x 2688	2688 x 1242
iPad Pro 2nd Gen.	12.9 inch	1200 x 1600	1600 x 1200
iPad Pro	10.5 inch	2048 x 2732	2732 x 2048
iPad	9.7 inch	2048 x 2732	2732 x 2048

Tab. 9: Screenshot Dimensions on iTunes
(Source: adapted from StoreMaven Academy 2018)[163]

In the *iTunes Media Manager*, you can simply check the box "use 5.5-Inch Display" to scale down the 1080x1920 creatives to match the sizes for the other devices. The iPhone X is the exception because it has other width-to-height-relations (886x1920 or 1920x886). For this model (and its variations), you need to create individual screenshot sets.

If you have an optimized iPad version of your app, you need screenshots in the matching format as well. Upload them for the 12.9-inch iPad and check the "use 12.9-Inch Display" box for the smaller iPad models. If you own a universal app that works on iPhone and iPad, you can pass on tablet screenshots if you do not want to invest the extra time.

Again, you can create individual sets for every phone type. In some cases, in-app footage looks different because of the size and shape of the devices' screens. More or less content can be viewable, or the navigation items might differ in size. In these cases, creating specific screenshot sets is useful, because it delivers a more honest preview. It comes with a lot of extra work, though.

On Google Play, you have more freedom in terms of size. Screenshots have to be between 320 and 3,840 pixels high. The same goes for their width. Within these limits, you are free to choose any size.

You can upload up to three sets: one for phones, one for 7-inch tablets, and one for 10-inch tablets. Only the first is mandatory. The two extra sets for tablets make sense if you have an optimized app version for these devices. If not, feel free to omit them.

Device Orientation

When you programmed your app, you had to make a decision about its orientation. You had three options to choose from: portrait mode, landscape mode or a flexible app that adjusts to both orientations, depending on the user behavior. For your screenshots, you have to make a similar decision. But this time the flexible version is no option, so you have to pick either portrait or landscape mode.

The simplest way is to choose the screenshot orientation that matches your app's orientation. It is also the most common approach in the app stores. Its advantage is that it minimizes the risk of confusing users.

If your app has a flexible layout, you should choose depending on which orientation you consider better for the SERP.

If you pick portrait, users will see three screenshots on iPhone and two on iPad. This orientation gives you the chance to present more content at first glance.

For landscape, only one complete screenshot will be visible on the SERP. But its height will be the same as for portrait screenshots. That means it will scale up, which makes it easier for viewers to read captions and notice small details.

Use landscape screenshots for visually appealing apps with a lot of details, especially games. For apps whose in-app footage focuses on functionality rather than beauty, portrait screenshots are the better choice.

By no means should you mix different orientations. It looks terrible in the gallery and users will have to rotate their devices several times to watch all screenshots in close-up. If you are eager to see a bad example, check the gallery of *Chem Pro: Chemistry Tutor*[164] on the next page.

If you plan to add a preview video, this might be a changer for the question about screenshot orientation (see page 170).

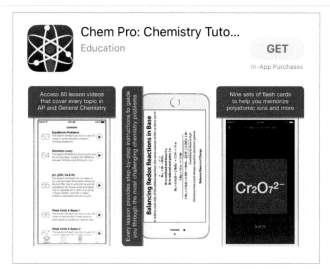

Fig. 79: SERP Screenshots Chem Pro
(Source: iTunes)

If 10 Screenshots are not enough

The mobile marketing company Moburst developed a smart strategy to maximize the space for content. They combined three portrait screenshots to one landscape creative. On SERPs, the user experience stays the same. And as the height for both orientations is the same, this approach does not harm the legibility.

The advantage is obvious: Developers can show the content of 30 portrait screenshots instead of only ten. Their space to present the app tripled. Have a look at the graphic on the next page to get a better understanding of this strategy.[165]

Go for this approach if the limit of ten portrait screenshots is not enough to show all the content you want to.

Another reason to follow this strategy is the length of captions. For complicated apps or features, four words might not be enough to explain them properly. In this case, use one-third of the landscape picture for your portrait screenshot (including the device frame). The rest of the space is for text elements.

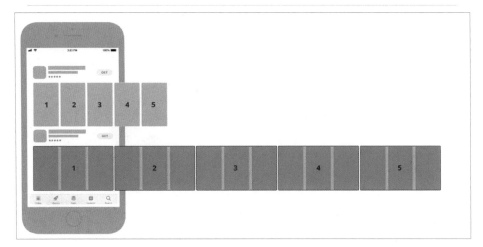

Fig. 80: Screenshot Orientations on the SERP
(Source: adapted from Bechar 2018)[166]

Step 1: Drafting a Story

Have you decided about device orientation? Great. Now develop a screenplay for your screenshot set. Write it down and draw rough drafts on paper.

First decide about the story you want to tell. It is perfectly reasonable to use the same one that you told in your description.

Decide which features you want to show. Base your decision on the importance of features. Also, take into consideration how unique they are. If your app has a useful function that your competitors do not have, prioritize showing it.

Choose the techniques which suit your story and your content best. Do you want to emphasize specific elements? Use partial devices or Augmentation. Does your app have social features or cross-platform functionalities? Consider multiple device screenshots. Do not overact though. There is no point in using techniques if they do not support your message, and sometimes less is more. Always remember the KISS principle.

Make your mind up about backgrounds. Can you use photos to support the subject of your app? Will connected backgrounds improve the user experience? Or will unicolor backgrounds do a better job? If so, which color is associated with the emotions that you want to create? Hint: You will learn about these associations in the bonus chapter about Color & Contrast (page 247).

Write down your captions. How many words do you need and how much space will they take? Again, keep it simple. Decide about caption colors and whether you need outlines or layers to provide a good contrast.

Determine how you can implement your brand into your screenshots. Where can you place your logo? Do you need a branding screenshot? Also consider a promotion screenshot with more text to highlight temporary offers.

Step 2: Preparing

Before capturing in-app footage, clean up your status bar. Close all notification alerts and disable Bluetooth and the vibration mode. Make sure that your battery is full and you have an excellent WiFi connection. A clean status bar simply looks better than a device in plane mode that is running low on battery.

Check the time. It is unlikely that productivity apps are used in the middle of the night. It makes sense to take screenshots at a time when people actually use the app. Or just reset the clock to this time.

I recommend taking one screenshot with a perfectly clean status bar, cutting it out and saving it, so you can copy and paste it into other screenshots later. In case users need to register themselves to use your app, prepare a test account with a neutral name. Pick a fake name, but not a ridiculous one. All content you want to present must be unlocked for this account. The last point is crucial if you wish to tell a Progression Story and compare content from different stages of the user journey.

If you want to use device frames, look up proper files on the Internet. Be aware, that the look of in-app footage can differ significantly depending on the device. For example, an HTC phone has different navigation elements than Samsung Galaxy devices. So look for mockups of the phone which you will actually use to capture the in-app footage.

Make sure all mockups are open PSD files. All elements (the device frame, reflections, shadows, etc.) must be single layers. Otherwise, you will not be able to manipulate the file afterward.

Browse for background art or pick up your camera and create it yourself. Check the section about graphics tools (page 277) to find sources for background photos as well as device frames.

Step 3: Creating In-App Footage

The next step is to create your in-app footage. Log in to the account you prepared and start shooting.

Depending on your device, the controls to do so vary. On iPhone 8 and older models you need to press the *Home* and *Standby* buttons at the same time. On the iPhone X, it is the button on the right side and the volume-up button. For Android devices, the shortcuts for creating screenshots differ from brand to brand. Look it up in the manual or ask Google if necessary.

Step 4: Editing

Now put together the single elements of your screenshots according to your drafts. First, replace the status bar with an optimized version (see step 2). Then insert the in-app footage into the device frames. Add captions and background art.

If you use professional graphics programs like Photoshop or GIMP, stick to these practices:

- Use an individual layer for every object (text element, logo, device frame, background art, in-app footage). Layers make it easier to rearrange or delete single elements. Also, it takes less time to create different localizations and test versions if you only need to replace one layer instead of the entire screenshot.

- Make sure to name all layers reasonably, so you recognize their content by their name. Use prefixes or suffixes that indicate their language (for example *en_* for English). If you delegate screenshot creation to a co-worker or an external partner, proper layer names will make your files more accessible for them.

Step 5: Exporting and Uploading the Screenshots

Export your final screenshots as JPEG files and upload them to the stores.

Make sure to use the right screenshots for each language. Double-check the set order after the upload is complete, especially when you use a connected design. Both iTunes and Google Play sometimes confuse the order of bulk uploads, so take special care.

Hit the Save button. Sounds obvious, but I admit, I forgot it once after uploading screenshots in more than 20 languages and five different sizes. Do not waste your time doing the upload twice as I did.

Chapter Summary

Congratulations, you made it to the end of the screenshot chapter. These are the key takeaways:

- Screenshots can raise users' interest and desire in your app and call them to action.
- The first two screenshots are the most important, because they also can attract attention.
- Before shooting in-app footage, clean your phone's status bar.
- The orientation of your screenshots should match your app's orientation.
- Never mix landscape and portrait orientation screenshots.
- Guide viewers' eyes with partial devices or Augmentation.
- Create a tutorial by showing people who use your app.
- Add background pictures that match the app category to beautify your screenshots and add relevance.
- Connect the fore- or background layers across your screenshots to support your story and beautify the set.
- Use highly relevant keywords to create on-point captions (four words max).
- Make sure captions are readable on product page and SERP (regarding size and contrast).
- Design branding screenshots without devices and in-app footage to introduce your brand. Use promotion screenshots for longer messages that are not related to in-app footage.

CHAPTER 11
THE APP PREVIEW VIDEO

Since 2014, app developers have been able to upload preview videos to their iOS product page. On Google Play, videos have been available even longer. Since then, they have become the most important visual creatives. About 25% of app store users consider videos crucial for their decision making.

Especially people younger than 25 value preview videos (15%). For men, they are more important than for women.[167]

Fig. 81: The Importance of Videos for Download Decisions
(Source: adapted from Koetsier 2018)[168]

According to StoreMaven, adding a video to your product page can increase the conversion rate by up to 35%.[169] One reason for this enormous potential is the fact that having preview videos still is not a matter of course. As of 2016, only 7% of all apps that rank in the top 150 for their category had a preview video on their product page.[170]

Clearly, these numbers are outdated, but many product pages still do not contain preview videos. So by adding a video to yours, your app will stand out against many competitors.

How Videos support the Three Columns

Videos have great potential to contribute to viewers' experience in terms of guidance, relevance, and beauty.

Guidance in Videos

Videos can tell your story in more detail than screenshots and in a more appealing way than the app description.

On iTunes, preview videos appear in the screenshot gallery. They take the first spots on the left, so screenshots are pushed to the right. In these prominent spots, preview videos can attract users' attention when appearing in search results. On devices that run iOS 11 (or a later version), they will start auto-playing as soon as they appear on the users' screens. So it is not even necessary that people engage with them actively. For that reason, the different components of the preview video can impact users in all stages of their decision-making process. We will discuss these components in more detail on the next pages.

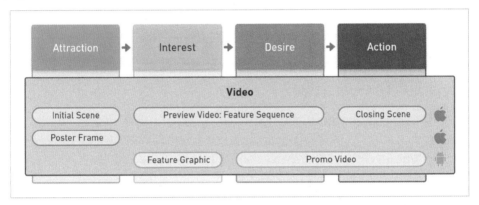

Fig. 82: Videos in the AIDA Funnel
(Source: Author's own illustration)

On Google Play, that is not the case. On the SERP, promotion videos are only visible if users do a brand search for the exact app name. But they will not appear in search results for generic keywords. For this reason, promotion videos cannot attract users' attention.

On product pages, videos show up in the first spot of the screenshot gallery, for both iOS and Android. So they catch visitors' eyes and have the potential to increase their interest as well as their desire to use the app. As Android users have to leave the product page to watch them, this ability is limited, though. In any case, videos can encourage viewers to take action and download the app.

Relevance in Videos

A video has great potential to connect your app to user needs. With moving pictures, you can emphasize this connection much better than with static texts or creatives. Besides, you can add a voiceover track to explain your app in more detail.

Beauty in Videos

In terms of beauty, videos have tremendous potential, as well. If your app has stunning graphics, you can show its beauty to its full extent. But even if it does not look extraordinary good, you have many options to create an engaging experience.

Guidelines for Video Content

Apple and Google both have rules for the content that you can show in your videos. They differ significantly, so we need to talk about them one by one.

Promotion Videos on Google Play

The promotion video on Google Play actually is a YouTube video. To add it to your product page, you place a link to its YouTube URL in the Google Play Console. The linked video may have a length of up to two minutes.

As its name says, the promotion video is primarily a marketing asset. Its purpose is to be both informative and entertaining. To serve this purpose, you are free to show whatever content you consider helpful. That includes in-app footage, people using your app or cinematic trailers. There is only one rule to follow: Your video must be appropriate for users of all ages.[171] So content including violence, nudity, vulgar language or harmful activities is not allowed. Check out the *YouTube Community Guidelines* for more details.[172]

Preview Videos on iTunes

On iOS, videos cannot be longer than 30 seconds. But you can upload up to three of them to your product page.

Besides the length restrictions, Apple has strict rules for content. Like for screenshots, the original idea behind preview videos was to present an honest experience of an app's look. Apple wanted them to be real previews and not just marketing proposals. This rule implied a strong focus on in-app footage, and Apple was very strict about it in the past.

The focus on an honest experience is still valid and vital. That is true especially for premium apps because users have no other chance to preview their look without paying for it.

Nowadays, Apple's guidelines are less strict, though. They encourage many design techniques that were forbidden in the past, for instance adding captions or voiceover tracks. But there are still some restrictions in place: Showing real people using the app or animated hands to indicate touch spots remains a no-go.[173] The same is true for cinematic trailers, at least in theory.

In practice, the enforcement of these guidelines is inconsistent. Many preview videos on iTunes violate the rules. So apparently, the approval or rejection of a video depends to a large degree on the reviewer's goodwill.

Let me be clear here: I am not encouraging you to break Apple's rules. But you can try to stretch them a little bit if it benefits the user experience. Just be prepared to have a version of your video ready that precisely follows the guidelines. In case Apple rejects your video, you can upload the backup version without losing too much time for adjustments.

How Videos affect Screenshots

When you add a preview video to your product page, the role of screenshots changes to some degree. Both are dependent on each other regarding content and orientation.

Redundant Content

When you add a video (and select its poster frame), some screenshots might become redundant.

For instance, if you use a branding poster frame, you do not need a branding screenshot. The same goes for promotion creatives. Instead, add more feature screenshots.

Also, do not duplicate the content related to features. Showing the same images and captions in videos and screenshots is boring to users. It is better to display different content.[174] So consider telling two stories instead of showing the same story twice. Pick one for your screenshots and another for your video. As the video offers more options to explain features, for instance a voiceover audio track, it makes sense to use it for introducing the most complex features.

Video Orientation is crucial

Besides the content, you need to take care of the orientation of screenshots and videos. For both, you can use either portrait or landscape orientation. Depending on how you combine them, you can create very different experiences.

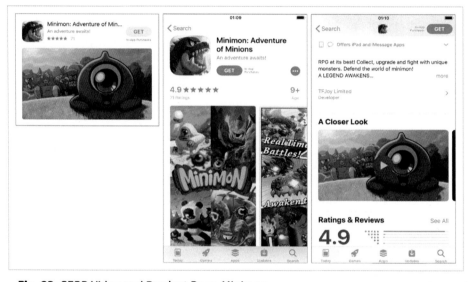

Fig. 83: SERP Video and Product Page *Minimon*
(Source: iTunes)[175]

Using the same orientation for videos and screenshots is the safe approach. Videos will simply integrate into the gallery. The only thing you have to consider is that one screenshot less will be visible on the SERP for every video you add.

When mixing orientations, the topic becomes more complicated.

If you combine a landscape video with portrait screenshots, something unexpected will happen: On your product page, the video will not appear in the screenshot gallery. Instead, a new section called *Closer Look* shows up between the app description and the reviews. Check out the product page of the game *Minimon: Adventure of Minions*, for example.

Another change is more interesting. On the SERP, users will only see the video. So the screenshots will have no chance to attract users' attention anymore. Consider carefully whether this behavior is beneficial for your app.

Under no circumstances should you combine portrait videos with landscape screenshots. Doing so creates a gallery in portrait orientation. But the screenshots will be rotated by 90 degrees—a very unpleasant experience for users. See an example from *Panzer Sturm* below.

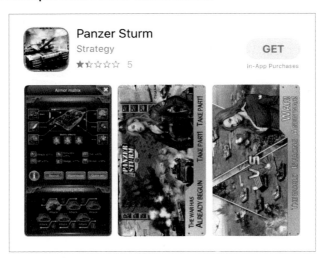

Fig. 84: SERP Video and Screenshots *Panzer Sturm* (Source: iTunes)[176]

The Preview Video's Structure

A video of 30 seconds on iOS (or two minutes on Google Play) gives you the chance to deliver a decent amount of information. But getting all this information across in the right way is a big challenge. In the area of social media, peoples' attention spans become shorter and shorter. On average, every five seconds after starting, about 10% of viewers quit watching a video. As a result, on iOS only 55% and on Google Play 45% watch preview videos until the end.[177]

You need to find a way to keep as many viewers as possible watching until the end. Otherwise, they will not receive all the information that you want to give them.

The solution to this problem is a proper video structure. As I said before, a video consists of various components that serve different purposes. Now it is time to have a closer look at these components:[178]

The fundamental component of each video is a *scene*. Scenes show an action at a specific time and place.

Scenes can include several *shots*. While all shots of a scene show the same action, the angles and fields of view differ.

Examples for different angles are:

- Low angle shots with the camera pointing up to the action.
- High angle shots with the camera pointing down.
- Eye level shots with the camera at the same level as the action.

Examples for fields of view are:

- Close-up shots that show details.
- Mid-range shots showing fewer details and more of the surrounding scenery.
- Long-range shots that present the entire scenery.

If the action progresses along multiple scenes, these scenes form a *sequence*. Sequences are narrative units that are connected by a continuity of time or location or both.

The following graphic illustrates the general structure of a video.

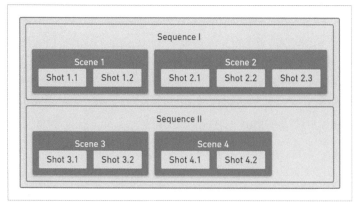

Fig. 85: Video Structure
(Source: Author's own illustration)

There is no best practice regarding the number of sequences, scenes, and shots per scene that works for all video types. They differ depending on the content and the emotions which the video shall create. Nevertheless, for an app preview of 30 seconds, a reasonable structure should include these components:

- An opening scene to attract attention.

- One or more sequences showing features to raise viewers' interest in and desire to use the app.

- A closing scene to call viewers to action.

- A poster frame to attract attention when the video does not auto-play on the SERP.

- Optional audio tracks can be applied to any part of the video.

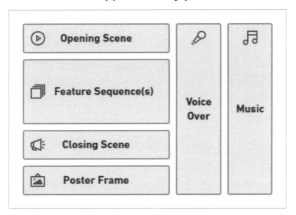

Fig. 86: Components of the Preview Video
(Source: Author's own illustration)

The Opening Scene

When users scroll down the SERP, the first three to five seconds of an auto-playing video are visible for them. This short segment is the opening scene. It is crucial for the success of every app preview for three reasons:

1. It is the part that attracts attention. If users scroll by and ignore the opening scene, the chance to grab their attention is gone.

2. The opening scene can raise the interest of explorers (check page 25 for a definition). If it does, those users' attention spans will expand. They will stay to watch the rest of the video or visit your product page.

3. The opening scene can encourage decisive users to take immediate action. If it convinces them, they will download the app directly from the SERP.

For these reasons, the opening scene is as essential to the video as the first paragraph is to the app description.

To take advantage of its full potential, your opening scene must be compelling. It is more about emotions than about information. Thus it is not the place for in-depth technical details. Instead, you need to impress your audience with the most exciting or most beautiful content. Hammer your core message and your central value proposition into viewers' brains. Convince them of your app's relevance by showing material that is connected to their problems.

For example, the opening scene of *Skoove*[179] shows the phrase "The easiest way to learn piano," followed by a person playing the piano. It focuses on relevance. For viewers, it is immediately clear what the app is about.

The Feature Sequence

When the opening scene succeeds raising users' interest, they will watch the rest of your video. At this point, your agenda needs to change. It is time to turn down the emotional tone and get more factual. The purpose of the second part of your video is to transform viewers' interest into the desire to use your app. You need to explain your app and how it can help users.

But presenting random features without any causal connection would confuse users. Let us watch the preview video of *Bookly*[180], an app to track reading behavior. The video makers show different aspects of the app in random order. They go from the stats screen to the goals section and back. Then they scroll down the "I've read" section, back up and down again, showing the same content multiple times.

Can you identify any central theme or storyline in their video? I cannot. And I have no idea what the message behind the video is.

Avoid confusing viewers with mistakes like this. Like for the description and the screenshot set, tell a congruent story for the feature sequence. We talked about the different alternatives earlier (see page 78):

- Transaction Story

- Progression Story

- Complexity Story

No matter which of these story types you pick, your preview video must explain your app's main functions. Be precise about how to use them. Where screenshots can only deliver static extracts from the user experience, a video can display all the details. Leverage this advantage. Show the single actions users have to perform, as well as the consequences of these actions.

The following examples show how to apply different story types for a preview video.

The Transaction Story

The app *Where to?*[181] helps people to find nearby places to eat, shop or relax. Its video follows the user journey step-by-step. It starts with picking a category and selecting a location. Then it shows the photo and the review section where users can get information about a place. Finally, the video demonstrates how to navigate to this place. It is a perfect tutorial for using the app with a clear outcome at the end. Although there is no payment involved, the Transaction Story is an excellent fit for this app.

The Progression Story

The makers of the drawing app *Linea Sketch*[182] use a Progression Story for their video that demonstrates how to create a comic character. They start by drawing the outlines, then add more details and colors, and finally present the complete character.

The Complexity Story

As its name suggests, *Scientific Calculator*[183] is a calculator app. In its preview video, you can see very basic functions like fractions and percentage calculation in the beginning. Toward the end, the video shows more and more complex operations like the polynomial solver and the graphing calculator. The video follows a Complexity Story although the presentation of some convenience features like the handwriting function interrupts it temporarily.

The Closing Scene

By the end of the video, viewers should have an understanding of your app. Ideally, they are convinced that it solves their problems, and they want to test it now. But some users need a final push to hit the download button. The purpose of the closing scene is to provide this push. Its goal is to convert users' desire for your app into action.

The closing scene should be short. One or two seconds are enough. It should contain a CTA like "Download now". You can also go for a claim that adds some Social Proof such as:

- "Join our community of 1,000,000 users."
- "Challenge hundreds of thousands of players."
- "Choose from 5,000 products now."
- "Test the best-rated productivity app on Google Play."

Also, include branding elements such as the brand logo and the app name. If you have a mascot or testimonial, put it in the closing scene as well, given it does not overload it.

The Poster Frame

The poster frame is a frozen picture taken from the preview video. It is visible on the product page and the SERP, but only as long as the video does not start playing. That is the case if users disable the auto-play function in their iTunes settings.

As the preview video appears in the gallery, the poster frame works like a screenshot. Because of this prominent placement, it is critical. Its primary purpose is to gain viewers' attention. Think of it as an invite: "Look here and watch my video."

A case study by StoreMaven underlines the importance of poster frames: For Kabam, a Canadian games publisher, optimizing their poster frame resulted in a conversion rate boost of 66%.[184]

Choosing the Poster Frame

So how can you make a poster frame a good experience? Surely not in the way the designers of *7mind* tried it. There is nothing relevant or beautiful in their poster frame. It is almost empty. This frame will neither attract the attention of users nor will it increase their interest in the app.

Do it better. Be aware that you can select any shot from your video as your poster frame. After uploading your video, simply fast forward it to the scene of your choice and set it as the poster frame.

If you design your closing scene according to the recommendations above, it should contain a decent poster frame.

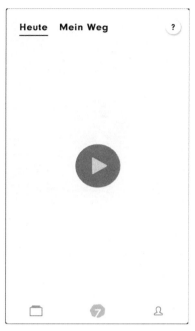

Fig. 87: Poster Frame *7mind* (Source: iTunes)[185]

Designing a new Poster Frame

In case no scene of your video qualifies as a poster frame, create a new one. Use a graphics program to design a static picture and add it into your video. When doing so, you have the same design options as for screenshots.

Branding poster frames without in-app footage are very common. They present the app's name, logo, mascot or testimonial. The poster frame of *TikTok* is a good example (see it on the next page).

Instead of a unicolor background, you can apply artwork or photos to beautify the poster frame. *ViewRanger* uses a nice picture of two hikers for this purpose.

You can also go for a promotion poster frame with your core marketing message like *Blinkist* does.

Social Proof is another alternative. And of course, you can mix this content with branding elements. Do you recall the video of *Where to?* that we discussed earlier (see page 175)? In their poster frame, they show quotes from media coverage about their app.

Fig. 88: Poster Frames *TikTok, ViewRanger, Blinkist*
(Source: iTunes)[186,187,188]

A great way to fit your poster frame into the gallery is the Connected Style. You can connect the poster frame to your screenshots like you connect screenshots to each other. *Mondly*, an app for learning languages, uses this approach.

Fig. 89: Poster Frame *Where To?* and Connected Poster Frame *Mondly*
(Source: iTunes)[189,190]

<u>Avoiding the Pitfalls</u>

When creating a poster frame, you will face some pitfalls. To avoid making mistakes, follow these guidelines:

- Too much content confuses viewers. So do not overload your poster frame. Keep it simple, so your audience gets the message.

- Make text elements readable in terms of size and contrast.

- Be aware, that the play button to start the preview video overlies your poster frame in the middle. If you place important content like your app logo in this spot, viewers cannot see it. *Tandem – Language Exchange* has this problem: The play button covers their logo. Recognizing it is hard. To avoid this issue, place your branding assets in the upper or lower third of the poster frame. Keep the middle section clean.

- In case you have more than one preview video, choose different poster frames for each of them. *Calzy 3* has very similar poster frames for their first two videos. That is a dull experience for users. It is better to create poster frames that differ from each other. For instance, consider a connected design with branding and promotional elements.

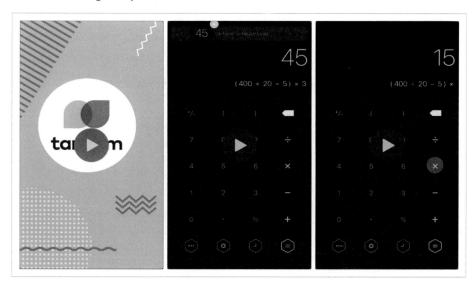

Fig. 90: Poster Frames *Tandem, Calzy 3*
(Source: iTunes)[191,192]

The Preview Video's Branding Power

A video offers plenty of options to introduce your brand. I already mentioned one of them: Showing your app logo and title in the closing scene, together with the CTA. This approach is reasonable. Viewers who watch the video until the end demonstrate a deep level of interest. If they liked it thus far, it is probable that they will remember your app after seeing the closing scene.

The problem with this approach is obvious. Only viewers who watch the entire video will see the branding assets. So does it make more sense to introduce your brand in the beginning instead?

Yes and no.

On the one hand, it makes sense to let people know who the messenger is before they perceive the message. That way, even someone who quits the video after a couple of seconds will see your logo and app name.

But on the other hand, the opening scene is crucial for catching viewers' attention. Only exciting content will spike their interest in the app and encourage them to keep watching. If they see a static picture of your app logo and name for three seconds, they will get bored rapidly.

So both approaches have advantages and disadvantages. If you want to enjoy the benefits of both and reduce the downside, go for a middle way:

Introduce your branding assets in the opening scene, but only very briefly. One second is enough. In the closing scene, present them again, but this time for longer. Showing your brand twice maximizes the chance that users keep it in mind. Have a look at the video by the dating app *Happn* for example.

If you do not want to waste time showing a steady scene, you can lay your branding elements over the in-app footage. Check the video of *Rodeo Stampede*. It starts with action scenes from the game right away. The logo overlies these scenes for a couple of seconds before it fades out.

Be aware that this approach is a bit risky. If the branding assets cover essential parts of the in-app footage, they can harm the story. So make sure that they are not too distracting.

Another reasonable approach is to show your logo during the entire video. Just put it in one of the four corners. Again, make sure it does not overlie any other important piece of in-app footage. Also take care about legibility. Logos with many details might be too small when scaled down.

The video editors of *Restaurant Dash – Gordon Ramsey* chose to present their logo very prominently. They put the in-app footage into a frame. Above that frame, they placed the app logo and the game's main character. They then added a red button with a CTA below the frame. For the purpose of branding, this approach is excellent.

This example video has a significant problem though: As the in-app footage is in landscape orientation, it had to be scaled down massively to fit into the portrait video. And at the new size, it is hard to recognize all the details. This combination of different orientations causes another issue: A lot of space was wasted, in particular around the app logo.

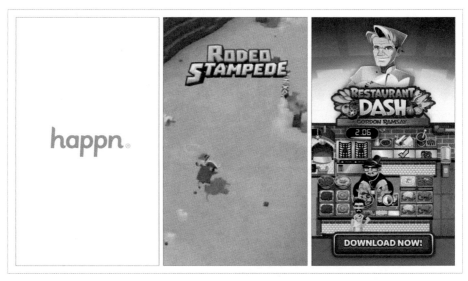

Fig. 91: Video-Screenshots of *Happn, Rodeo Stampede, Restaurant Dash* (Source: iTunes)[193,194,195]

It is smarter to choose a video orientation that matches the orientation of the in-app footage. Use landscape footage in landscape videos and portrait footage in portrait videos. Scale it down just a bit so you have enough space to create a framework including your branding assets.

Video Composition

Moving pictures offer more chances than static creatives, but they also carry a bigger risk of overwhelming users.

Screenshots can overwhelm users if they contain too much content in limited space. For videos the same is true. But in addition to the limited space, time is a crucial factor too.

Viewers have only a limited amount of time to gather the information they see in a video. Thus you need to orchestrate carefully which content pieces you show when and for how long.

In this context, you must consider three parameters: Speed, Pace, and Rhythm.

Parameter I: Speed

Speed refers to the number of events that are presented within a scene. These events include tabs, swipes, typing, and other user actions, but also content fading in, popping up or disappearing.

Here is an example for clarification: Let us say you want to record a scene demonstrating the search mechanism of a marketplace app. You type in a search term and filter the results by price, by the seller's location, and by the product color. In total, you have to perform at least six actions:

- Typing the keyword.
- Applying to start the search.
- Adjusting the filters (three times).
- Applying again.

Additionally, viewers will see two changes in the scenery:

- The SERP showing up after the first search.
- The SERP updating after applying the filters.

If you show these eight actions within 20 seconds, the speed of the scene will be very low. But if you choose to present the same procedure within only 3 seconds, the scene's speed will be extremely high.

Speed is crucial when it comes to making your video understandable. Every time something happens on the screen, people need a moment to process the new information in the context of the overall story. If too many actions happen at the same time (or in a short period of time), viewers might miss some of them. In the worst case, they do not understand the message at all and quit watching the video.

On the other hand, a lack of speed creates a dull experience. It can drive your audience away to something more interesting.

Thus it is essential to adjust the speed of every scene carefully. Every viewer must have the chance to recognize the relevant actions and yet feel engaged.

Let us compare a couple of example videos:

The video of the travel app *Flightscom – Cheap Flights & Airfare Search*[196] shows the process of booking a flight and a hotel. The video consists of only one scene. But in this scene, viewers can see much content fading in and out, including the search mask, various filters, and the SERPs for flights and hotels. Most of these elements appear for split seconds only. Viewers have way too little time to investigate them. Also, it is almost impossible to follow the actions. The reason is the lack of an action indicator that shows where the presenter tabs or swipes.

Now watch the preview of *Elk Travel Currency Converter*[197]. Its speed is much lower. Especially the scene with the exchange rate table for HDK to USD is timed terribly. For more than five seconds, nothing happens at all. At this point of the video, viewers might think that it is already over and quit.

My Scans PRO[198] does it better. Any time the scenery switches or a caption fades in, the action slows down. The viewer can gather all the new information and follow the course of events without problems. But the video never gets too boring, because after the short pause at a new scene's beginning, the action speeds up again.

Setting the Speed while Recording In-App Footage

You initially set the speed of your video when capturing your in-app footage. It is determined by the frequency of actions such as the number of tabs per second and the intensity of these actions.

You can, for instance, scroll down a list with one very powerful swipe that takes you right to the bottom. In this case, most users will identify only the first and the last elements in this list. The items between will not be readable because they disappear too fast. If you wanted to emphasize the variety of your app, that would be a problem. It would be better to perform multiple less intense swipes to allow users to read more of the list items. Watch a good example in the preview video of the cooking app *Hippie Lane*[199].

So before capturing your in-app footage, determine which details viewers have to see to understand the video's message. Make sure to emphasize these details with properly timed actions.

Increasing the Speed with Fast Motion

Although you set the speed while capturing in-app footage, you can alter it later, at least to some degree.

One way to do so is fast motion. In some apps, user journeys are very long. They include many time-consuming actions to get to the desired outcome. Showing this journey in real time would not only take too long for a video of 30 seconds, it would also bore viewers to death. By speeding up actions with fast motion, you can solve both of these problems: meeting the time limit and avoiding boredom.

An excellent example of this technique is the preview video of *Sim City BuildIt*[200]. The editors sped up several scenes to show how the virtual city changes over time while playing the game. In real time, this development would take too long, but speeding up makes it easier to tell the game's Progression Story. It also allows viewers to see more of the beautiful graphics.

Lowering the Speed with Slow Motion

The opposite of fast motion is slow motion. This technique is useful to reduce a scene's speed. Check the video of the racing game *Asphalt 9: Legends*[201]. When cars perform a stunt or are involved in a crash, the video slows down significantly for a couple of moments. This slow motion gives viewers more time to follow the action and enjoy the great visual effects.

In this particular case, the slow-motion shots are not the result of editing. Instead, they are part of the actual gameplay. Nevertheless, they are a great example of proper use of slow motion.

Parameter II: Pace

The interplay between different scenes (and shots) determines a video's pace. This refers to the number of scenes within a video.

A video of 30 seconds with 30 different scenes has a high pace. Most scenes will not display for more than one second. So viewers have only little time to get their content. If, in contrast, the video contained only three scenes, the average screen time would be about 10 seconds. The pace would be very low.

The number and length of the in-app scenes you initially shoot will define a framework for your video's pace. But you have many options to adjust it in the editing process. If you do it right, you will create an emotional setting that supports your message.

A high pace (many cuts and low screen time per scene) communicates thrill and excitement. It creates a dynamic and vital vibe. But if the pace is too high, it can also make a video hectic and hard to understand.

A low pace (few cuts and high screen time per scene) creates a relaxed and thoughtful atmosphere. A pace that is too low can be boring for viewers, though.[202]

The interplay of both speed and pace determines which of the possible effects sets it. Let us watch some more videos to understand the outcome of different combinations of speed and pace.

High Speed and High Pace

Hungry Shark World[203] shows a lot of action in its video. The player's character (the shark) eats different objects and causes explosions and other visual effects. Its actions add points to the score counter and text elements pop up (for instance "Health Critical" or "Good Doggo!"). Because of all these actions, the speed of the single scenes is high. And so is the video's pace. In about 15 seconds the viewer sees more than ten different scenes. The combination of high speed and high pace makes the video a thrilling and breath-taking experience.

<u>Low Speed and Low Pace</u>

The app preview of *Wildfulness 2 – Nature Sounds*[204] is the exact opposite. There is not much action going in the various scenes, so its speed is low. With 11 scenes in 26 seconds (including caption interstitials), the average screen time is about 2.5 seconds. For a video consisting of low-speed scenes, that is a rather low pace. The combination of both creates a calm and relaxing experience.

How to soften Extreme Compositions

Combining high pace and high speed or low pace and low speed creates extreme feelings. But going for these extremes always carries the risk of going one step too far. The difference between exciting and confusing is small, and so is the margin between relaxing and boring.

To reduce the risk of making your video a bad experience, mix high speed with low pace, or vice versa. A higher pace makes scenes with low speed more exciting and decreases the chance of boring people. On the other hand, lowering the pace of high-speed scenes prevents confusion by giving viewers more time to recognize all the content.

<u>High Speed with Low Pace</u>

Just like the *Hungry Shark World* video, the in-app scenes of *Thunderdogs*[205] contain a lot of action and visual effects. Their speed is very high. But the video contains only seven scenes (if we ignore the sequence showing several loot boxes at the end). Their average screen time is above three seconds. So the video's pace is relatively low in comparison to videos of other action games. The length of the single scenes gives users enough time to explore the content and read the captions. As a result, the overall experience is less hectic than the video of *Hungry Shark World*.

In general, low pace with high-speed scenes is a rare combination. But it is a suitable approach to show detailed in-app footage with a lot of action going on.

<u>Low Speed with High Pace</u>

Combining high pace with low-speed scenes is great to present an app's variety of features or products. Check out the video of *AirPano Travel Books*[206]. Focus on the sequence, that starts with the caption "50+ places." It shows a series of very short scenes with landscape motifs. These scenes are just static pictures, so there is no action going on at all. Their speed is zero. But as the sequence shows about 15 motifs in less than five seconds, its pace is extremely high.

The initial caption indicates that the purpose of this sequence is to show the app's variety. The sequence supports this message, although viewers are not able to identify the locations in the single scenes. In this case, it is only important that they can distinguish them, and the color contrast between the various landscapes enables them to do so.

Imagine each of the 15 motifs would show up for two seconds. The sequence would be dull to watch. But the high pace allows the editors of *AirPano* to present their low-speed content in an engaging form.

Parameter III: Rhythm

So far, we have looked at four steady combinations of speed and pace and the emotions they create. But it is not a must to keep the same combination from the first to the last second. Variations in speed and pace create a rhythm that raises emotions, builds tension, and creates moments of surprise.

Let me illustrate the concept of rhythm with the example of a speech. If a speaker talks in the same tonality and at the same speed, the audience will get bored quickly. His lecture will be much more exciting if he speaks faster, pauses, raises his voice or accentuates single words once in a while. These variations in tonality, speed, and volume create emotional spikes. And emotions help to keep the audience engaged. With rhythm in videos, it is the same.[207]

The video of *Iron Throne*[208] is an excellent example of an engaging rhythm. It starts with a long scene showing a dragon flying over the player's castle. Then, landscape shots demonstrate the impressive graphics of the game. The speed is rather low, and the pace is average.

The next sequence emphasizes the game's variety. It contains a mix of low-speed scenes showing the main characters. Each of them is presented only for split seconds, so the pace is very high.

Then the pace decreases again to introduce the battles. Viewers get slowly pulled into the action. At first, the settings are clear. A few soldiers prepare for battle and approach each other. In the following scenes, intensity increases, and the fights start. Visual effects emphasize the chaos on the battlefield. The cuts appear faster than before, and the average screen time per scene decreases. Finally, the video shows long shots of huge armies moving on burning maps. Dragons hover above them and spit fire. The action is so thrilling that it is hard to recognize every detail in the various battle scenes. That is not necessary though, because the main purpose of this section is to create emotions.

The *Iron Throne* video ends with a sword falling and the game logo—a big bang at the climax of the tension.

Playing with Expectations

Each segment in the *Iron Throne* video follows one of the four ways to combine speed and pace that we discussed earlier. And each of them is linked to a specific emotion. These patterns are common. For instance, many videos build tension by gradually increasing pace to end with a big bang, like our last example. Some viewers might recognize these patterns and expect a specific course of events following them.

You can play with this expectation to create even stronger emotions. If your video uses a familiar pattern but results in an unexpected climax, it will surprise viewers, and this surprise will create a bigger emotional spike than the expected ending. This experience will stick in people's minds, and it will increase the chances that they download your app, or at least remember your brand.

The video of *Donut County*[209] cleverly plays with viewers' emotions like this. In the beginning, it presents the basic gameplay by showing in-app footage and caption interstitials. Then the pace slowly increases; the cuts appear faster and faster. The in-game action gets more intense as well, and the sceneries become more impressive. The course of action indicates that the video moves toward a jaw-dropping climax. But the bang does not come. The video cuts to a very calm campfire scene with characters from the game having a snappy dialogue. Instead of the expected big bang action shot, the video ends with humor. Although this ending does not fit the expectation of viewers, it is an emotional spike, and it is even better because it comes by surprise.

How Repetition affects Pace

The video of *Donut County* has another interesting aspect. It repeats the interstitial containing the "Bigger" caption multiple times. Each time, it appears shorter than the last time. As it contains only one word, short screen times are reasonable anyway. But even for longer captions, the increasing pace would be fine. The reason is that viewers already know the wording and thus need less time to process it.

Keep that in mind: The more often you show the same motif or text element, the shorter you need to keep it on screen.

The right Rhythm for each Vertical

You may have noticed that most of the examples we have discussed in this chapter are games. Games are supposed to spike emotions and entertain people. Especially racing, action, strategy, and role-playing are genres that rely on thrill and tension to attract players. Thus an engaging rhythm is crucial for gaming videos.

That does not mean that other apps cannot spike emotions. But depending on your app's category, it makes more or less sense to aim for a video that creates extreme feelings.

For traveling, cooking, lifestyle, entertainment, music or sports, emotions are relevant. People are passionate about these hobbies, and apps need to add to their fun. Therefore, an engaging rhythm is crucial for a preview video in these categories. But information is equally important to communicate your app's benefits properly. So a preview video should be a well-balanced mix of both emotions and information.

In contrast, tools, finance or efficiency apps are not linked to strong emotions. The same goes for other apps that are used in a professional context. People expect that they will solve a problem, but they do not expect to be entertained. For these apps, varying speed or pace does not make much sense. So focus on explaining features rather than creating emotions. Fast motion to show complex features or high-paced segments to emphasize variety might be useful, though.

Cutting

For the feeling of a proper rhythm, the cuts between shots and scenes are a decisive factor. Bad cuts draw attention away from the story because they happen abruptly and are unexpected. A functional interplay between varied pace and speed can be destroyed by poor cutting. In contrast, good cuts feel natural, and they create a seamless experience. In the best case, viewers do not even notice that they happen.

Let us resume the example with our speaker again to explain cuts in more detail. In this context, cutting is comparable to changing topics. If the speaker explained one topic, but switched to another in the middle of a sentence, that would feel odd. This unpredictable change would leave the audience confused. The right way would be to finish the sentence and then make a logical transition to the next topic.[210]

There are many ways to lead from one shot to the next. You will learn about the most common techniques on the following pages.

Straight Cuts

When one scene suddenly ends and the other starts immediately, that is called a *straight cut*. The human brain is familiar with this abrupt form of transition because this is the way it processes visual input from the eyes. Nevertheless, straight cuts can be confusing if the new scenery is not distinguishable from the old. In any case, straight cuts create a feeling of immediacy and are a good match for high-paced videos.[211]

Jump Cuts

Jump cuts divide two shots in the same scene. Their views differ a bit because they are taken from a slightly different angle. Sometimes, the characters or objects in the scene have other positions, but the general scenery is similar. For that reason, these cuts appear like jumps forward in time. Jump cuts are a good technique to create a feeling of hecticness or nervousness.[212] They are great to show in-app footage from different stages of a game—a perfect match for Progression Stories.

In the preview video of *Dawn of Titans*[213], one scene shows the player's kingdom and its development. While the camera slowly flies over the region, four different shots appear successively. Each one shows more and bigger buildings. For transitions, the editors used jump cuts and created a time-lapse sequence.

The Dissolve

A *dissolve* describes the transition of one scene gradually fading into the next. During this transition, the scenes overlap for a moment and details of both are visible at the same time. The dissolve indicates a change of place, time or both. It is a good fit for low-paced videos that aim to relax the viewer.[214]

CSI: Hidden Crimes[215] uses the dissolve multiple times to cut between scenes. The game is about criminal investigations, which is a fascinating theme but usually not full of action. Thus the dissolve is a proper approach.

Fades

A *fade-out* (or *fade-in*) is a special form of the dissolve. In case of a fade-out, the scene fades to a one-color screen. A fade-in is the opposite with an initial uni-color screen that fades to a new scene. Both the fade-in and the fade-out are time-consuming cuts that slow down the pace of a video. So they are fine for low-tense videos, but not appropriate for sequences full of action.[216]

The video preview for *Apollo Justice Ace Attorney*[217] contains both variants of the fading technique. The initial scene fades out to a white screen and immediately fades back in, and the next scene starts. This unicolor extra screen makes the cut less hectic and clearer to users.

Wipes

Wipes are widespread cuts for changes of locations. The new scene replaces the old scene gradually in a geometric pattern. The contents of both scenes appear next to each other but never overlap. Think of it as a curtain with the new scene printed on it. The curtain gets pulled in front of the old scenery so that the replacement starts on the left side and progresses to the right (or vice versa). Wipes can also follow vertical (top-to-bottom), diagonal, circular or even more complex patterns.[218]

Horizontal wipes are used, for example, in the video of *Scanbot Scanner App*[219] to get from in-app footage to caption interstitials.

Adjusting the Cutting Technique to support Pace

Finding the right cut is vital to support a video's pace, its rhythm, and the emotions it creates.

A great example of the interplay between cutting and pace is *Blade Reborn*[220]. In the beginning, the video's pace is not very high. The first scenes show the graphics of different progression levels and introduce the main character. Dissolves are used for transitions. Then the action speeds up. The video shows battle scenes with multiple enemy fighters and impressive graphic effects. The more intense the action gets, the more the pace increases. To support this dynamic atmosphere, the editors switch from using dissolves to straight cuts.

For our next example, we will go into more detail. *Asphalt Xtreme*[221] is another racing game of the *Asphalt* series. Its initial scene shows the countdown to the race's start in three different shots. The camera moves around various cars waiting at the starting line. Besides the numbers counting down, there is no action at all. Note that the fades from and to a black screen are very smooth. The power of this intro lies in the expectation it creates. Every racing fan knows the countdown is the prelude to an event full of action and adrenalin. It is the calm before the storm. Because of this expectation, the initial scene builds up the tension, although both pace and speed are low.

The following sequence is much more thrilling. It shows racing scenes with high speed. The pace in this segment is variable though. Some scenes are visible just for split seconds, while others stay on the screen for up to three seconds. The straight cuts emphasize the action.

In the next sequence, the speed drops again. Four flyover shots show different scenes without any racing action. Viewers can relax for a moment and enjoy the beautiful graphics.

The third sequence begins with a mid-speed scene consisting of two long shots of the same car. Afterward, the speed increases rapidly. Racing scenes in close-up third-person style, overtaking maneuvers with multiple cars involved, breathtaking stunts, and weather effects draw the viewer in. At the same time, the pace rises. While the frequency of cuts increases, the screen time per scene goes down to split seconds. The transitions get more and more hectic. At the peak of this thrill, the video ends with a short slow-motion shot that dissolves to the poster frame with the app logo.

Let us recap the different changes of pace again:

- A smooth starting scene with low speed and low pace.
- Racing scenes with high speed and various pace.
- Scenery shots with low speed and low pace.
- Long shots of one single car, medium speed, low pace.
- Racing scenes full of action, high speed, very high pace.
- A slow motion shot dissolving to the poster frame.

The numerous changes in speed and race create an engaging rhythm that spikes viewers' emotions. This experience has excellent potential to stick in their minds and raise their desire to play the game.

Adding Captions

A couple of pages ago, we discussed the video preview of *Bookly* (page 174) and concluded that it is hard to understand the message its producers want to get across. While the main point of the critique was the confusing and repetitive order of content, the video has another problem: It does not contain any captions to explain the in-app footage.

Just like in screenshots, adding text to videos helps explain the content and creates guidance.

Apple encourages adding captions to your video. Their reason for doing so is the auto-play function, or more precisely the fact that videos auto-play in silent mode. Explaining the video content with voiceover is no help for auto-play viewers, but captions are.

Another reason for using captions is equally important: Captions add relevance. You have already read this in the chapter about screenshots, but as it is valid for videos too, let me repeat it: Users who see their keyword in your video after searching for it feel assured of your app's relevance for their problem. So captions with the right keywords will increase your conversion rate.

Reading Time

Text elements in videos come with a unique challenge that is connected to speed and pace. When you show text elements in a video, you must give viewers enough time to read them. But how much time is enough? To make a reasonable decision about this, we need to consider *reading time.*

A person who reads on a regular basis can gather between 200 and 250 words per minute. That equals three to four words per second. For unpracticed readers, it is even less.[222]

To make your captions readable for as many people as possible, go for the lower end. Give viewers at least one second reading time per three words. For instance, if you put a CTA of nine words into your video, it should be visible for three seconds or more.

As text elements drive viewers' attention away from your in-app footage, they are a form of distraction. In order to minimize distractions, you should try to keep text elements short. Three seconds of screen time for a caption of nine words would consume 10% of the video's length. That is too much. It is better to commit less time to text elements and show more in-app footage instead. Just like in screenshots, aim to use not more than two to four words per caption. In most cases, it is possible to explain the in-app footage with this small amount of words.

The length of captions also impacts pace. Committing much screen time to text elements will reduce it significantly. This might be harmful to the emotions you want to create. So you need to consider how captions change your video's rhythm and adjust them if necessary.

Ensuring Readability

Besides the screen time, the size and contrast of captions are crucial for readability. You must make sure that all text elements are big enough and have good contrast to the background, so users can read them easily before they disappear.

In general, you have two different options to implement captions into your video. You can lay them over the in-app footage of an existing scene. Or you can create a new interstitial scene reserved only for text.

Overlaying Feature Scenes

In the first case, you must pay special attention to where you place captions. Make sure text does not overlie essential elements of the in-app footage. For example, if you want to explain a specific function, do not cover the crucial navigation elements for this function.

For this approach, readability is the key. In-app footage is an uneasy background. Make sure to pick a caption color that provides a good contrast. Text outlines or one-color layers behind the text can help you. Check the correspondent section in the screenshot chapter for details (page 142).

Interstitial Scenes for Captions

The alternative is creating a new scene that consists only of the captions and a static background art.

An interstitial scene like that has some advantages. As in-app footage and text elements are separated from each other, viewers can focus on either one. No one element will distract viewers from the others. So you can determine precisely what people see at which time.

Furthermore, it is easy to make captions readable. As you can use the entire screen to scale your text, you are not limited regarding font size. You are also free to pick background art that provides great contrast.

But interstitials also have one big downside: Depending on the number of interstitials and the length of your captions, they will consume a significant amount of time. So when using caption interstitials, you will reduce the time to show in-app footage.

The video editors of *Todoist*[223] added interstitials with a one-color background to display their captions. They managed to make the new screens more dynamic than static frames by fading the captions in gradually. Nevertheless, all text is readable on both the product page and the SERP.

Instead of unicolor screens, you can also add background photos to your interstitials. Just make sure that contrast is good, so the text is readable.

Adding Audio Tracks

To support your visual material, you can add audio tracks to your video. Before you do so, remember this fact, though: Many users watch app store videos in silent mode, so audio will not have any impact on them. For this reason, your video must be engaging and understandable without sound. Audio is just a bonus for a small portion of viewers. For them, you can add two different kinds of audio tracks: voiceover and music.

Adding Guidance with Voiceover

A voiceover track is a good way to provide additional guidance. Written captions are limited by the screen size and by viewers' reading time. Audio tracks are not. So you can explain the visual content in more detail. For this reason, a voiceover is in particular useful to explain complex features.

Voiceover can also add relevance. If the speaker mentions important keywords while explaining features this will help to convince viewers that your app is the solution to their problems.

Finally, the right voiceover track can also create acoustic beauty. Speakers who engage the audience can intensify their emotions and support your story.

Do not overuse it, though. A monologue of 30 seconds will rather annoy viewers. The spoken explanations must be short and on point, so users can focus on what they see instead of what they hear.

The Impact of the Voice's Theme

As we are talking about speakers, let us stay with that topic for a moment.

The emotions you want to create are strongly connected to the theme of the voice actor. If they do not match, the audio will confuse users instead of supporting the emotions that you want to create. For instance, a high, squeaky voice is not the right fit for the video of a horror game. It cannot create a thrilling and scary atmosphere like a deep and smoky voice can.

On the other hand, the deep theme is inappropriate if you want to generate a lighthearted vibe, for instance for a travel app.

In general, people find lighter voices to be more trustworthy and friendlier. Deeper voices are perceived to be aggressive and dominant.[224]

In this context, the voice actor's gender is an important aspect. Men tend to have deeper voices than women. So if you need a dominant or aggressive voice, a male speaker is probably the right fit. But for creating trust, warmth or friendliness, a female actor might be the better pick.

When deciding about the voice actor's gender, also think about your audience. A study in *The Journal of Advertising* found that female voices can promote any product. It does not matter if the target audience is male, female or mixed. In contrast, male actors are useful to address male and neutral viewers, but not to address a female audience. Women rely more on other women's advice, especially on gender-specific products such as hygiene articles or fashion. So hiring a male speaker is not the best idea, if your app is made for women.[225]

Speaking naturally

Make sure your voiceover track sounds natural. The following tips will help you (or your voice actor) to reach this goal:[226]

- Choose a small room to record in. The smaller the room, the lower the chance that your voice will create an unpleasant echo or reverb. Furniture, curtains, and other fixtures can help to prevent echoes. If you record at home, read your text aloud in each room to find the best spot before you start recording.

- Stand up straight while speaking. Your voice will sound much better than when you lounge in an armchair or lean against the wall.

- Show the face that matches the emotion you want to create. Smile, for instance, to sound happy and joyful. Even if your audience does not see your face, your voice will reflect your facial expression.

- Use your hands like you would do when talking to someone face-to-face. Natural gestures will also make your voice sound more natural.

- Talk a bit slower and louder than you usually do. Make sure that your pronunciation is clear.

- You will get better results with a slightly wet mouth. So have a glass of water nearby. Alternatively, take a bite from an apple from time to time.[227]

The right Equipment for Recording

If you record the voice track yourself, you will need equipment:

- A microphone is most important. Do not be too cheap here. Your laptop's built-in microphone will not produce a pleasant recording, and your smart-phone's headset will not either.

- A pop filter is a shield between the microphone and the speaker's mouth. It helps to avoid popping and hissing noises that you might create accidentally while speaking.[228] Do a test recording to determine whether you need a pop shield or not.

- Wearing a decent headset and listening to your voice while recording can help get a better feeling for volume and pronunciation. It also helps identify issues like side noises.[229]

- A stand (or a similar device) allows you to place your text notes on it, so your hands are free while speaking. It will enable you to gesture naturally. Furthermore, if you do not hold papers in your hand, you will not produce rustling noises.[230]

Do not settle with the First Recording

To make sure you have at least one proper recording, you should take multiple takes for each voiceover segment. Vary the speed and tonality to have different options for the editing process. It is much easier to record three or four versions of your audio track than to spend hours with editing later.

Supporting Emotions with Music

Unlike voiceover, music does not provide additional guidance, nor can it increase a video's relevance. But it can support the creation of emotions.

To find a proper piece of music for your video, you need to be aware of the emotions that you want to create. The video for an action game must express its thrill and excitement. For that, powerful music, for example, performed by a classical orchestra or a rock band, might be a good match. For a meditation app, a less vigorous piece would be a better fit.

Although your music should support the emotional tone of the visual content, it should neither define nor change it. So even without the music, the emotions created by the video should be the same.

Dealing with Copyrights

Copyrights are a pitfall when it comes to music. You cannot use the latest chart hits for your preview video. You must have the right to do so and this right usually comes with royalties to pay. Using music without having the right to do so can result in nerve-racking and costly lawsuits.

The safe method to avoid this mess is to compose your music yourself. Composing means to actually create a new piece of music. Covering existing music and using it in your video would also be a copyright violation.

In case you are not a talented musician, you can find many sources for royalty-free music on the Internet. You can use these pieces in private and commercial projects without any bureaucratic hurdles. Check the websites I recommend in the Tools & Sources section of this book (page 278).

Google Play Promotion Videos

So far, we have focused on the iOS app preview video. The reason is that the content guidelines on iOS are much stricter than on Google Play.

When creating the Google Play promotion video, you can include whatever content you want. You can show devices, people using your app, and you even can forego in-app footage and create a cinematic trailer.

As you have up to two minutes for your video, you can also add much more content than in the iOS preview. Unfortunately, this also means that it is more difficult to keep users watching until the end.

For this reason, composing an exciting story is even more critical, and so is the video's rhythm.

You have to decide whether you want to tell one long storyline with more details or instead go for multiple shorter stories.

Besides these differences, the best practices I laid out for iOS videos apply for Google videos too.

The Feature Graphic

On iOS, one frame from your video will be the poster frame, which is visible when the video is not playing. On your Google Play product page, you also have a poster frame, but it is not taken from your video footage. Instead, it is a separate graphic called *feature graphic.*

The feature graphic has a size of 1024x500 pixels in landscape orientation. Many users browse the Play Store in portrait mode, though. So the feature graphic will be scaled down massively to fit their screen. That makes it hard to recognize its small details. For this reason, showing in-app content usually is not a good idea. Check the feature graphic of the game *2048* on the next page, which shows three devices with in-app footage. This footage is way too small. Recognizing its details is hard.

Keep the feature graphic simple and focus on branding. Show the brand name and logo together. Include characters or testimonials, if you have them.

For the background, use a simple artwork (unicolor or color gradient) or a blurred photo that relates to your app's category. Watch the contrast carefully.

A play button will overlie the middle of the feature graphic. So do not place any critical elements there. An excellent approach is to put branding elements on one side of the creative and characters and the other, so the middle stays free.

The feature graphic of *DAZN*, a streaming service for sports events, shows its logo on the left side. They placed it on a black unicolor background to make sure the contrast is excellent. Also, the logo is protected, because there are no disturbing elements nearby. Pictures of famous athletes fill the rest of the creative. Although the play button overlies the photos, it does not cover essential elements like the players' faces.

The designers of *Fallout Shelter* followed a similar pattern. They put the game's mascot on the right and placed the app's name left-aligned in the upper part of the creative.

The *UFC* app has an exciting feature graphic, promoting their next fights by presenting one fighter on the left and the other on the right. That is a great design because it fits the one-on-one character of ultimate fighting. But it is not perfect: The play button covers the fighters' names in the middle. This mistake takes away some of the graphic's promotion power.

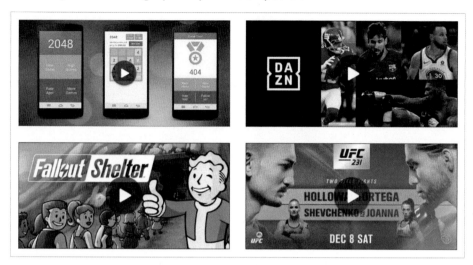

Fig. 92: Feature Graphics *2048, DAZN, Fallout Shelter, UFC* (Source: Google Play)[231,232,233,234]

Video Analysis

We have talked about many single aspects of preview videos. Now it is time to look at some examples to analyze how these aspects work in practice. I picked two iOS videos for this purpose.

Example A: Journi Print

Our first example is the video of *Journi Print – Photo Book*[235], an app for creating photo books.

It starts with a branding screen, showing the app logo together with multiple photo books. So it presents the outcome of the app right in the beginning and connected to branding assets.

The next sequence demonstrates the user journey. It starts with selecting photos and goes via editing the layout to the final result. During this process, many pictures with happy people and beautiful scenes appear. These motifs support the mood of joy and easiness that matches the app's purpose: saving precious memories.

The video's final sequence focuses on variety. It shows more photo books made for various occasions.

Every scene is introduced with a caption interstitial. But the text elements do not explain the screenshots following them. Instead, they emphasize the convenience of the app. Some of them even point out what users do *not* have to do with the app ("no photo-cropping"). While this information might be valuable to users, this approach lacks explanatory guidance. In this case, that is not a big problem though, because it is clear what the app does.

The timing in the *Journi Print* video is precise. All scenes are long enough to allow viewers to get every detail. Also, the text elements are short and crisp so people can read them easily within the given time. The pace is smooth but still engaging.

But there is a small downside. The arrangement of some of the scenes is not optimal. They contain a lot of empty space without any relevant content. Especially in the last segment, the editors are wasteful with the space. The photo books and captions cover only a small portion of the screen. It would have been better to enlarge the content to make it easier for viewers to see all the details.

In conclusion, *Journi Print*'s video does not focus on explaining the app, but on emphasizing its outcome. With the presented motifs and a decent rhythm, it points out the fun character of the app.

Example B: Food Street – Restaurant Game

The next example for our recap is *Food Street*[236]. This game lets the player build a restaurant, grow crops, cook meals, and take care of customers.

The first scene focuses on the building aspect of the game. It starts by showing the main character of the game standing in a kitchen. The camera zooms out while new rooms and furnishings pop up. This zoom out allows viewers to see more rooms and shows the variety of items players can build in the game. The action in this scene is limited to the expansion of the restaurant, so its speed is low.

The second part shows more steps in the player's journey. It is about growing and harvesting ingredients, cooking, and serving meals. The action focuses on the character. There is no "side action" to distract the viewer, so the speed is still low, and it is no problem for viewers to follow the course of events.

The third sequence presents another feature: raising pets. It is not really clear how this function fits into the restaurant story. And the scene lacks explanatory guidance that sets it in context to the rest of the game. That makes it a little bit confusing. Probably the purpose of this part of the video is to make people fall in love with the cute pet characters.

The first three segments are seven, ten, and four seconds long, so the pace is low. Their speed is also low, creating a calm and relaxed mood, just like it should be for a peaceful building game like *Food Street*.

To present a large variety of rich late-game content, the pace increases for the next segment. Scenes appear more rapidly after each other, with less screen time per scene. Also, the speed of the single shots increases, because they contain more characters. It is harder to get every single detail. But as we learned before, for the purpose of showing variety, that is acceptable.

The closing scene of the video is a recognizable branding screen. It includes the app logo, two characters, and background artwork.

The story of *Food Street*'s video follows a progression pattern. It emphasizes the user journey from a small kitchen to a large and successful restaurant. But it is broken by the pet scene, which does not fit into it, because it has no relevant connection to the app's story.

A fascinating detail is the behavior of the main character throughout the video. In the beginning, she looks into the camera and waves, like she is greeting the people who are watching. In the next scenes, she repeats similar actions. It seems like she involves viewers—a cute detail to engage them.

All captions displayed in the video contain four words maximum. They show up for several seconds, and their font size is big enough to be readable. The outlining and the red background layer ensure that the contrast is fine too.

There is only one weakness regarding the captions: In the second scene, the three different text strings appear one after another. Unlike the first caption "Harvest your crops", the other two do not fly into the screen. Instead, a dissolve is used to bring them in. But that dissolve only affects captions, not the rest of the scene. In this case, this technique draws too little attention. When focused on the character, viewers might miss the change of text elements. So this approach takes the risk of wasting the potential to guide users.

Despite its flaws, *Food Street*'s video is a pleasant experience for viewers. It emphasizes the game's calm atmosphere and the cuteness of its characters, but it does not follow a clear storyline consequently.

Step-by-Step: Creating a Video

After learning about the different techniques for video creation, you are now ready to go to work. So let us check the technical requirements that you need to match.

Just like the screenshots, preview videos on iOS are device-specific (see page 158). A video of 1080 x 1920 pixels (or 1920 x 1080) is a must-have. This version works for all devices with the aspect ratio of 16:9. iPads and the iPhone X have other aspect ratios. So if you want users who own these devices to see a preview, you have to create individual versions for them. See the following table for the individual dimensions of each device type:

Device	Screen size	Portrait	Landscape	Aspect Ratio
iPhone 6+/ 7+/8+	5.5 inch	1080 x 1920	1920 x 1080	16:9
iPhone 6 / 7 / 8	4.7 inch	750 x 1334	1334 x 750	16:9
iPhone 5	4.0 inch	1080 x 1920	1920 x 1080	16:9
iPhone 4	3.5 inch	1080 x 1920	1920 x 1080	16:9
iPhone X	5.8 inch	886 x 1920	1920 x 886	
iPad Pro 2nd Gen.	12.9 inch	1200 x 1600 900 x 1200	1600 x 1200 1200 x 900	4:3
iPad Pro	10.5 inch	1200 x 1600	1600 x 1200	4:3
iPad	9.7 inch	900 x 1200	1200 x 900	4:3

Tab. 10: Video Dimensions on iTunes
(Source: adapted from App Store Connect Help)[237]

The iOS preview video has to be 15 to 30 seconds long. And there is no reason not to go for the upper limit. About its orientation, follow my recommendations on page 170.

Google recommends using videos in landscape orientation, with a length between 30 seconds and two minutes on their platform.[238] You should definitely follow this recommendation, at least regarding the orientation. As you have to upload your promo video to YouTube, users will always see it in landscape orientation. That is true even if you upload your video in portrait mode. To adjust a portrait video to the screen, YouTube would display two big black bars left and right of the content, making it a very unpleasant experience for viewers.[239]

Thus you should go for a landscape orientation video of 1920 x 1080 pixels. Google Play will automatically adjust it to other screen sizes.

Now that we have clarified the technical requirements let us go through the process of creating a video.

Step 1: Drafting a Script

First thing, you need a plan, or more precisely, a script.

Use the storyline you developed as the basis for this script. Make it precise. It should contain the following information:

- The single scenes and their elements (features, characters, captions, etc.),
- the purpose of each scene according to the AIDA principle,
- the information each scene will contain and the emotions it appeals to,
- the screen time of each scene,
- the cutting techniques you want to use for the transitions,
- the voiceover text for each scene,
- and the music you want to add.

Take your planning seriously. It can save you a lot of time and work later. Create a timeline and indicate where the different segments of your video start and end. Mark the speed and pace you want to apply to each segment, and also the changes of rhythm.

Pay particular attention to timing. Figure out how much time you need for each scene and the transitions between them. Make sure to include the right reading time for captions. Speak your voiceover text aloud to understand how to time it properly.

Do not compromise on timing, speed or pace. If you cannot fit all the content into the 30-seconds limit, cut out the least important scenes. Remember you can upload up to three videos to iTunes, so rather create two videos than one which is poorly timed.

As on Google Play the maximum length is two minutes, you will not face timing issues with promotion videos.

Step 2: Preparing

Before you start recording, clean up your status bar (see page 163 for details).

To provide better guidance for users, you should show your touches and swipes while recording. On iOS, you need to activate *Assistive Touch* for this purpose:[240]

- Go to your device's general settings, and click *Accessibility*.
- Click *Assistive Touch* and enable it.
- Click *Create New Gesture*.
- Tab on the screen once, save, and name the new gesture.
- You will now see a new round button on the screen. When you start recording, select *Custom* and then your new gesture.

Alternatively, add the libraries *Fingertips*[241] or *Touchpose*[242] to your app code.

On Android, there is also a native feature to record touches, but it is hidden. Here is how to reveal it:

- Go to the settings menu and click *About Phone*.
- Hit *Build number* multiple times until you get the message "You are a developer now."
- Click back to settings. Now you can see the *Developer Options*, right above the *Legal information*. Click it and set the toggle to *on*.
- Activate the function *Show touches* in the *Input* section.

Step 3: Creating the Raw Material

Now it is time to record the in-app footage.

It should go without saying, but let me emphasize it anyhow: You cannot show iOS footage in Android videos (and vice versa). So you have to capture Android and iOS footage separately.

There are many ways to do so. For an Apple device, the easiest way is to use the native screen capturing function. This function is available on iOS 11 or later versions, and you need to enable it in the settings. Afterward, you can start recording by tapping the red button in the *Control Center*.[243]

On Android, there is no native function, so you have to use a third party recording app. And of course, you can do the same for iOS as well. Check the section about Video Tools for suggestions (page 278).

Do not capture all the footage in one run. Instead, record it scene by scene. Add one or two seconds without performing any action (tabs, swipes, etc.) to the beginning and the end of every shot. These margins make it easier to cut and edit your material later. Record two or three different versions of each scene if you are unsure about timing.

Design the captions or caption interstitials as well as the poster frame you want to use. Download matching music or create it yourself.

Step 4: Editing

The editing is the part of the process that will consume the most time. Work along with your script.

Start by adjusting the single scenes separately before putting them together. That allows you to reorder them later, when creating additional versions for testing.

Implement the text elements. Be aware that you must add a disclaimer to scenes that include premium content. If users need to pay for features, you must tell them in your video. A short phrase like "available with in-app purchase" does the job.[244]

When you have finished all the scenes, connect them. Adjust their lengths and the transitions. Add the poster frame if it is a separate file.

Step 5: Adding Audio

Now it is time to add audio. You might have realized that I have not mentioned voice recording for step 3. The reason is simple: It is much easier to time your words when you can see the final video while recording. The same is true for a voice actor if you prefer to hire one.

Last but not least, add music and adjust its volume. When the speaker talks, tune down the music's volume. When the voice track is silent, you can play it louder.

Step 6: Exporting and uploading your video

Finalize your video and export it as a MPEG, MOV or M4V file. All these formats are compatible with iTunes and Google Play. For iTunes, make sure the file's data weight is below 500 megabytes.

For more detailed specifications, check *App Store Connect Help*[245] (iOS) or *YouTube Support*[246] (Android).

Upload your preview video to iTunes. Note that you can only do so using the *Safari* browser. It will not work on *Google Chrome* or another Internet browser. Do not forget to select your poster frame.

Submit your Android video to your YouTube channel. If you want it to be undetectable via the YouTube search, set its status to *unlisted*.

Copy the video link and place it on the Google Play Console. Make sure to use the complete link (http://www.youtube.com/...) and not the short version (https://www.youtu.be/...).

Congratulations, your product page now contains a preview video.

Chapter Summary

As usual at the end of a chapter, here is a summary of our insights about videos:

- Follow the AIDA concept and address all stages in your video.

- Use the first five seconds to draw attention to the video.

- Raise viewers' interest by showing the most impressive content in the beginning.

- Present your key story after the opening scene.

- Save the last frame for a CTA.

- Create a poster frame that is capable of attracting attention.

- If you use branding (or promotion) poster frames, do not use screenshots containing the same content.

- Speed refers to the level of action within a scene.

- High speed creates thrill and tension, but too high speed makes a scene hard to understand.

- Low speed is relaxing, but too low speed is boring.

- Use fast motion to increase speed and slow motion to decrease it.

- Pace refers to the number of scenes in a video and the screen time per scene.

- Reduce the pace to give users the chance to enjoy high-speed scenes. Increase the pace for low-speed scenes to show the app's variety.

- Varying speed and pace creates rhythm and makes a video more engaging.

- Pick the right types of cuts to support your video's rhythm.

- Make sure all captions are readable. Take care about reading time (one second per three words).

- Use only two to four words per caption.

- Use interstitials, outlines or layers to ensure a good contrast.

- Explain your content further with voiceover.

- Implement music to intensify the emotions you want to create.

CHAPTER 12
THE APP ICON

Besides screenshots and videos, the app icon is the third of the prominent visual metadata elements. It is a must-have for your product page. Releasing an app without an icon is neither possible on iOS nor on Android.

Be aware that the icon is not the same as your logo. A logo that appears on your website or your business letters can have any shape. But the icon always is a square image, and typically, you only use it in the app stores.

In users' opinions, the app icon is not extraordinary important when making a download decision. Only 18% of them call the icon the convincing factor for their decision-making process.[247] That is not surprising, as the app icon is tiny and limited in terms of its content. Other metadata elements can transport much more useful information.

Although the app icon is not users' favorite piece of metadata, you should not ignore it for two reasons:

1. It appears in all conversion opportunities. It does not matter if people come across your app in the search results, in a feature or in another way, the first contact with your app always includes the icon.

2. If users install the app, the icon will appear on their devices' home screen. So even after they decide to download the app, they will face this metadata element on a regular basis. That fact makes the icon an excellent tool for creating brand awareness. Users who recognize your icon easily will remember your app.

How Icons support the Three Columns

Let us find out how the app icon can contribute to the product page.

Guidance in Icons

Again, all users will see the app icon, no matter how they find your app. Thus the icon can attract people's attention.

Unfortunately, it cannot add much value beyond the attention stage. Because of its limited size, it is tough to provide a higher level of guidance with it.

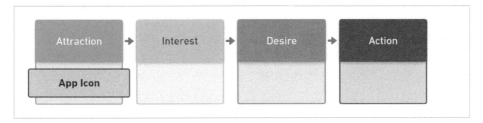

Fig. 93: The App Icon in the AIDA Funnel
(Source: Author's own illustration)

Relevance in Icons

The icon can add relevance to your product page, at least on a basic level. A proper motif can draw a connection between users' problems and the solutions your app provides.

Beauty in Icons

It is evident that your app needs to be pleasant to look at, right? That means the colors should harmonize with each other. But it also implies that the icon is recognizable, so viewers do not have problems identifying its components. As the app icon is the first point of contact, beauty is the key to creating a decent first impression.

The Icon's Branding Power

The app icon is a great branding tool. With a well-known brand, it makes perfect sense to design the icon similar to the brand's logo. Users who know and trust the brand will recognize the icon and be more likely to download the app.

That approach requires a decent level of popularity across the target audience, though. People need to be aware of the products or services that are connected with the brand name or logo.

Trivago, a service for booking flights and hotels, relies solely on the branding power of its logo. This strategy works fine for them, because they have created a substantial level of brand awareness by advertising their services. In their target markets, they run ads across many channels, including offline media such as TV. Thus people are aware of what *Trivago* does.

The educational app *Duolingo* also uses its logo in the icon. But their designers added a second branding component: their mascot. The cute little owl makes the icon unique and helps users recognize *Duolingo* across platforms. Note that the mascot is very simple: It lacks details like legs or feather. For this reason, the mascot is a good fit even for small creatives like the app icon. More details could have made it hard for the viewer to identify it.

For comparison, have a look at *Learn Russian Free*. They also have an owl as their mascot, but it has much more detail. Close up, you can identify single feathers in different color shades. But if you see the icon at a smaller size in the app store, the experience is worse. The owl and the book with the Russian flag on its cover are much harder to identify than *Duolingo*'s mascot.

Fig. 94: App Icons *Trivago, Duolingo, Learn Russian Free*
(Source: Google Play)[248,249,250]

Only use your mascot for your app icon if it is a simple one. Viewers must be able to recognize it without problems anywhere the icon appears.

The last example emphasizes the biggest problem of app icons: their limited size. Often, it is not possible to implement a perfect copy of the logo into an icon. As a consequence, many companies use a partial brand logo instead. Still, substantial popularity of the brand must be the basis for this approach. Actually, it requires an even bigger level of familiarity than the full logo approach. Check out the following examples for well-recognizable app icons.

  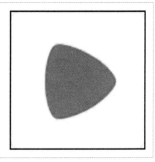

Fig. 95: App Icons *McDonalds*, *Netflix*, *Zalando*
(Source: Google Play)[251,252,253]

The golden M belongs to the fast food empire *McDonald's*, and the red N stands for the streaming platform *Netflix*. Note that the latter is not the official logo of the brand (the red *Netflix*-lettering is). Nevertheless, people recognize it.

The last icon without alphabetic letters is probably the hardest to identify, especially if you are not situated in Europe. The orange triangle belongs to the online fashion shop *Zalando*. *Zalando* is very present in the online world and also advertises through many other channels such as TV and print media. Therefore the brand and its triangle are well-established. It makes perfect sense to transfer this symbol's popularity to their app by using it as the icon.

None of these three icons have significant relevance for their category, though. Someone who does not know *McDonald's* will not associate the golden M with food, the red N has no apparent connection to TV shows or movies, and the orange triangle is not relevant for fashion. All these icons only work because the brands behind them are well-known and people recognize them.

Making the Icon relevant

If your app has not gained much traction yet, a branding icon will most likely not work very well. The reason is that users cannot connect it to their problem or the solution to it. To catch the attention of users, your priority should therefore not be branding. Instead, outline your app's relevance.

For most apps, it is easy to find at least one motif that is relevant for users and easy to cognize. One-color pictograms of these motifs are very common for all app categories.

For instance, *Flush* is an app that shows users the way to the nearest public toilet. They put a roll of toilet paper into their icon, which is a relevant symbol for sure. This motif has a major problem though: It is not unique. A surprisingly high number of apps have rolls of toilet paper in their icons too (see the examples below). Many of them are games, some belong to other categories, but no app offers a similar service as *Flush* does. While it is good for a company to provide a unique service, an ordinary icon is a problem. In this case, users who see it might connect it rather to a game than to a navigation app, and they might be disappointed when their expectation is not met.

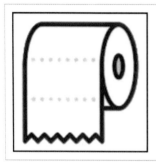

Fig. 96: App Icons *Flush, Toilet Paper, Toilet Paper Racing*
(Source: Google Play)[254,255,256]

Many other app icons lack distinguishing features. A heart, for instance, is the most-used symbol in the icons of dating apps. Its relevance is perfectly clear. But the capability to create a recognizable memory for viewers is minimal.

The designers of *SwissDating* realized this issue and decided to customize the heart in their icon. They added a white cross to the heart. A white cross and a red background are also the components of Switzerland's ensign. As the app targets Swiss users, this design is perfect to distinguish the icon from other dating apps. At the same time, it provides additional relevance.

If you want to create an icon, that is relevant, recognizable, and distinguishable, combining two pictograms is a great approach. Here are some more examples of apps following that pattern. All of them provide a good level of relevance for users.

Lieferando.de is a food delivery app. Its icon contains a cutlery set of knife and fork embedded in a house. The cutlery set is a common symbol for food apps, and a house is used by many apps related to real estate. But the combination of the house and the cutlery set is unique, and it is very relevant because it indicates that users eat at home.

Another good example for relevant icons is *Skyscanner*. The app gives users the ability to compare flights across multiple airlines. Their icon consists of two pictograms as well. A cloud symbolizes the sky and a wave that looks like a WiFi symbol stands for the scanning process. Both symbols are merged into each other, giving the app icon a very distinctive look.

Fig. 97: App Icons *SwissDating, Lieferando.de, Skyscanner* (Source: Google Play)[257,258,259]

Combining Branding Power and Relevance

In addition to the unique pictogram, *Skyscanner* also included their brand name in the app icon. So they go for a combination of both the branding strategy and the relevance approach. This middle way is great to attract new users and increase brand awareness. Let us see some more examples.

Look at the icon of *Fender Play*, an app to learn to play the guitar. It combines a guitar pick with the *Fender* logo. In combination with the unique font type, this motif is relevant and recognizable as well.

The icon of the music and podcast player *Deezer* also consists of the app's name and a pictogram. The five colored pillars look like the graphical interface of an equalizer (a tool used for audio editing). The pictogram creates relevance for the app, while the brand name makes it unique.

The designers of *Banggood* used a shopping cart to emphasize the category it belongs to. Besides, the logo has great potential for recognition. The two "gs" in the app name and the curved line below form a smile—a very catchy and unique design.

Fig. 98: App Icons *Fender Play, Deezer, Banggood*
(Source: iTunes, Google Play)[260,261,262]

You do not need text elements to create branding effects. Colors and color gradients can do so as well. The *Instagram* icon is a famous example. It contains the pictogram of a camera, which is relevant for the app and the category. But it also creates enormous branding power because of its background. The orange-to-violet gradient is unique and recognizable in the app stores. Well, actually this is wrong. It *was* unique. When *Instagram*'s user base grew, and people started associating the color gradient with the app, other developers began to copy it. Nowadays you can find dozens of icons in the app stores with the very same background color scheme.

Fig. 99: App Icons *Instagram* and Color Scheme Copycats
(Source: Google Play)[263,264,265,266,267]

Do not get me wrong here. I am not encouraging you to copy the icons or single design aspects of popular apps. You should instead try to create your own individual and recognizable background design.

Portfolio Branding

Of course, the purpose of your icon is primarily to represent your app. But it can do more. If you own multiple apps (or plan to build more apps in the future), you can use congruent icon designs to cross-promote them.

Let us have a look at the apps by Leap Fitness Group[268]. Many of them follow the same design scheme. They combine a red background with a black-and-white character. Additionally, they include a little badge with the number 30 to indicate the length of their training programs. This congruent design is great for cross-promotion: People who like one of the company's apps will recognize the design of the others and be more likely to download them.

Fig. 100: App Icons of Leap Fitness Group's Portfolio
(Source: Google Play)[269,270,271,272,273]

Another excellent example of a congruent design scheme is the Adobe portfolio[274]. Adobe has about 30 apps on Google Play, and most of them have a similar design for their app icons. The background is always black. For the foreground, the designers created either two character text elements or pictograms. Each icon also has a frame in the same color as the foreground elements. Although the colors differ for every icon, the overall design sticks in the mind.

Fig. 101: App Icons of Adobe's Portfolio
(Source: Google Play)[275,276,277,278,279]

CHAPTER 12

Chrome and other apps by Google also use the same colors in their logos: blue, yellow, red, and green. The motifs have different shapes, but the color scheme is congruent and recognizable.

Fig. 102: App Icons of Google's Portfolio
(Source: Google Play)[280,281,282,283,284]

Even for app icons that do not share a specific shape or color scheme, you can create a portfolio branding. Especially across game publishers, it is common to add the company logo to all app icons.

Fig. 103: App Icons of Electronic Arts' Portfolio
(Source: Google Play)[285,286,287,288,289]

Electronic Arts[290] does so with the initials of their company name. Among players, this logo is well-known and therefore this is a great approach to strengthen the brand.

GameLoft[291] does it similar with the squiggled letter G, which is their logo.

Fig. 104: App Icons of GameLoft's Portfolio
(Source: Google Play)[292,293,294,295,296]

Amazon[297] uses a more subtle approach. They have a curved orange arrow in their company logo and use it in their app icon as well. But the same arrow is also part of many other icons in their app portfolio. Its color differs from icon to icon, but the shape is always the same. Besides the arrow, Amazon's app icons also share another similarity: They never use capital letters for their product names.

Fig. 105: App Icons of Amazon's Portfolio
(Source: Google Play)[298,299,300,301,302]

If you plan to publish more than one app, think about how to build a brand up front. When designing the first icon, you should already have a plan for branding your future portfolio. A memorable design will give you a big strategic advantage over competitors.

Promotional Icons

You have already learned about promotion screenshots (page 154), whose purpose is to communicate special offers, Social Proof, and other messages that are not related directly to app features. Unfortunately, you cannot apply the same variety of promotional messages to app icons. These are the reasons:

- The icon is too small to transport text messages that go beyond the brand name.

- Your icon must be recognizable. Of course, you should optimize the icon and test different versions to get the best results. But in general, the design should be consistent over time. Otherwise, the icon loses its potential to create brand awareness. Promotional messages tend to have a date of expiry, so they change frequently. Thus the app icon usually is not the best place for promotional content.

However, there are ways to modify your icon in a promotional sense. One option is to change small details to match a seasonal setting.[303] The icon of *The Simpsons: Tapped Out* changes on a regular basis, depending on the time of the year. For example, in December 2018, the designers replaced the original icon with a Christmas-themed version.

Many occasions are good fits for this kind of promotional adjustment:

- Seasons (summer/vacation time, winter)
- Bank holidays (Christmas, Thanksgiving, Independence Day)
- Special days (Halloween, Valentine's Day, New Year's Eve)
- Cultural and Sports events (Carnival, Olympic Games, Soccer World Cup)

The other opportunity is an app update that adds significant new content. Here is another example from *The Simpsons*: With the big update in summer 2018, a zoo was added to the app's virtual city of Springfield. To emphasize this update, the designers changed the app icon. They gave their main character Homer a new hat that said "Springfield Zookeeper".

Fig. 106: App Icons *The Simpsons*
(Source: SimpsonsWiki.com, Google Play)[304,305]

As Homer is a well-known figure, all of these variations of the icon work well. For a less popular app, the changes should be less drastic, though.

No matter which approach you choose, vary your app icon only rarely. Too many changes will confuse users and harm the icon's branding power.

In-App Footage in Icons

An easy way to create an icon is using in-app footage. You do not need great design skills to do so. Just shoot the motif from the app and cut out the content you want to show, so it fits the icon dimensions. A simple graphics program like *Microsoft Paint* is all you need to do this.

Fleet Battle – Sea Battle uses a small piece of the game's board for the icon. That is a great idea for two reasons:

- First, the game Fleet Battle is popular around the world as a board game.

- Second, its board usually looks very similar. So many people will recognize the small cut-out from the in-app footage.

Minesweeper is another great example. If you have been a *Microsoft Windows* user anytime in your life, you are familiar with this name, right? Probably a picture of the game's board comes to your mind. Have a look at the app icon below. I bet it matches the picture in your mind. If it works this way, it also works the other way: If you saw the icon first, you would instantly think of the game.

Using in-app footage for your icon can go wrong, though. Have a look at the icon of *Art of War 3*. It contains a lot of content, including tanks, soldiers, buildings, trees, and visual effects like flames. To make all these content pieces fit into the icon, the designer had to scale it down massively. As a result, it is impossible to recognize anything without putting the icon right in front of your eye.

Again, simplicity is key.

Fig. 107: App Icons *Fleet Battle, Minesweeper, Art of War 3*
(Source: Google Play)[306,307,308]

Photos in Icons

Across the app stores, you can find several icons that contain photographic content. Like icons with in-app footage, they are easy to create.

You can find millions of photos for free in online stocks. And if you prefer an individual picture, you can simply take it yourself. With a graphics program, you can cut them to the right dimensions within minutes.

But is it a good idea to use photos for app icons? The examples on the next page are the best answers to this question.

The icon of *Accurate Altimeter* contains a picture of a mountain for the background and an altimeter for the foreground. The background picture probably is not a photo but hand-drawn. But as it looks like a blurred photo, I put it into the photo category anyway.

This app icon has two major problems:

1. The details of the altimeter are hard to identify. The numbers are too small to be readable, and the contrast between the needle and the altimeter's body is bad. The light and shadow effects make the experience even worse.

2. The other problem is that the styles of the back- and the foreground do not fit together. On the one hand, the altimeter has a very clean appearance. But the dark, dull colors give it an unpleasant look. On the other hand, the artsy and colorful background picture distracts the viewer from the foreground. Why would anyone even try to identify the altimeter's details if the background is more pleasant to look at? This discrepancy creates unintentional visual guidance, but it draws viewers to the wrong content.

The second example is the app *Ghost in Photo*. It has a (manipulated) photo in its icon to demonstrate what the outcome of using the app is. This photo contains many elements: A woman sitting on a bench next to a ghost, with a piece of lawn and various plants behind them.

Like many other photo icons, this one is difficult to understand. The various details such as the girl's colorful appearance distract viewers. So they might miss the crucial element of the icon: the ghost. The fact that the ghost is semi-transparent makes it even harder to identify it.

The icon by *Collage Maker Pro* is overloaded in the same way. It shows the final result of editing a photo, after several filters and tools were used to manipulate it. But it has way too many details to be recognizable when appearing on a SERP.

Fig. 108: App Icons *Accurate Altimeter, Ghost in Photo, Collage Maker Pro* (Source: Google Play)[309,310,311]

So the answer to our initial question is clear: No. Stay away from photos when designing your app icon. Icons are simply too small for the amount of detail a photo contains.

Icon Analysis

To conclude this chapter, let us analyze some more app icons based on what we have discussed so far.

Example A: Vivitar Smart Home Security

Vivitar Smart Home Security is our first example. Their icon shows a combination of three pictograms. The biggest one is a shield. Inside it, you see a house. Actually, the house is cut out of the shield, so you could argue that it is just one pictogram with a house-shaped cutting. However, let us call the house a discrete pictogram. Concentric lines filling the house are the third component of the icon.

Fig. 109: App Icon *Vivitar* (Source: Google Play)[312]

The shield is a common symbol for all kinds of products and services concerning security. The house specifies the security aspect: It clarifies that the app is about home security. The concentric lines represent radio waves or WiFi and emphasize the *Smart* aspect of the app. The combination of the three pictograms creates a high level of relevance, and it also makes the icon unique in comparison to the many apps containing either a shield or a house. That is true although the single elements are simple and contain only a few details.

As the designers cut out the house instead of inking it separately, they were able to keep the number of colors low. With just two colors (white and the background color gradient), they avoided running into contrast problems. The lack of branding power is the only weak point of the *Vivitar* icon. As the design is in line with the KISS principle, it would be possible to include the app name. Even in addition to the existing pictograms, it would not overload the icon.

Example B: Boxing Round Interval Timer

Fig. 110: App Icon *Interval Timer* (Source: Google Play)[313]

Our next example is *Boxing Round Interval Timer*, an app that provides a countdown clock for boxing competitions. The icon contains three pictograms as well: a clock, a sandbag, and the silhouette of a boxer. Although the boxer overlaps the other two components, all of them are perfectly recognizable. The reason is that they do not contain any unnecessary details. Besides, with the exception of the clock, they are monochrome. The thick outlines ensure that viewers can distinguish them from each other as well as from the background.

The combination of the three pictograms is highly relevant. Users who search for terms related to boxing (or martial arts in general) immediately will see the connection to their search.

The design is also unique. Dozens of apps on Google Play offer the same features as *Boxing Round Interval Timer*. Many of them include a clock or boxing gloves, but no one shows a similar combination of pictograms.

Like the *Vivitar* icon, the *Interval Timer* icon lacks branding power, though (and the same goes for the app title). It seems the developers did not really care about the recognition value of the app. That is a pity because the icon's relevance and uniqueness is fantastic.

Example C: Boxing Round

Fig. 111: App Icon *Boxing Round* (Source: Google Play)[314]

We will stay with boxing for our last example, but this time we have a look at a game: *Boxing Round*. Its icon shows a character with very many details. Close up, you can identify the muscles, the unique hairstyle, and even the tape on the gloves. Behind the athlete, you can see a ring of steel with flames in it. The icon has two captions: One states the app name and another one in the upper right corner says "3D Game". Both are written in shiny golden capital letters.

Now check out the same icon on the SERP after searching for the app name. Downscaled to this size, it is tough to read the captions. The golden fonts with the glowing and the 3D-effect make them very illegible. In front of the background (which is uncomfortable as well) it lacks contrast.

The character is not optimal either. The single details are too small to be recognizable, and the dynamics of light and shadow increase this problem. Fewer details would be better, especially for users seeing the icon on the SERP. Emphasizing the game's 3D graphics to stand out against competitors without this feature is not a bad idea. But the caption "3D game" is too long to put in an icon. "3D" alone would work better.

In sum, the icon clearly contains too much content, even for a game. The visual effects like glowing, light, and shadow should be reduced drastically for all components, but especially for the captions, so they become more readable. An outline would be a much better option than the current 3D effect.

Chapter Summary

That is it about icons. I have not written a step-by-step guideline for this chapter, because the process of creating icons is very simple: Read my advices, decide about the motif, and create the icon.

Here are the key findings of this chapter in brief:

- Unless you have a significant awareness across your target audience, focus on providing relevance rather than branding.
- Use pictograms that are connected to the purpose of your app to do so.
- Combinations of multiple pictograms provide more relevance than single pictograms. They also make your app icon unique, so it is distinguishable from competitors.
- Use only simple characters or mascots with few details in your icon.
- Beyond your app name, do not add text elements.
- Try to limit the number of components (pictograms, mascots, text elements) to three. Make them all perfectly identifiable and readable.
- Stay away from photos.
- Use unicolor or color-gradient backgrounds.
- Make sure that all colors in your icon create good contrast.
- Vary your icon only rarely, for seasonal promotions or when providing a big update.
- Create a consistent design scheme across all app icons in your portfolio to create long-term branding effects.

CHAPTER 13
THE TITLE & OTHER TEXT ELEMENTS

The App Title

The app title is only a small piece of metadata, and in users' eyes, it is not essential. Only 15% of women and 22% of men name it the most important element of the product page.[315]

Fig. 112: The Importance of App Titles for Download Decisions
(Source: adapted from Koetsier 2018)[316]

For you as the app owner, the title is crucial, though. We have already talked about its enormous potential to create visibility for your app (see page 53).

But the app title has another important purpose: It creates relevance. Users who see their keyword in the title after a search will consider your app a solution to their problem. So a title that contains relevant keywords attracts users' attention.

Fig. 113: The App Title in the AIDA Funnel
(Source: Author's own illustration)

Besides, the title appears in all conversion opportunities, so all users who come across your app will face it. That makes it the perfect metadata to introduce your brand and build brand awareness.

The best practice is to optimize it for both branding and relevance. Put your brand name together with two to five keywords in the title. Use terms that describe your most popular functions or the outcomes of using your app.

I recommend separating the brand name visually from the keywords so readers are able to distinguish them. Use one of the following formats:

- Brand – Keywords

  The brand name stands first. The dash separates it from the keywords. For this format, two extra characters (one dash plus one space after it) are necessary, which is a reasonable number. *Badoo*[317] is an example for this format:

  Badoo – The Dating App

- Brand: Keywords

  With a colon instead of a dash, you can save one character, because it needs no extra space. The visual separation is less obvious though. Here is how it looks for the cooking app *Fooby*[318]:

  FOOBY: Recipes & More

- Keywords by Brand

  This format is a good choice if you prefer to put your keywords first. The visual separation with a preposition is not as clear as with a dash or a colon, but it looks smoother. However, it will take more characters away from keywords.

  Instead of "by", you can also use other prepositions like "at", "with" or "on". *JoyTunes*[319] and *eBay*[320] are great examples for this format:

  Simply Piano by JoyTunes

  Shop top brands at eBay

No matter which approach you pick, do not waste characters for the word "and". Use the ampersand (&) instead.

Title Length on iOS

Although you can use up to 30 characters, it can be beneficial if you do not. In some cases, the app title is too long to be displayed entirely on the SERP, so it gets cut off. That is a bad experience for users. Depending on the title format you picked, it might also hurt its relevance, because if keywords are not displayed, they cannot attract people who search for them.

Whether a title gets cut off or not depends on its length, but also on the characters it contains. Have a look at the following SERP screenshots, taken with an iPhone 8 Plus.

In the title of the app *CodeCheck: Food & Cosmetics*, half of the word *Cosmetics* is cut off and not readable.

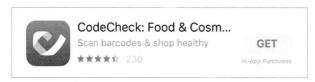

Fig. 114: App Title *CodeCheck*
(Source: iTunes)[321]

But the title of *8fit Workout & Meal Planner* is completely visible, although it has the same length of 27 characters. The reason is that the title contains more slim letters such as l, i and t.

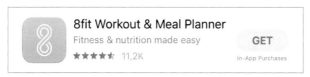

Fig. 115: App Title *8fit*
(Source: iTunes)[322]

Aim for a title that is completely visible on the SERP, even if you do not use all the 30 characters.

Title Length on Google Play

On Google Play, you have the same chances but also the same issues as on iOS. On the SERP, titles longer than about 25 to 30 characters are cut off. In features, users will see even less; text beyond about 20 characters is invisible. The full title of 50 characters appears only on the product page.

Fig. 116: App Titles in Google Play Features
(Source: Google Play)

I recommend ignoring this problem on Android. Use all of the 50 characters. Combine your brand name with lots of relevant keywords. Separate both with a dash or a colon, as I suggested for the iOS app title.

Make sure that the first 20 characters include your brand name and the most relevant keyword, so both are visible no matter where and how users come across your app.

The Subtitle

Arranging the iOS subtitle is easier than compiling the title. There is no need to include branding elements, so go for keywords only.

Besides, you do not have to worry about the subtitle's length. Even if you use all the 30 characters, it will not get cut off. So implement as many terms as possible.

Focus on relevant keywords which did not make it into the title. Avoid articles and conjunctions. A comma-separated list naming the essential features is fine.

The "What's new" Section

Both iTunes and Google Play provide a section called *What's New* on their product pages. In this section, you can provide information about the latest update of your app. These update notes usually include:

- New features added to the app.

- Bugs that you fixed.

- General improvements to the app's stability and performance.

The *What's New* section is not indexed, so it has no impact on visibility. But it can help increase the conversion rate.

Make updates to your app on a regular basis and document it in the *What's New* section. Users will appreciate that you care about their convenience and their feedback. Especially if you solve problems, about which people complained in reviews, you should mention the bug fixes in your update notes.

In case an update does not contain critical bug fixes or new features, go for general statements. Here are some examples:

- "minor bug fixes"

- "performance improvements"

In any case, keep the *What's New* section rather short. On the iOS product page, only the first three lines are visible. If your notes are longer, users have to enlarge the section by clicking *more*.

The Promotional Text

The promotional text is a metadata element that is available on the iOS product page, but not on Google Play. It is a text of up to 170 characters, and it appears on the product page above the first paragraph of the description. As it has no clear optical outline, some users might confuse it with the actual description.

Just like the *What's new* section, the promotional text is not indexed, so it does not create visibility. But it can be used to provide additional information to help increase conversion. Check the graphic that illustrates the app description's purpose again (page 94).

The promotional text is the only metadata element you can change without uploading a new app version. Thus it makes sense to use it to communicate more frequently with users. Tell them the latest news about your app, announce future functions, and promote limited-time offers.

CHAPTER 14
TESTING METADATA

No matter which techniques and approaches you choose for your metadata, the purpose is the same: You want to increase the conversion rate. But your initial ideas might not be the best to achieve this goal. Tastes are different, and users might not agree with your opinion on design. Thus you should always judge your efforts based on data.

The easiest way is to compare conversion rates before and after adjusting your metadata. Unfortunately, comparisons of old and new versions are never accurate. Many factors can cause a rise or drop in the number of downloads and the conversion rate. Here are some of them:

- Competition: Competitors' marketing activities (including ASO) might hurt your download numbers.

- Seasons and weather: During summertime, people are usually less likely to use apps than in winter.

- Events and holidays: Bank holidays tend to increase the traffic for leisure apps and games. For instance on Christmas, when people set up their new devices, download numbers spike across all categories. Other events can push traffic for specific categories. For example, during the soccer World Cup, apps related to sports might be very successful.

All these external factors can falsify the results of a before-and-after test.

How A/B Testing works

A great way to minimize the influence of these external factors is an A/B test, also called split-testing. For an A/B experiment, you run different versions of your metadata against each other at the same time. This way you can test the original metadata against one new version, but also two new variations against each other. During the test, the audience splits: 50% of product page visitors see version A, while the other half sees version B. The version that generates more downloads wins the test.

Of course, you can test more than two alternatives against each other. Simply add version C or D. You should not use more than four versions for one test, though.

This setup ensures that external factors impact both versions. So the results are more reliable than for a before-and-after test.

All variations must address the same aspect of your metadata. If you want to optimize the background art of your screenshots, do not vary other elements. Keep the foreground motifs and the captions congruent for all test versions. If you want to test rich formatting for your description, make sure the wording stays the same. Vary only one variable per experiment to get precise results.

Even more critical: Run only one test at once. If you start a screenshot test before the description experiment is finished, you will falsify the results for both tests.

How to do A/B Tests on Google Play

Doing A/B tests for your Android product page is easy. The Google Play console offers a native feature for this purpose that is called *Experiments*. It allows you to test up to four different versions against each other.

Google Play will automatically split your audience, according to your test settings. It will take about 24 hours before you see the first results. But it can take several weeks until the data sample size is big enough to judge fairly which version is the winner. Google will display the hint that more data is needed until then.

As soon as it is clear which version is the winner, you can select this version as your new default with just one click.

How to do A/B Tests on iOS

Apple does not offer a native function for split-tests. Therefore you need a third party solution to do A/B tests. Companies offering these solutions create a duplicate of your product page for every version you want to test. By sending users to these duplicates, you can judge which version performs best. After the test, you need to manually adjust your actual product page, so it matches the test winner. Check the Tools & Sources chapter to learn about potential partners for A/B tests (page 281).

Of course, these services are not free, so if you decide to hire them for running A/B tests, be prepared to pay them. In case you are not able or willing to do so, consider running tests only on Google Play, and copy the results to iTunes.

How to set up Test Series

No matter how clear the result of your first A/B test is, you need to continue testing. Testing is a never-ending process. So your first test is just the start of a series of experiments. Based on its winning version, start another test addressing the same variable.

Begin your series with general ideas. Then narrow down the subjects to more specific aspects. Even a small detail can lead to a conversion rate increase of a tenth of a percent, and this small increase can result in thousands of extra downloads in the long run. So do not be afraid to test ideas that seem to be absurd at first glance.

A series of Google Play experiments to improve your app description could look like this (underlined subjects are the winners of the experiments in this made-up example):

Test #	Subject	Version A	Version B
1	Text Structure	Paragraph Style	Bullet-Point Style
2	Paragraph Style	with Header	without Header
3	Header Style	All Cap	Non All Cap
4	Header Style 2	Bold Fonts	Plain Fonts
5	Header Style 3	with Emojis	without Emojis
6	...	...	...

Tab. 11: Test Series Example
(Source: Author's own illustration)

CHAPTER 15
CONVERSION SUMMARY

Let us briefly summarize our learnings about conversion rate optimization.

A good product page stands on three columns: guidance, relevance, and beauty. All metadata elements support at least one of these columns. The following graphic summarizes their abilities.

Fig. 117: The Three Columns and supporting Metadata Elements
(Source: Author's own illustration)

The potential impact is not the same for all metadata, though. It differs because of their attributes (size, length, number, etc.). The table on the next page specifies the individual level of impact for each element.

	Guidance	Relevance	Beauty
Ratings and Reviews	+	+	
Description	+++	+++	+
Videos	+++	+++	+++
Screenshots	++	+++	+++
App Icon		+	++
App Title		++	

Tab. 12: Metadata's Ability to Support the Three Columns
(Source: Author's own illustration)

Metadata elements differ not only regarding their level of impact on the three columns. They also impact users in different stages of their decision-making process. These stages are:

- Attracting attention
- Raising interest
- Awakening desire
- Calling to action

Only if you manage to address users properly on all these stages, you will convince them of downloading your app. The next figure summarizes which stage you can address with your metadata. Be aware that blue elements refer to iOS while green elements stand for Android. White and gray elements are valid for both iOS and Android.

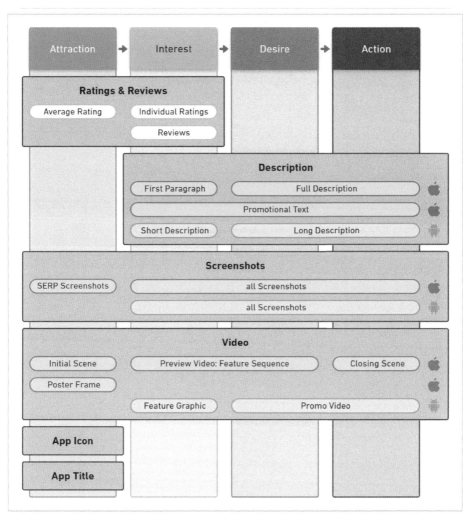

Fig. 118: Metadata Elements in the AIDA Funnel
(Source: Author's own illustration)

PART IV

BONUS CONTENT

CHAPTER 16
LOCALIZATION

For apps that are distributed worldwide, English is by far the most important language. The reason is simple: English is the most widespread language in the world. 371 million people speak English as their first language. And around the world, one billion people speak it in total.[323]

Even more important, many people in industrial nations speak English. It is the official language of the United States and Great Britain, which are ranked #1 and #5 in the list of the biggest economies. In other wealthy countries such as Germany or France, children learn English at school. So most of their citizens understand it at least on a basic level.

In all these countries, a large portion of the population owns smartphones and has access to the Internet. Also, people are used to shopping online and paying for digital goods like IAPs.

So an English product page opens the door to address an enormous number of potential users. Nevertheless, you should consider translating it into other languages.

We have already talked about one reason for localizing your product page: boosting your visibility (page 61).

But localizations can also help increase conversion rate. If English is not the official language in a country, a localization will make your app more accessible. Approaching people in their native language will make it easier for them to understand what your app is about. And thus, the chance that they download it will increase.

Localizing your product page is a complex process, because it is not only about translating words. Think about localization in three different layers.

The First Layer: Translation

The basic layer is the simple translation of words. Although it is the simplest form of localization, it carries some risks. These risks are valid for all metadata elements that contain text.

One Word, many Meanings

Some words in other languages have several meanings, although they translate to the same English term. In the context of a phrase, one incorrectly translated word can destroy its relevance.

For instance, the word *Goal* means *target*. But it also describes the object that soccer players try to hit in order to score. The German translation for goal depends on the meaning: *Tor* means *soccer goal*, and *Ziel* means *target*. In the context of a soccer app, the wrong translation *Ziel* would make no sense to readers.

Online translation programs are especially prone to errors like this. You can reduce the risk, though: Translate entire phrases or paragraphs instead of single terms. In any case, you should double-check the results.

Local Vocabulary and Syntax

Depending on their home country, people might spell terms differently, although they speak the same language. English is the best example: Americans write *color*, but Brits spell the same word *colour*. Many terms differ in a similar way.

While these differences are only cosmetic, others are more crucial. The afore-mentioned *soccer* is an American term. In Britain, people call the same sport *football*. If you do not exchange terms in cases like this, people will misunder-stand what you talk about.

In multilingual countries, local languages can be even more confusing. In Switzerland, for instance, both German and French are official languages. But even people whose native language is German use the French word *Merci* to say *Thank you.*

Be aware of little differences like this to give readers the impression that you really care about them.

Formal and Informal Language

A more crucial issue is the differentiation between formal and informal language. In English, it is only marginal; the vocabulary is nearly the same. So for your product page, this differentiation is not relevant.

In other languages, speakers differ more strictly. Let us stay with the German language. To address someone informally, Germans use the second-person singular. But for formal speech, people talk in third-person plural. So depending on whether you use formal or informal language, the same message needs different wording.

To pick the right form, you need to know which version is appropriate in which context. In German, it is common to address people formally in a professional context. So if your app belongs to the finance or productivity category, this approach is fine. In entertainment or gaming, informal language is acceptable, though.

In other languages, the rules are stricter. For the French, it is a no-go to address any stranger informally, no matter what the context is.

To avoid being impolite or even rude, find out what style is typical for the languages you translate into as well as for the context of your app.

Numbers, Measures and Scales

Numbers are easy to overlook when localizing the product page. They are only a minor factor, and for many apps, they are not relevant at all. But if you state numbers in texts or graphics, you should localize them.

Use the proper syntax for decimal markers and thousands delimiters. For example, in the United States and the United Kingdom, the comma is the delimiter and the point marks the decimals. In France, Germany or Spain, it is the exact opposite. In Switzerland, the apostrophe is used for delimiting thousands and the point for decimals. As a result, the same number looks different depending on the language and the country:

- 1,499.99 : English (UK / US)

- 1.499,99 : German (Germany)

- 1'499.99 : German (Switzerland)

Besides the syntax of numbers, also take care of measures and scales. Europeans count distances in centimeters, meters, and kilometers. Americans use inches, feet, yards, and miles. Across the world, different units exist for many other measures, and they differ not only between the US and Europe. Here are some more examples:

- Speed: Kilometers per hour vs. Miles per hour
- Areas: Square Meters vs. Square Feet
- Volumes: Liters vs. Gallons
- Weights: Kilograms & Grams vs. Pounds & Ounces
- Temperatures: Degrees Celsius vs. Degrees Fahrenheit
- Dress sizes
- Currencies

Especially for apps that rely on measurements (sports, maps, travel, cooking, weather, shopping, etc.), make sure to show users the units they know.

The Second Layer: Arrangement

The second level of localization deals with the arrangement of text elements.

Text Length

In some languages, speakers need more and longer words to express the same message. Therefore localized texts can become much longer than the English original. This might cause the need to adjust them.

Let us pretend one of your screenshots contains the following caption: "Try our app now." In English, it is only 15 characters long, including spaces. In French, the same phrase translates to: "Essayez notre application maintenant." With 36 characters, the translation is over twice as long as the original phrase. To make it fit into your screenshot, you have two options: Either you reduce the size of the captions (which harms the readability) or you shorten it by replacing or cutting words.

In texts like the description, you only have the latter option. In order to stay within the 4,000 character limit, you might need to rephrase text segments. Use shorter synonyms and cut words that are not crucial for the message. Of course, this task is very hard without the help of a native speaker. When in doubt, cut a whole paragraph (i.e. the technical requirements) instead of creating terrible kludge.

Reading Directions

Another challenge with visual creatives arises from reading directions. Languages based on the Latin or the Cyrillic alphabet, that are predominant in Europe, read from left to right. But Semitic languages like Arabic and Hebrew read from right to left. Some Asian languages like Japanese, Korean, and Chinese offer more than one option. It is possible to write them from left to right, but also from top to bottom.

In screenshots or videos, this can be a problem. The change of the reading direction can overload one side of an image. It also can harm guidance, because eye-catchers might not work anymore.

By reordering content, you can avoid these problems. Ideally, you create designs that work for all reading directions in the first place.

The Third Layer: Culturalization

The third and most complex layer of localization is culturalization. Based on their culture, history, and religion, people from different countries perceive your message differently. To pay tribute to these unique traits, you should adjust your localized product page. So double-check whether there is a need to localize the visual content in your icon, screenshots, and videos.

Regional Content for Regional Audiences

Especially in screenshots, you can address people with local content that they know. Check how *Google Maps* does it on iTunes. Their screenshots show the Statue of Liberty and the skyline of New York City for American English. But the French localization displays the Eiffel Tower and the Louvre Museum. In the Italian versions, you can see the Colosseum and the Leaning Tower of Pisa. And for German, they present the Berlin Gate (see examples on the next page).

You can also celebrate local holidays and events by adjusting your localizations. Think of the U.S. Independence Day, Chinese New Year, Brazilian Carnival or

Royal Weddings in the United Kingdom. Localized content gives people the impression that your app is made especially for them.

Fig. 119: Screenshots *Google Maps*
(Source: iTunes)[324]

Sensitivity for Cultural Manners

In some cases, changes are not only helpful but absolutely necessary to avoid offending people. For example, if your app is a farming game, you should not show pigs in your Arabic screenshots. In many Arabic countries, these animals are considered to be impure and showing them might offend people.

Also, check your characters and emojis. Gestures and symbols can have different meanings depending on the culture. The OK emoji, for instance, is a sign of approval in most European countries. But in Brazil, the same gesture is a terrible insult. The same is true for a thumbs-up in Arab countries and parts of Africa and South America.

The Cultural Meaning of Colors

Finally, take care about the colors in your visual metadata. Citizens of one country might connect a color to a positive characteristic, while people from another part of the world associate it with a negative meaning. Check the chapter about Color & Contrast for more details (page 254).

Which Localizations are for your App?

Localizing your product page requires a lot of time and work. So you need to choose wisely which languages are worth your efforts. Base your decision upon two criteria: the size of the audience and the relevance of your app for these audiences.

The Size of the Audience

Let us talk about audience size first. If you want to increase your user base significantly, focus on languages with many native speakers. These are the world's most popular languages (English excluded):[325]

- Chinese: 1.1 billion speakers worldwide
- Spanish: 572 million
- Hindi: 544 million
- Arabic: 422 million
- Malay / Indonesian: 281 million
- French: 233 million
- Portuguese: 229 million
- Bengali: 224 million
- Russian: 201 million
- Japanese: 140 million
- German: 128 million

Of course, the number of speakers is not sufficient to base your decision on. If people do not have access to smartphones or the Internet, they cannot use your app. Thus it does not make sense to create a localization for them.

Also consider education levels, especially regarding the languages that are available in your apps. As mentioned before, Germans must learn English at school. So it is reasonable to translate your product page into German, even if your app is only available in English. But if your app is only translated into Hindi, German metadata does not make any sense. People could not understand your app, even if they liked the product page.

Your App's Relevance in the Context of Language

You must also take into account whether your app is relevant for specific cultures or countries. It is unlikely that an app about ice hockey will be successful in Spain or Latin America. The sport is not popular there, so it makes no sense to localize the product page into Spanish.

In countries like Russia, Canada, and Switzerland, people love ice hockey, though. With these target markets in mind, it would be reasonable to translate the product page into Russian. This step would open the door to approach around 200 million Russians. A French translation could attract the seven million native speakers in Canada and 1.6 million Swiss. A German localization would make sense too, because it is the most popular language in Switzerland, with 5.5 million speakers.

Before picking up your dictionary, make yourself aware where your potential users are and which languages they speak.

Chapter Summary

Here is the summary about our learnings regarding localization:

- Localizing your product page makes your app more accessible for people that do not speak English as their first language.
- Localization has three layers: Translation, Arrangement, Culturalization.
- Translation affects terms, syntax, and scales. It is also important to distinguish between formal and informal language.
- A change of the reading direction might require adjusting the arrangement of visual creatives.
- Content or colors can have different meanings in different cultures.
- Localizing only makes sense if the audience you address with the new localization is big enough and interested in your app.

CHAPTER 17
COLOR & CONTRAST

Colors and color schemes are a crucial factor in marketing. They attract people's attention, and they transport messages and emotions on a subconscious level. They also have great branding power: According to a study by the University of Loyola, color increases brand recognition by up to 80%.[326]

As ASO is a form of marketing, colors are essential for your product page as well. This chapter will teach you how to use colors to create great user experiences and emotions that support your app's message.

What is Color?

To understand how we can use colors to enforce our messages, we need to dive into color theory for a moment. Let us start by defining what color is.

From an artistic point of view, color is "produced when light, striking an object, is reflected back to the eye."[327]

Physicists specify this explanation more technically. They define visible light as a form of electromagnetic radiation. Its wavelength determines its color. The human eye can distinguish colors with wavelengths between 390 nanometers (violet) and 700 nanometers (red). Wavelengths below or above are invisible to us.[328]

Color Properties

Colors have three different properties that define how they appear: hue, value, and saturation.

Hue refers to the wavelength of a color. When we talk about colors like *red* or *blue*, we actually talk about hues.[329]

Artists and educators distinguish twelve different hues. The color wheel, a visualization tool developed by Sir Isaac Newton, shows them in relation to each other.

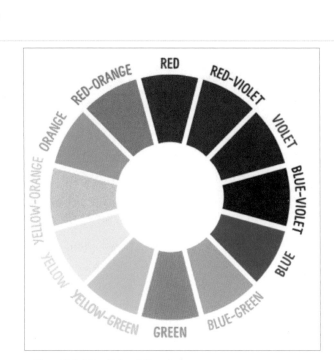

Fig. 120: The Color Wheel
(Source: Presentitude 2015)[330]

The second property of color is *value*. Value describes the lightness (or darkness) of a hue. High-value colors are lighter than low-value colors. The lightest color in the visible spectrum is white, while the darkest one is black.

You can make any hue appear lighter by adding white to it. The result is called a *tint*. The opposite is a *shade*: a darker variant, created by combining the original hue with black.[331]

The third property of every color is saturation—how the color appears under particular lighting conditions. Other terms for saturation are intensity or chroma. A hue is a pure color with maximum saturation because it does not contain black or white. It appears very strong and bright. In contrast, low saturation colors like pastels appear pale.

By adding gray to a hue, you lower its saturation and create a *tone*. A tone appears duller and softer than the original hue.[332]

The graphic on the next page shows an extended version of the Color Wheel, including tints, tones, and shades.

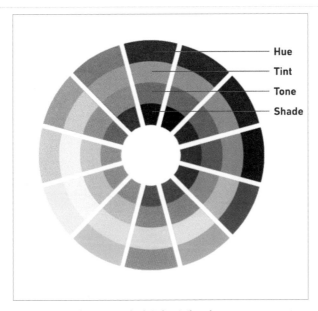

Fig. 121: The Extended Color Wheel
(Source: adapted from Presentitude 2015)[333]

Color Categories

Sorting colors into categories makes it easier to understand their relationships. It is common to do so based on their generation or their temperature.

Color Generations

We can classify the pure hues shown in the color wheel into three categories: primary, secondary, and tertiary colors.

Red, yellow, and blue are the *primary colors*. By mixing these three, you can compose all other colors. Thus they are also called *additive colors*. You can think of primary colors as "the parents of all the future generations of colors."[334]

Secondary colors are the children generation of the color family. They are the results of mixing equal parts of two primary colors. The three secondary colors are:

- Orange = Red + Yellow
- Green = Blue + Yellow
- Violet = Red + Blue

The grandchildren generation consists of the *tertiary colors*. They are created by mixing a primary color with one of its secondary color neighbors. The possible mixtures are:

- Amber = Yellow + Orange
- Chartreuse = Yellow + Green
- Aquamarine = Blue + Green
- Indigo = Blue + Violet
- Magenta = Red + Violet
- Vermillion = Red + Orange

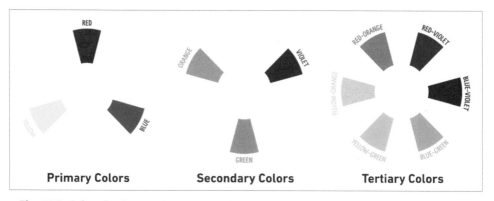

Fig. 122: Colors by Generation
(Source: adapted from Presentitude 2015)[335]

Color Temperature

Colors can also be classified by their temperature. Color temperature depends on the wavelength of a hue (page 247). In general, we distinguish three temperature classes.[336]

- Yellow, orange, and red are *warm colors.* They arouse feelings from optimism to violence, and rev viewers up.
- *Cool colors* tend to calm people down. They range from impersonal and antiseptic to comforting and nurturing. Blue, green, and purple belong to the cool side of the spectrum.

- *Neutral colors* are flexible. Depending on the surrounding colors, they can have warm or cool attributes, but they are more subtle. In some cases, they help to put the focus on adjacent colors. But they also can tone down their environment to avoid overpowering viewers.[337] Neutral colors include black, white, gray, silver, gold, brown, tan, and beige.

The Impact of Color

Colors are not just decorative. They have meanings. People learn from society to connect colors with specific attributes and values, and these associations unconsciously influence their evaluation of products and marketing materials. So colors impact consumer behavior.

Furthermore, colors also have physiological impacts. They can influence mental activity, the nervous system, hunger, and they can even cause pain. Their effects on the mind and the body are a crucial factor for marketing.

What we associate with Color

Most colors can have several positive or negative meanings, depending on the context. The categories of warm, cool, and neutral colors already gave you a broad idea about these meanings.

Let us be a bit more specific at least for the most common primary, secondary, and neutral colors. Note that the following pages discuss colors in the context of Western societies like the United States or Europe. For other cultures, the meanings of colors might differ.

Blue

Blue is a color that calms viewers and sets them into a state of inner balance. It is associated with trust, wisdom, and stability. That is why many logos in the banking and finance industry, as well as the seals of government authorities, contain blue. Think of Deutsche Bank, PayPal, the FBI, or the United States Department of Defense.

Furthermore, blue is the color of masculinity. Thus people dress their newborn baby boys in blue. But blue can also stand for sadness and melancholy.[338]

Red

Red is an intense and stimulating color that grabs viewers' attention and activates their internal alarm system. Therefore it is used in our daily life to point to danger and also to indicate prohibitions, for example in traffic signs.[339]

Red symbolizes a broad spectrum of emotions, from love and passion to aggression and rage. Many companies in the tourism industry like American Airlines or Air Emirates use red as a symbol of the passion for travel.

Yellow

Positivity, happiness, and joy are feelings that are connected to yellow. It is a warm color that stimulates the nervous system and increases mental activity. Logos in the food industry often contain yellow, because it also affects hunger. The logos of McDonald's, Subway or Burger King are famous examples.

Just like red, yellow is an attention-grabbing color that appears on many traffic signs. But it also has negative associations: Yellow stands for unreliability, cowardice, and deceit.[340]

Violet

Violet (or purple) is the royal color. It stands for wealth, luxury, nobility, and trustworthiness. As it is rare in nature, it is also connected to exclusivity and extravagance. Violet calms the mind and enhances spirituality and creativity. It represents feminine energy and romantic feelings, but also frustration.[341]

Companies from different industries use purple to emphasize their exclusivity, like the London-based jeweler Asprey.[342]

Orange

Orange is the result of mixing red and yellow, and it also combines many of their positive attitudes. Orange stands for warmth, fun, freedom, and a general sense of wellness. While it grabs viewers' attention almost as well as red, it is less aggressive and obtrusive. Orange stimulates mental activity and hunger. It leads to a higher level of confidence, and it helps to overcome disappointments.[343]

Orange is common for logos in the entertainment industry. Examples are the movie company 20th Century Fox or the German TV station ZDF.

Green

Green is relaxing and calming for viewers. Because this color is omnipresent in nature, we associate it with life, youth, and health. Thus green is popular in the medical industry (Healthcare Services of America), but also used to promote eco-friendly products like renewable energy (SolarCity) or recycling technologies (Waste Management Inc.).

But green is associated with negative attributes like greed and jealousy too.[344]

Black

Technically speaking, black is not a color, but the absence of color. It is mysterious and often connected to the unknown. Black can spike negative emotions such as sadness, emptiness or fear. But it also visualizes power, strength, and elegance, and it is perceived as professional and serious.[345]

Luxury brands like Rolex, Chanel or Gucci use black to emphasize their prestige.

White

White is an inherently positive color. It is clean, simple, and pure, and it stands for innocence, goodness, safety, and peace. White helps to create mental clarity and provides a feeling of renewal to viewers. But if it is too bright, it can also be painful to view and even cause a headache.[346]

Many logos across different industries contain white. Because of its association with peace, it is common in the logos of nonprofit organizations like WWF, UNICEF, and PETA.

Gray

Gray is a neutral, timeless color. It stands for conservatism and sophistication. Companies and organisations from all industries use gray to emphasize their reliability. Prominent examples are Apple and Wikipedia.

Gray tends to have negative associations with emotions like loss and depression. But in general, it is rather emotionless. Dark variants of gray communicate the same messages of strength and mystery as black, while lighter versions are more accessible.[347]

Brown

Just like green, brown symbolizes nature. It is the color of earth and wood, and it symbolizes wholesomeness, home, and stability. Brown stimulates the appetite and creates cozy feelings of warmth and relaxation.[348]

Brown is a common branding color for companies that offer agricultural products, like Nespresso, Sunfood or Organic Valley.

Gold

Gold stands for wealth and prosperity. It indicates extravagance, glamour, and excess. Depending on its saturation, gold can appear cheerful or traditional.[349]

Various luxury brands have gold in their logo. Some of them are Porsche and Lamborghini (cars), Patek Philippe (watches), and Roberto Cavalli (accessories).

Silver

Silver is elegant and sophisticated. Like gold, it stands for wealth and riches. It is also associated with adjectives like modern, industrial, and high-tech.[350]

In the car industry, many companies such as Audi, Lexus or Mazda use silver to emphasize their vehicles' quality.

Colors and Culture

As mentioned before, all the examples for the meanings, feelings, and attributes of colors descend from Western cultures. These associations can differ for viewers from other cultural backgrounds.

For example, black is a color of grief in the United States and many European countries. It is common to wear "mourning black" when attending funerals. But in South Africa, people wear red for the same occasion. The reasons are historical: Red represents the bloodshed suffered during the Apartheid era. In Buddhist societies like Cambodia, people believe that loved ones will be reincarnated after their death. To express this hope in a never-ending circle of life, they wear white mourning.[351]

Using color in the wrong cultural context can not only negate the desired positive effect, it can even be offensive to the target audience.

The following table gives you an overview of the meanings of colors in different parts of the world. Be aware that it is only a rough roundup on a continental level. Many countries have unique understandings of color. So before you localize creatives for a specific market, do your own research. Make sure to understand cultural interpretations of the colors you want to use.

	Europe / USA	Asia	Middle East	Latin America
Red	Love Passion Danger	Happiness Joy Celebration	Caution Danger Evil	Passion Religion Fire
Yellow	Warmth Happiness Caution	Sacred Royalty Courage	Happiness Strength Mourning	Sorrow Death Mourning
Blue	Trust Authority Masculinity	Strength Femininity Immortality	Holiness Spirituality Protection	Trust Religion Serenity
Green	Nature Luck Greed	Nature Youth Infidelity	Luck Fertility Strength	Nature Death Danger
Purple	Wealth Fame Royalty	Wealth Nobility Mourning	Wealth Virtue Omen	Sorrow Death Mourning

Tab. 13: Meanings of Colors in different Cultures
(Source: Globalme.net)[352]

Colors in Language

Western languages reflect the connections between colors and attributes, especially in idioms. For instance, the term *yellow press* refers to unreliable media. In contrast, the stocks of stable and trustworthy companies are called *blue chips*. The owner of a *black belt* is an acknowledged authority in martial arts, while *greenness* refers to a lack of experience. A *red flag* is a warning signal, but items on a *white list* are considered harmless.

Many similar expressions exist in the English language as well as culturally adjusted translations in other languages. If you learn about these expressions, you will get a better feeling for the meanings of colors.

Define for your app which emotions you want to connect to it. Then find color-related expressions that communicate these emotions. The results of your research will not only give you an idea about the colors that fit your app's purpose, they can also lead you to pictograms and other visual elements that support your message. Use these elements in your logo, app icon or screenshots to create additional relevance.

Colors and Demographics

In addition to the psychological meaning of colors, the preferences of specific demographics should be a factor in your designing process.

Color Preferences by Gender

The likes and dislikes of men and women regarding color show some similarities. Blue is the most popular color. For 57% of men and 35% of women, it is their favorite. Significant portions of both groups also like green, black, and red.

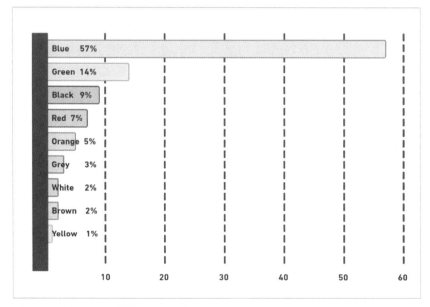

Fig. 123: Favorite Colors of Males
(Source: adapted from Joe Hallock)[353]

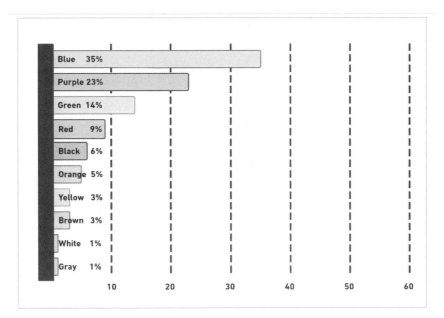

Fig. 124: Favorite Colors of Females
(Source: adapted from Joe Hallock)[354]

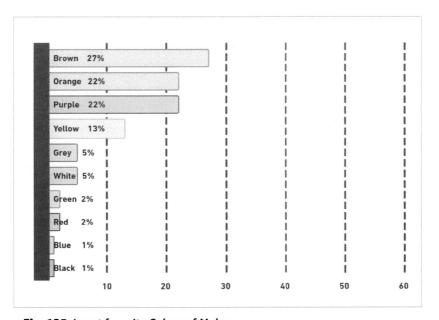

Fig. 125: Least favorite Colors of Males
(Source: adapted from Joe Hallock)[355]

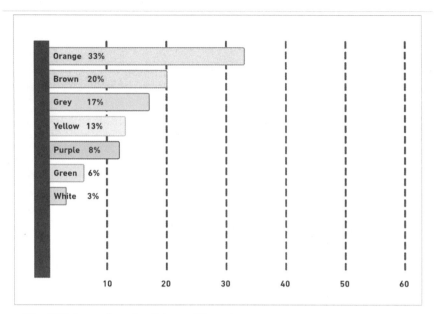

Fig. 126: Least favorite Colors of Females
(Source: adapted from Joe Hallock)[356]

But the opinions about purple differ. 23% of women call purple their favorite, making it the second most liked color among females. On the other hand, 8% of women name purple their most disliked color. Men do not love purple all at: 22% put it on top of their dislike ranking.

Other colors, such as brown, orange, and yellow, are disliked by both men and women.

If your app addresses a specific gender, you should take these preferences into consideration

Color Preferences by Age

Color preferences are not only different for men and women, but also for age groups. According to their phase of life, colors affect people differently.

Bright colors are exciting and stimulating for children, who start exploring the world. They prefer warm colors such as red, orange, and yellow.[357]

Teenagers, who struggle with adolescence, tend toward darker colors, including black.[358] On their way to adulthood, they also develop an interest in pastel colors.[359] The perception of colors changes further due to social conditioning.

The older people get, the more they reject colors that are associated with negative meanings.[360]

Finally, elders prefer compositions with darker and less saturated colors.[361]

Visual Harmony

No matter who your target audience is, the harmony of colors in your creatives is crucial.

So far we have looked at colors individually. But when you design your meta-data, you need a palette of multiple colors. Which colors you pick and how they look together affects the user experience significantly.

Visual experiences must be harmonious to engage viewers. Harmony pleases the human eye because it is orderly and balanced. This order helps the brain to process the visual information it receives and makes the experience understandable.

A lack of harmony is either under- or overstimulating for viewers. In the first case, the experience is boring, and the brain refuses to engage with it. In contrast, an overdone composition is chaotic. The brain rejects this chaos too, because it cannot organize the information. Both under- and overstimulating arrangements cause viewers to feel put off.

The solution is a middle way: a logical, yet challenging structure. Composing the right colors in an enjoyable color scheme creates this structure.[362] For this purpose, color relations matter.

Contrast

One aspect of visual harmony is contrast. Contrast describes "the difference in luminance between two adjacent colors."[363] But why is contrast important?

An essential function of the human eye is to identify indicators for danger. For this reason, dramatic changes in our environment attract our attention. Color contrast is one of these triggers.[364]

Color contrast also helps distinguish objects of interest, such as ripe fruit. Red apples stand out against the green leaves around them, and therefore they attract our attention.

When designing the visual metadata elements of your product page, you can leverage this condition. By applying colors with good contrast, you can highlight interesting components in your images. Additionally, you can use them to manipulate the harmony of a visual experience (and the emotions it creates).

Creating a Color Scheme

The relationships between two (or more) colors determine the harmony of a color scheme, and these relationships depend on their distance on the color wheel. For example, the distance between red and blue is four steps (also see the figure on the next page):

0. Red
1. Magenta
2. Violet
3. Indigo
4. Blue

Each color scheme rests upon a dominant hue. This base color sets the general mood and defines the emotions that the scheme creates. For instance, a warm base color will create a warm color scheme, and using a dominant color with high saturation will result in an intensive palette. In contrast, picking a pale base color will result in a less energetic composition.

All other colors of the scheme are supportive colors. They are picked based on their relationship to (or distance from) the dominant hue.

On the next pages, I will introduce you to the most common color schemes.

Monochromatic Schemes

A monochromatic color scheme contains different variations of only one hue. They can vary in value and saturation.[365]

Monochromatic schemes are elegant and comfortable. But they fail to create sufficient contrast for complex creatives. Setting highlights to emphasize specific elements of a picture is not possible.[366]

Analogous Schemes

Analogous colors are direct neighbors in the color wheel. For example, the neighbors of red are vermilion (red-orange) and magenta (red-purple). The three of them create an analogous color scheme.

Analogous color schemes are slightly richer than monochromatic designs. You can find them often in nature. They appear calm and comfortable, but they also lack contrast.[367]

If you choose this scheme, pick one of the neighbor colors to support the base color. The third color should only be used in small portions to set accents.[368]

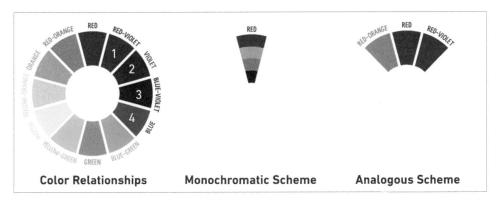

Fig. 127: Color Relationships, Monochromatic, and Analogous Color Scheme (Source: adapted from Presentitude 2015)[369]

Complementary Schemes

Complementary colors oppose each other in the color wheel, so they have the largest possible distance between them. Although a complementary scheme includes only two hues, it contains all three primary colors. For instance, red and green are complementary colors. As green is a mix of blue and yellow, all primary colors are needed to create this scheme.

A complementary color scheme creates maximum contrast. That comes with a downside: Especially high saturation colors tend to create unpleasant vibration effects. Thus complementary schemes should be applied in small doses only. They are fine for emphasizing singular aspects of an image, but they are a bad choice for larger areas or text.[370]

Split-Complementary Schemes

With a little adjustment, you can create a variation of the complementary scheme that provides a similar level of contrast but produces less tension. Split-complementary schemes consist of one base color and two supportive colors of the opposite temperature. So it is one warm base color with two cool supportive colors (or vice versa). Instead of the complementary color, you use its left and right neighbors as secondary colors.

If a split-complementary palette has the base color red, the proper supportive colors are chartreuse (yellow-green) and aquamarine (blue-green).

A split-complementary scheme is a smart pick for new designers. It is almost impossible to create a bad visual experience.[371] However, define the purpose of the supportive colors precisely. Use them for accents and highlights.[372]

Triad Schemes

The triad color scheme is a unique variation of the split-complementary scheme. It combines three colors that are evenly spaced around the color wheel. That means they are four steps away from each other and create a triangle, like the three primary colors red, blue, and yellow.

Just like complementary colors, the triad scheme tends to vibrate. As triad colors are evenly distributed around the color wheel, it is also hard to work out the dominant color.[373] Thus you need to balance them with care. Use the secondary colors for emphasizing only small aspects of your pictures.[374]

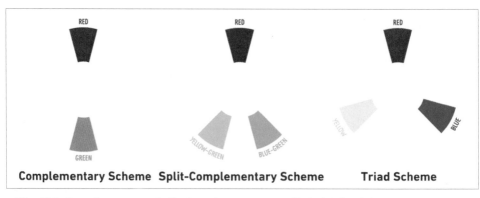

Fig. 128: Complementary, Split-Complementary, and Triad Color Schemes (Source: adapted from Presentitude 2015)[375]

Double-Complementary Schemes

Schemes of four colors offer even more options for design variations. They consist of two pairs of complementary colors, so they include two base colors and two supportive colors. Four-color schemes are hard to handle because they appear more nervous than three-color palettes.[376]

The double-complementary scheme uses color pairs that are neighbors on the color wheel. For example, red forms a complementary pair with green. Their neighbor pair is magenta (red-violet) and chartreuse (yellow-green), or alternatively vermillion (red-orange) and aquamarine (blue-green).[377]

Double-complementary colors create the least tension of all four-color schemes. Still, it is important to keep a good balance between warm and cool colors.

Rectangle Schemes

Another variant of the four-color scheme consists of two complementary pairs with a distance of two steps. In combination, they form a rectangle scheme. For red and green, the matching pairs are violet and yellow or orange and blue.[378]

Rectangle palettes create more tension than double complementary compositions. Again, keeping the warm-cool-balance is key.

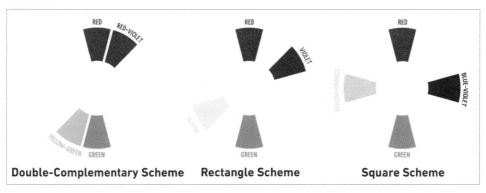

Double-Complementary Scheme   **Rectangle Scheme**   **Square Scheme**

Fig. 129: Double-Complementary, Rectangle, and Square Color Schemes (Source: adapted from Presentitude 2015)[379]

Square Schemes

The square color scheme is the third variation of the four-color scheme. It also uses two pairs of complementary colors, but their distance on the color wheel is three steps. That means the four colors are evenly distributed. For red and green, the matching pair for a square scheme is indigo (blue-violet) and amber (yellow-orange).

The square scheme is the most aggressive of all schemes. Defining dominant colors is difficult, and so is finding the proper balance between warm and cool colors. Unless you are an experienced designer, you should avoid this scheme.[380]

Amplifying a Color Scheme

Even four colors are usually not enough to create harmonious experiences. For a complex image, containing background, foreground, and text elements, schemes with only four pure hues are not flexible enough.

Adding Shades, Tones and Tints

To set highlights, provide better contrast or set a specific mood, you need lighter or darker color variations. Thus you should add shades, tones, and tints of your base and supportive colors to your palette.

Adding Neutral Colors

You may have noticed that all schemes we discussed only include warm and cool colors. Of course, neutral colors can be part of a color scheme as well. Especially if you use text elements in an image, they absolutely should.

You can add black, white, and most variants of gray to any scheme. Brown, off-white, beige, and tan are a little more challenging to fit in. Dark brown can be a good alternative for black, and the same goes for off-white as a replacement for white. For other colors, you have to try them out individually.[381]

Working with Graphics Software

The color model based on the three primary colors red, yellow, and blue is called the RYB model. It is great to learn color theory, but for practical work in a digital environment, it is inappropriate. A graphics software like Photoshop uses another model.

The RGB Model

The RGB model is based upon the hues red, green and blue. For each of them, the model knows 256 different levels of intensity. 0 is the least intense and 255 the most intense level.

Every color in the RGB model is the combination of one specific variant each of red, green, and blue. For instance, pure red consists of level-255 red, level-0 green, and level-0 blue. Its syntax in the RGB model is (255,0,0). Accordingly, the syntax for pure green is (0,255,0), and it is (0,0,255) for pure blue. Adding the maximum levels of red, green, and blue results in white (255,255,255), while the combined minimum levels deliver black (0,0,0). With the same technique, you can define every other color, including all tints, shades, and tones.

The Hexadecimal System

Three numbers in brackets, separated by commas, look somewhat bulky. Thus many graphics programs also know an alternative nomination system.

The hexadecimal system translates the RGB numbers from 0 to 255 into 2-digit codes. Each code consists of the numbers 0 to 9 and the letters A to F. So every color can be defined by a unique six-character string.[382]

This list shows the RGB values and hex codes for the basic hues:

Hue	RGB Value	Hexadecimal Code
Red	(255,0,0)	#FF0000
Green	(0,255,0)	#00FF00
Blue	(0,0,255)	#0000FF
Purple	(128,0,128)	#800080
Orange	(255,165,0)	#FFA500
Yellow	(255,255,0)	#FFFF00
White	(255,255,255)	#FFFFFF
Black	(0,0,0)	#000000

Tab. 14: RGB and Hexadecimal Values for the Main Hues
(Source: Author's own illustration)

Chapter Summary

Let us round up what we have learned:

- The appearance of a color is determined by hue, value, and saturation.
- Hues are pure colors, mixed from the three primary colors red, yellow, and blue.
- Value defines the lightness of a color.
- Saturation determines the purity or brilliance of a color.
- Hue + black = darker shade.
- Hue + white = lighter tint.
- Hue + gray = duller tone.
- Warm colors like red, orange, and yellow raise emotions.
- Cool colors like purple, blue, and green calm viewers down.
- Neutral colors like black, white, and brown can have both effects, depending on the adjacent colors.
- People associate specific characteristics and feelings with colors. These meanings vary depending on viewers' cultural background.
- Color preferences differ by gender and age.
- Harmonious color schemes are based on color relations (their distance in the color wheel).
- Schemes can consist of one to four hues on the cool-warm-spectrum.
- Shades, tints, tones, and neutral colors make palettes more flexible.
- For practical work, RGB or hexadecimal numbers are necessary to define a color.

CHAPTER 18
BLACK HAT ASO

Millions of apps compete for the highest rankings in the SERPs, the top positions in charts, and the prominent features. With the knowledge you have gained thus far, you have a good chance to end up as a winner in this competition, at least for search results.

But as in most competitions, some participants do not play by the rules. They try to create advantages for their apps by tricking users and the stores' algorithms with shady measures.

These measures are called *Black Hat ASO*.

On the following pages, I will introduce you to some of the most common black hat tactics. Be aware that fraudsters use many other shady tactics to create advantages for themselves, and they constantly develop more.

I strongly recommend not getting involved in this game. Black hat measures violate the guidelines of both Google and Apple, and using them can result in your app being banned. Besides, their benefits are limited, so it is absolutely not worth taking this risk. Stick to the permitted measures to increase visibility and improve the conversion rate which we discussed in this book.

Keyword Stuffing

On Google Play, you have to implement keywords into your app description. Some publishers do this excessively, but not in the form of a grammatically correct running text. Instead, they create large comma-separated lists that are a violation of Google's guidelines and also create a bad user experience.[383]

Targeting irrelevant Trending Keywords

As search volume is a crucial factor, it is a good idea to target trending keywords in iTunes, right? As long as these terms are relevant for your app, this tactic is great. But some developers do so although the trending keywords are not relevant for their apps, and that is a black hat measure.[384]

Targeting Competitors' Brands

A similar approach is to target brand keywords to benefit from competitors' popularity. This tactic violates the store guidelines on both Google Play and iTunes, but it also has little potential to create traffic because brand keywords are only valuable for the brand owner.

Copying popular Apps

Another shady way to take advantage of another app's fame is copying their title or icon. The graphic below shows a collection of example apps that look very similar to the popular *Adobe Flash Player*.

In many cases, these copycats are dangerous, because they steal users' personal data or install malware on their devices.

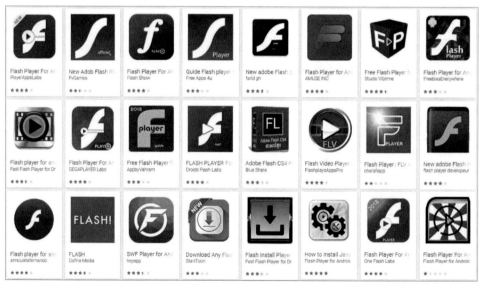

Fig. 130: Adobe Flash Player Copycats
(Source: Stefanko 2018)[385]

Buying Search Traffic to manipulate SERPs

Incentivized search traffic is another black hat tactic that targets SERPs. Some companies pay users to search for a specific keyword and download an app afterward. Alternatively, they use computer programs, so-called *bots*, to simulate the same process. By doing so, they improve the app's ranking for this keyword. Apple and Google consider incentivized search traffic a manipulation of their algorithm. That makes it a violation of their terms and conditions.[386]

Buying Bot Traffic to manipulate Top Listings

Instead of trying to get into SERPs, some fraudsters target the category or overall charts. To get to the top ranks, a vast number of downloads is necessary. Fraudsters try to create these by buying incentivized downloads or bot traffic.[387]

While it was possible to get into top ranks using this tactic in the past, today it is almost impossible. The store algorithms changed. Today, they value traffic quality much more than before, so user retention and engagement matter. With bot traffic, you cannot create either of the two.

Generating Fake Revenue to manipulate Grossing Rankings

Another black hat tactic is the manipulation of the top grossing charts. The grossing chart is the list of apps that generate the most revenue. It includes both premium apps and freemium apps with IAPs. On iTunes, this chart existed only until the introduction of iOS 11. So today, this tactic targets Google Play only.

It works like this: The fraudsters raise the price of their app to an unreasonably high level for a short time. Then their accomplices purchase the app multiple times to push it into the grossing charts. As soon as they accomplish this goal, the fraudsters reset the price back to the original amount. Finally, the accomplices claim refunds, which the fraudsters grant. To browsing users, the app now appears to be very successful, because it is on the top of the grossing charts, although no real user actually purchased it.[388]

Manipulating Ratings and Reviews

We have discussed that Social Proof is crucial for users' decision-making process (page 85). Thus fraudsters try to manipulate ratings and reviews. For instance, they incentivize users for giving reviews, or they buy them directly from services that have specialized in creating user feedback. Other black hat measures include reviewing one's own app and giving competitors negative reviews.[389]

Using misleading Publisher Names

On Google Play, publisher names appear in search results. This fact makes this metadata element the target of some fraudsters too. These publishers try to mislead people by using fake Social Proof instead of real company names to suggest their apps are very popular. See some examples in the screenshot below.[390]

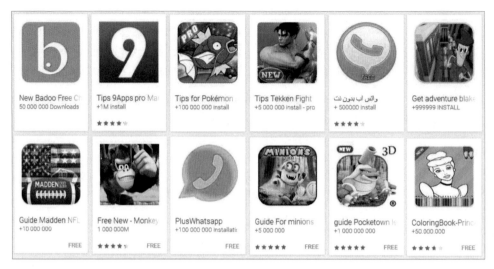

Fig. 131: Apps with misleading Publisher Names
(Source: Stefanko 2018)[391]

Again, black hat measures violate Google's and Apple's guidelines. Their outcome is not worth taking the risk of a rejection or ban of your app. Thus you should stay away from them.

CHAPTER 19
TOOLS & SOURCES

The number of tasks accompanying ASO can be overwhelming. Some of them take a lot of time or require very specific skills.

The good news is: You do not have to perform all of them manually. Many great tools and websites can save you time and work. In this chapter, I will introduce you to some of them. Be aware that this collection includes premium tools that you need to pay for. If you are on a tight budget, look for the free tools.

Keyword Tools

The following tools and sources help you to find keywords based on the behavior of users.

Synonyms Sources

Synonyms are terms with a similar meaning to a keyword. To find promising synonyms, check out these free websites:

*   *Thesaurus.com*:

    https://www.thesaurus.com/

*   *Oxford Dictionaries*:

    https:/www.Oxforddictionaries.com/thesaurus

*   *One Look Thesaurus*:

    https://www.onelook.com/thesaurus/

Keyword Suggestion Tools

To take the manual work out of finding new keyword suggestions, try these free tools:

*   *Apptweak* delivers keyword suggestions by country for Google Play or iTunes:

    https://www.apptweak.com/free-aso-tools/keyword-auto-suggestions

- *Appkeywords.net* gives suggestions only for Google Play, but in seven different languages:

  http://www.appkeywords.net/

- *Soovle.com* suggests keywords for web search engines like Google or Yahoo, as well as for Wikipedia and popular e-commerce platforms like Amazon or eBay. Note that soovle.com is not related to apps and only delivers English terms. Nevertheless, the site might give you some good ideas:

  https://soovle.com/

- *Apple Search Ads* suggests keywords including volume estimations (page 51):

  https://searchads.apple.com/

- *Google Trends* gives you a broad idea about trending web searches:

  https://trends.google.de/trends/

- The purpose of *Google Keyword Planner* is to assist customers of *Google Ads* in setting up campaigns. But keyword suggestions might be valuable for ASO as well:

  https://ads.google.com/home/tools/keyword-planner/

Keyword Evaluation Tools

For evaluating your keywords regarding volume and competition, check out these tools:

TheTool

https://thetool.io/

TheTool was originally developed to make the work of Spanish ASO agency *PickASO* easier. But it turned out to be so good that its developers decided to make it available to the public in early 2017. Since then they have improved TheTool constantly and added a ton of useful features.

TheTool has much more to offer than just the basic features. It allows you to analyze the quantity and quality of ratings for your app and your competitors. In addition, it has a feature called *ASO Score*, which scans your product page and highlights the potential for improvement.

AppTweak

https://www.apptweak.com/

AppTweak, located in Belgium, released its keyword tool in 2014. Features beyond the basic functions are added and optimized frequently. One of these is the *ASO Checklist*. This feature offers advice on how to optimize your product page, just like TheTool's *ASO Score*. Another component of AppTweak's portfolio is *Search Ads Intelligence*. It provides detailed information about popular search terms on Apple Search Ads.

Other functions include extensive keyword suggestion features or an overall visibility score, showing you the results of your keyword research.

SensorTower

https://sensortower.com/

Being in the industry since 2013, SensorTower is the grandfather of keyword tools. The basic keyword features are combined in a product called *App Intelligence*.

SensorTower offers even more useful tools, for which they charge separately:

- *Store Intelligence* gives you the ability to keep track of the most popular and most successful apps in the stores. It lets you analyze how many downloads are necessary to gain top rankings. Also, it offers insights about competition and profitability of different categories and countries.

- *Ad Intelligence* provides functions to analyze your competitors' advertising campaigns. You can use it to find out how much money they spend and which creatives they use.

- *Usage Intelligence* lets you track users' demographics and their behavior.

Working around Tracking Limits

If you buy one of the cheap or free plans, the limit on trackable keywords will restrict your ability to do research. You will not be able to track all promising terms permanently. That is a problem. At least for your initial evaluation, you need data for all your keyword candidates. Here is a workaround for this issue:

Each of the mentioned tools has functions for importing and exporting keywords. The former allows you to add many terms at once, so you do not need to type them in manually. The latter lets you download a keyword list including search volumes, difficulty, and your app's SERP rank for each term.

You can use these functions to work around the tracking limit of your plan. All you need in addition is a spreadsheet. If you followed my advice about brain-storming, you already have such a file. To fill it with the required data, follow these steps:

- Order the keywords in your spreadsheet alphabetically.

- Make sure the number of terms per column does not exceed your tool's limit of trackable keywords. Split columns to match the limit if necessary.

- Add three new columns on the right of each keyword column: one for volumes, one for difficulty, and one for ranks.

- Copy the terms in the first column and import them into your keyword tool.

- Wait until the tool has calculated volumes, difficulty, and ranks for each term.

- Export the list, including all data.

- Make sure the data columns in the export file match the columns' order in your keyword sheet.

- Copy the data from the export file into your spreadsheet.

- Clear all keywords from your keyword tool.

- Repeat the process for the other columns.

This whole process is very time-consuming. If you repeat it for all your single and long-tail keywords, it will take a couple of hours at least. But in the end, you will have an excellent database for your decisions, so it is worth the time.

Be aware that this approach is fine for a first-time evaluation of potential keywords. But for long-term monitoring, it is not appropriate.

Tools for Ratings and Reviews

As discussed, third party tools can help you gather user feedback, and they offer some advantages over the native solutions:

- *Instabug*: https://instabug.com/
- *Helpshift*: https://www.helpshift.com/
- *Apptentive*: https://www.apptentive.com/

Feedback Analytics Tools

If you receive a lot of feedback from users, scanning it and replying will take a lot of time. With the following tools, you can speed up this process:

- *AppBot*: https://appbot.co/
- *AppFollow*: https://appfollow.io/

App Review Services

Your app has no Social Proof yet? Approach the owners of these app review sites and ask them to write a piece about your app:

- https://feedmyapp.com/ (Android & iOS)
- https://web.appstorm.net/ (Android & iOS)
- http://www.appsafari.com (iOS only)
- https://fanappic.com/ (Android & iOS)
- https://pocketfullofapps.com/ (iOS only)
- https://www.theiphoneappreview.com/ (iPhone only)

Tools for the Description

The basic tool you need to draft an app description is a word processing program. Microsoft Word is fine, but you can also try one of the free alternatives:

- *Free Office*: http://www.freeoffice.com/
- *LifeOffice*: https://www.libreoffice.org/
- *AbiWord*: https://www.abisource.com/

Spell and Grammar Checking Tools

If the word processing program of your choice does not include a spell checker (or if you want to double-check), these online tools will do the job. All their basic versions are free:

- *JSpell*: https://www.jspell.com/public-spell-checker.html
- *Online Spellcheck*: https://www.online-spellcheck.com/
- *Grammarly*: https://www.grammarly.com/

Writing Style Analyzing Tools

The *Hemingway Editor* is great to make your texts easier to read and more accessible. It will find bulky phrases and vocabulary as well as overuse of adverbs and passive voice. The online version of Hemingway is free:

- http://www.hemingwayapp.com/

Emoji Collections

If you want to add emojis to your Google Play description, you will find large collections to copy and paste here:

- https://getemoji.com/
- https://www.emojicopy.com/

HTML Preview Tools

Before uploading your description to Google Play, preview it, especially if it includes emojis or rich formatting. The following websites allow you to upload your text including HTML tags, so you can check its look. Be aware that colors and emojis might appear a little different in Google Play. So previews will not be 100% accurate. However, they are sufficient to check your text's readability. They will also help you to discover errors such as missing closing tags. Here are three free services to choose from:

- https://htmledit.squarefree.com/
- http://htmlcodeeditor.com/
- https://www.onlinehtmleditor.net/

Graphics Tools

To create screenshots or icons from scratch, you need a graphics tool. For professional techniques such as Augmentation, blurred background art or connected creatives, it is a must-have. *Photoshop* is the most popular tool:

* https://www.adobe.com/products/photoshop.html

If you prefer a free tool, try *GIMP*. It is as powerful as Photoshop, but you will need some time to learn how to unleash its power. As GIMP has a great community, you will find tons of useful tutorials to learn about it.

* https://www.gimp.org/

Device Frames

To create screenshots with Photoshop or GIMP, you need device frames in which you can embed your in-app footage. Apple provides an up-to-date collection of their latest devices:

* https://developer.apple.com/app-store/marketing/guidelines/#section-products

For other devices and orientations (including Android phones and tablets), check out these free third party sources:

* https://mockuphone.com
* https://applypixels.com/
* http://goodmockups.com/
* https://placeit.net/

Background Art

To find great background photos, have a look on the following websites that contain a great variety of royalty-free stock images:

* *Unsplash*: https://unsplash.com/
* *Pexels*: https://www.pexels.com/
* *iStock*: https://www.istockphoto.com/
* *FreePhotos*: https://freephotos.cc/

Screenshot Tools

You might not want to invest the time and work to learn Photoshop or GIMP. In this case, use a screenshot tool. These web-tools allow you to upload your in-app footage and manipulate it afterward. For instance, you can choose a device orientation and add captions and background art.

Most of these tools are premium tools, but they offer a free version with limited functions. No matter which version you choose, the results will be decent—but only decent. Using professional techniques such as Augmentation is not possible.

If you want to test them nevertheless, check these tools:

- *Appure*: https://appure.io/

- *AppLaunchpad*: https://theapplaunchpad.com/

- *DaVinci Apps*: https://davinciapps.com/

If you want to take the manual work out of capturing in-app footage, try *Fastlane*. This open source tool enables you to create screenshots for many device sizes and languages automatically. Be aware that you need programming skills to take advantage of the power of *Fastlane*. You can find it here:

- https://fastlane.tools/

Video Tools

The creation of videos includes many more tasks than designing static images. Thus you will need additional tools and sources.

Screen Recording Tools

As said, iOS offers a native function for recording in-app footage. But for Android, you need a third party program. Here are some apps for this purpose that also include editing tools:

- *DU Recorder*[392] (free app)

- *AZ Screen Recorder*[393] (freemium app)

- *Mobizen*[394] (freemium app)

Instead of capturing your in-app footage with a mobile app, you can plug your device to a computer and record its screen with the proper software. Like the formerly mentioned mobile apps, most of them offer editing tools.

- *Quicktime* for Windows and Mac OS (free):

  Windows: https://support.apple.com/kb/DL837

  Mac OS: https://support.apple.com/kb/DL923

- *Reflector 3* for Windows and Mac OS (free 7-day trial):

  https://www.airsquirrels.com/reflector

Editing Tools

For editing raw video footage, check out these mobile apps:

- *Kinemaster* for Android[395] or iOS[396] (freemium app)

- *PowerDirector* for Android[397] (freemium app)

- *iMovie* for iOS[398] (free app)

If you prefer to do the editing on your computer, try these programs:

- *OpenShot* for Windows and Mac OS (free):

  https://www.openshot.org/

- *iMovie* for Mac OS (free):

  https://itunes.apple.com/app/id408981434?mt=12

- *ScreenFlow* for Mac OS:

  https://www.telestream.net/screenflow/

- *Movavi Video Editor* for Windows:

  https://www.movavi.com/videoeditor/

- *Filmora* for Windows and Mac OS:

  https://filmora.wondershare.com/

- *Final Cut Pro X* for Mac OS (free 30 days trial):

  https://www.apple.com/final-cut-pro/

Audio Recording Tools

These tools are great for recording voiceovers:

- *Audacity* for Windows and Mac OC (free):

  https://www.audacityteam.org/

- *Adobe Audition CC* for Windows and Mac OC (free):

  https://www.adobe.com/products/audition.html

- *Final Cut Pro X* (see in the editing tools section)

Voice Acting Services

If you do not want to speak the voiceover track yourself, consider hiring voice actors. You will find them on these websites:

- *Voices.com*: https://www.voices.com/
- *VoiceBunny*: https://www.voicebunny.com
- *Voice123*: https://voice123.com/

Music Sources

In case you want to add music to your video, check out the following websites. Most of them offer royalty-free music. But for a small subscription fee, you will get better quality songs and a bigger inventory to pick from.

- *Musopen*: https://musopen.org/
- *Audioblocks*: https://www.audioblocks.com/
- *Melodyloops*: https://www.melodyloops.com/
- *PremiumBeat*: https://www.premiumbeat.com/

Video Creation Services

As video creation is one of the most intensive parts of ASO, you might want to outsource the entire process. Check out these companies for this purpose:

- *AppTamin*: https://www.apptamin.com
- *Online Video Maker*: https://onlinevideomaker.net

A/B Testing Services

Apple does not provide a native function for A/B tests like Google, so you need an external partner for testing your iOS metadata:

- *SplitMetrics*: https://splitmetrics.com/
- *StoreMaven*: https://www.storemaven.com/

Localization Services

If you need help localizing your metadata, find a freelancer on these platforms:

- *Fiverr*: https://www.fiverr.com/
- *Gengo*: https://gengo.com/
- *Upwork*: https://www.upwork.com/
- *Workgenius*: https://www.workgenius.com/

Color Tools

In the chapter about colors, I pointed out the importance of harmonious color schemes. The following tools are very helpful to compose your scheme.

Color Scheme Builders

You might already know which main color you want to use for your scheme. In this case, a palette builder will help you find the matching supportive colors:

- The color-picker by *htmlcolorcodes.com* gives you the matching colors for your main hue. It supports most of the standard schemes. It also suggests a palette of tints, shades, and tones for your main and supportive colors.

  https://htmlcolorcodes.com/color-picker/

- *Paletton* is a similar tool. It is more intuitive to use as it works with a virtual color wheel. Since you can adjust supportive colors as well as tones, tints, and shades, you have more freedom to compose an individual scheme. Besides, Paletton creates sample websites so you can preview your colors.

  https://paletton.com/

- In case, you prefer to use schemes by experienced designers, check out *Color-Hex*. It contains more than 50,000 user-crafted color schemes. They come with hex codes so that you can use them immediately in your graphics program.

  If you have not decided about your base color yet, search their database to find color schemes that match your keywords.

  http://www.color-hex.com/color-palettes/

- On *Canva*, you can find 100 schemes, containing four colors each. For each scheme, the site shows a sample image containing the scheme's colors to give you a better impression of its appearance. The gallery includes hex codes and the color names.

  https://www.canva.com/learn/100-color-combinations/

Color Grabbing Tools

Photographs transport emotions superbly. Therefore they are a good starting point for creating a color scheme. If you own a beautiful picture related to your app, use it to craft your palette. These tools will help you:

- *ImageColorPicture.com* lets you extract one specific color from any uploaded photo:

  https://imagecolorpicker.com/en

- *Canva* offers a similar feature, but you do not have to pick colors manually. Instead, Canva gives you a complete color scheme including hex codes, automatically.

  https://www.canva.com/color-palette/

- Another tool with the same functions is *Adobe Color CC*. In comparison to Canva, it allows more freedom. If you do not like the automatic color selection for a photo, you can pick them manually.

  https://color.adobe.com/create/image/

  The mobile version of this program is available for iOS[399] and Android[400]. It works with every photo from your phone's gallery.

Contrast Checking Tools

Finally, you need a tool to check the accessibility of your final creatives.

- *ContrastChecker* checks the contrast of two colors based on six criteria. You can input hex codes or RGB values, or upload your creative and pick colors from it.

  https://contrastchecker.com/

- On *Contrast-Ratio.com*, you can input either color names or hex codes to check contrast:

  https://contrast-ratio.com/

- The *Color Contrast Analyser* is a desktop program with similar functions. A unique feature of the Windows version is the simulation of visual conditions. This function lets you check how colorblind people experience your content.

  https://developer.paciellogroup.com/resources/contrastanalyser/

CHAPTER 20

CONCLUSION

You see, ASO is a complex topic with numerous aspects that you need to consider. Keyword Research and Conversion Rate Optimization are connected in many ways. Before jumping into it, make your mind up about these questions:

- What is your app's USP and what makes it special?
- What attributes and values does it stand for?
- Who is your target audience?
- What kind of story do you want to tell?

The answers to these questions will provide the basement for your work.

Where to start?

All the options you have to optimize your product page might be a little overwhelming at first sight. To funnel your efforts reasonably, consider the efforts for each metadata element as well as their impacts.

Indicators for a significant impact are:

- Indexed Metadata. The Google Play long description is indexed and thus has a bigger effect than the description on iOS.
- Users' opinion on metadata importance.
- The number of conversion opportunities a metadata element appears on. For instance, the icon appears on all opportunities, but the description shows up only on the product page.
- The number of actions users have to perform to see the element. To see the icon, users only need to perform a search. To read the description, they additionally have to visit the product page and click *show me more*.

The required effort also depends on several factors:

- Whether they address only visibility or conversion or both. Optimizing the Google Play description for both visibility and conversion requires more work than optimizing the iOS description only for conversion.

- Their number or length. An app title needs less work than a description.

- The number of tools you require to create them. For video creation, you need software for capturing the in-app footage, recording voiceover, and editing. For static visuals such as icons, you only need one graphics program.

It makes sense to start with the low-hanging fruit: The metadata elements that promise the biggest impact while you only need to invest little effort. In the figures below, you can find them in the upper right sections.

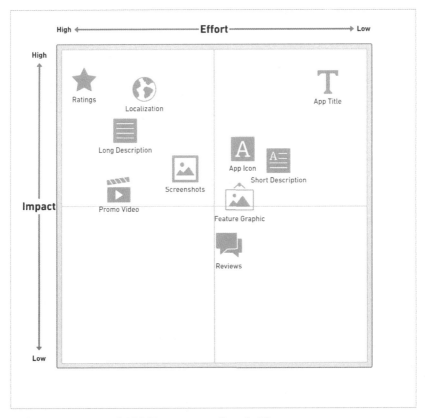

Fig. 132: Impact of ASO Measures on Google Play
(Source: adapted from Kwakyi 2017)[401]

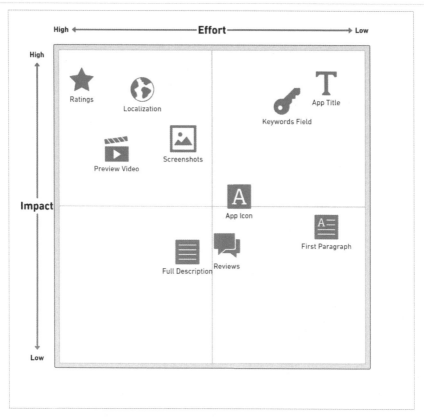

Fig. 133: Impact of ASO Measures on iOS
(Source: adapted from Kwakyi 2017)[402]

Final Words

That is it. Congratulations, you have made it through.

You have gained detailed insights about the basics of ASO, about keyword research, and about optimizing your app's metadata for conversion. Furthermore, you have learned how to properly localize your product page to attract people all around the world, how to use colors in the right way, and how you can make your daily ASO work easier with the proper tools.

You are now prepared to start your own ASO journey. I sincerely hope that the knowledge from this book will help you make your app successful on iTunes and Google Play.

If you want to share your success story, or if you have questions or comments regarding this book, I would love to hear from you. Send me a message to feedback@aso-ebook.com or visit www.mobile-marketing-masterclass.com and use the contact form. Alternatively, you can also ping me on LinkedIn: www.linkedin.com/in/oliverhoss.

Please tell your friends and colleagues about this book and consider leaving a review on Amazon.

Thank you for reading and best of luck for your ASO journey.

— Oliver

NOTES

1. "iPhone 3G on Sale Tomorrow", Apple Newsroom, July 10, 2008, https://www.apple.com/newsroom/2008/07/10iPhone-3G-on-Sale-Tomorrow/, accessed June 2018.

2. "Android Market: Now available for users", Android Developers Blog (blog), October 22, 2008, https://android-developers.googleblog.com/2008/10/android-market-now-available-for-users.html, accessed June 2018.

3. "Store Stats", 42matters.com, https://www.42matters.com/stats, accessed June 2018.

4. Ellis Hamburger, "Indie smash hit 'Flappy Bird' racks up $50K per day in ad revenue", TheVerge.com, February 5, 2014, https://www.theverge.com/2014/2/5/5383708/flappy-bird-revenue-50-k-per-day-dong-nguyen-interview, accessed June 2018.

5. Artyom Dogtiev, "Mobile App Advertising Rates (2018)", BusinessofApps.com, July 10, 2018, http://www.businessofapps.com/guide/mobile-app-advertising-cpm-rates/, accessed December 2018.

6. "App Store Optimization", TheTool.io, https://thetool.io/aso-app-store-optimization, accessed August 2018.

7. Cambridge Dictionary, s.v. "app", https://dictionary.cambridge.org/us/dictionary/english/app, accessed June 2018.

8. "Definition - What does Operating System (OS) mean?", Techopedia.com, https://www.techopedia.com/definition/3515/operating-system-os, accessed June 2018.

9. "Threema", iTunes, https://itunes.apple.com/us/app/id578665578?mt=8, accessed December 2018.

10. "Minecraft", iTunes, https://itunes.apple.com/us/app/id479516143?mt=8, accessed December 2018.

11. "Messenger", iTunes, https://itunes.apple.com/us/app/id454638411?mt=8, accessed December 2018.

12. "Clash of Clans", iTunes, https://itunes.apple.com/us/app/id529479190?mt=8, accessed December 2018.

13. "Veggie Weekend", iTunes, https://itunes.apple.com/us/app/id625161325?mt=8, accessed June 2018.

14. "USA TODAY", iTunes, https://itunes.apple.com/us/app/id504631398?mt=8, accessed June 2018.

15. Gerard Gordon, "App Store ASO vs. Google Play ASO in 2018 – Meet All the Differences!", ASO Blog (blog), TheTool.io, August 31, 2018, https://thetool.io/2018/aso-app-store-vs-aso-google-play, accessed September 2018.

16. Ibid.

17. Ibid.

18. John Koetsier, "How People Make Download Decisions on Google Play and the App Store", TUNE, 2018, downloaded from https://mkt.tune.com/rs/210-BFY-977/images/TMC-WP-App-Store-Optimization-How-People-Make-Download-Decisions-on-Google-Play-and-the-App-Store.pdf, accessed June 2018, 2-3.

19. John Koetsier, "App store optimization: How to win Google Play and App Store search", TUNE Blog (blog), September 24, 2016, https://www.tune.com/blog/app-store-optimization-win-google-play-app-store-search/, accessed June 2018.

20. Gad Maor, "How to Design the Perfect App Store Product Page", ASO-blog (blog), StoreMaven.com, October 22, 2015, https://www.storemaven.com/how-to-design-the-perfect-app-store-product-page/, accessed July 2018.

21. "Deconstructing the Mobile Marketing Funnel", TUNE, downloaded from https://mkt.tune.com/tmc-deconstructing-mobile-marketing-funnel.html, accessed June 2018, 3.

22. Ibid.

23. "What is an impression?", BrickMarketing.com, http://www.brickmarketing.com/define-impression.htm, accessed June 2018.

24. Peter Fodor, "Increasing Visibility Through Getting Featured", in: Advanced App Store Optimization - A complete Guide to ASO, edited by Moritz Daan and Gabe Kwakyi (Phiture & Incipica, 2018), 106-112.

25. "Twitter", iTunes, https://itunes.apple.com/us/app/id333903271?mt=8, accessed December 2018.

26. Rowan Emsilie, "The Complete Guide To App Store Categories", Priori Data (blog), August 1, 2017, https://blog.prioridata.com/the-complete-guide-to-app-store-categories, accessed June 2018.

27. John Koetsier, "App store optimization: How to win Google Play and App Store search", TUNE Blog (blog), September 24, 2016, https://www.tune.com/blog/app-store-optimization-win-google-play-app-store-search/, accessed June 2018.

28. Collins English Dictionary, s.v. "keyword", https://www.collinsdictionary.com/dictionary/english/keyword, accessed June 2018.

29. "Why Every App Publisher Must Use Long-Tail ASO Keywords", Mobile Action Blog (blog), August 9, 2018, https://www.mobileaction.co/blog/app-store-optimization/long-tail-aso-keywords/, accessed August 2018.

30. Ryan Weber, "App Store Optimization (ASO) Whitepaper Part 1: Breaking the Discovery Code- How to Achieve Top Search Rankings" (2016), downloaded from http://nativex.com/wp-content/uploads/2016/06/Whitepaper_ASO.pdf, accessed July 2018, 15.

31. Elisa Gabbert, "The 3 Types of Search Queries & How You Should Target Them", The Wordstream Blog (blog), December 10, 2012, https://www.wordstream.com/blog/ws/2012/12/10/three-types-of-search-queries, accessed June 2018.

32. "The App Store Factors Your Users Really Care About", TUNE, downloaded from https://mkt.tune.com/tmc-app-store-factors-users-really-care-about.html, accessed June 2018, 9.

33. John Koetsier, "App store optimization: How to win Google Play and App Store search", TUNE Blog (blog), September 24, 2016, https://www.tune.com/blog/app-store-optimization-win-google-play-app-store-search/, accessed June 2018.

34. "The App Store Factors Your Users Really Care About", TUNE, downloaded from https://mkt.tune.com/tmc-app-store-factors-users-really-care-about.html, accessed June 2018, 9.

35. Ryan Weber, "App Store Optimization (ASO) Whitepaper Part 1: Breaking the Discovery Code- How to Achieve Top Search Rankings" (2016), downloaded from http://nativex.com/wp-content/uploads/2016/06/Whitepaper_ASO.pdf, accessed July 2018, 11.

36. Alex Klein, "Organic Acquisition", in: The Complete Guide to App Marketing (TUNE 2014), downloaded from https://mkt.tune.com/tmc-complete-guide-app-marketing.html, accessed July 2018, 30.

37. Ryan Weber, "App Store Optimization (ASO) Whitepaper Part 1: Breaking the Discovery Code- How to Achieve Top Search Rankings" (2016), downloaded from http://nativex.com/wp-content/uploads/2016/06/Whitepaper_ASO.pdf, accessed July 2018, 9-10.

38. "Apple Search Ads Search Popularity for ASO", Chrome Web Store, https://chrome.google.com/webstore/detail/apple-search-ads-search-p/ihggdihemilfdammomlckdocaodobcbb, accessed June 2018.

39. "Search Ads Volume Tool for ASO", Chrome Web Store, https://chrome.google.com/webstore/detail/search-ads-volume-tool-fo/emaienkonoepeghlpppkjlidnmklkdao, accessed July 2018.

40. "The Ultimate Guide to Keyword Research", TUNE, downloaded from https://mkt.tune.com/tmc-ultimate-guide-keyword-research.html, accessed June 2018, 8.

41. Alex Klein, "Organic Acquisition", in: The Complete Guide to App Marketing (TUNE 2014), downloaded from https://mkt.tune.com/tmc-complete-guide-app-marketing.html, accessed July 2018, 25.

42. "Mobile & Tablet iOS Version Market Share Worldwide", StatCounter.com, http://gs.statcounter.com/ios-version-market-share/mobile-tablet/worldwide, accessed June 2018.

43. Gabe Kwakyi, "How to Optimize for Promoted IAP (In App Purchases)", Incipia Blog (blog), November 19, 2017, https://incipia.co/post/app-marketing/how-to-optimize-for-promoted-iap-in-app-purchases/, accessed June 2018.

44. "Add an in-app purchase to promote (iOS)", App Store Connect Help, https://help.apple.com/app-store-connect/#/deve3105860f, accessed June 2018.

45. "Promoting Your In-App Purchases", Apple Developer, https://developer.apple.com/app-store/promoting-in-app-purchases/, accessed June 2018.

46. "My Little Pony Rainbow Runners", iTunes, https://itunes.apple.com/us/app/id1195841989?mt=8, accessed July 2018.

47. "Jetpack Joyride", iTunes, https://itunes.apple.com/us/app/id457446957?mt=8, accessed July 2018.

48. Moritz Daan, "Increasing the Number of Keywords in App Store Optimization by Localization", ASO Stack, June 28, 2016, https://asostack.com/increasing-the-number-of-keywords-in-app-store-optimization-by-localization-daa02ffd8946, accessed January 2019.

49. Moritz Daan and Gabe Kwakyi, "Localization", in: Advanced App Store Optimization - A complete Guide to ASO, edited by Moritz Daan and Gabe Kwakyi (Phiture & Incipia, 2018), 273-274.

50. Moritz Daan, "Increasing the Number of Keywords in App Store Optimization by Localization", ASO Stack, June 28, 2016, https://asostack.com/increasing-the-number-of-keywords-in-app-store-optimization-by-localization-daa02ffd8946, accessed January 2019.

51. "Super Mario Run", Apps on Google Play, https://play.google.com/store/apps/details?id=com.nintendo.zara&hl=en, accessed December 2018.

52. Daniel Peris, "URL / Package as a Search Ranking Factor in Google Play Store [ASO—App Store Optimization]", Medium.com, April 6, 2017, https://medium.com/@DanielPeris/google-play-aso-url-package-search-ranking-factor-35c4ce938bdc, accessed August 2018.

53. "Last Day on Earth: Survival", Apps on Google Play, https://play.google.com/store/apps/details?id=zombie.survival.craft.z&hl=en, accessed December 2018.

54. John Koetsier, "How People Make Download Decisions on Google Play and the App Store", TUNE, 2018, downloaded from https://mkt.tune.com/rs/210-BFY-977/images/TMC-WP-App-Store-Optimization-How-People-Make-Download-Decisions-on-Google-Play-and-the-App-Store.pdf, accessed June 2018, 6.

55. Ibid.

56. "AIDA: Attention-Interest-Desire-Action", Mindtools.com, https://www.mindtools.com/pages/article/AIDA.htm, accessed June 2018.

57. Raaf Sundquist, "Copywriting 101: What's In It For Me?", Telepathy Business (blog), https://www.dtelepathy.com/blog/business/copywriting, accessed June 2018.

58. "Keep It Simple Stupid Principle (KISS Principle)", Technopedia.com, https://www.techopedia.com/definition/20262/keep-it-simple-stupid-principle-kiss-principle, accessed June 2018.

59. "How to manage your Brand's Reputation on Mobile", AppTentive, 2016, downloaded from https://go.apptentive.com/2016-03MobileBrandRepMgmt_ThankYouLandingPage.html?aliId=2532340, accessed July 2018, 2.

60. John Koetsier, "How People Make Download Decisions on Google Play and the App Store", TUNE, 2018, downloaded from https://mkt.tune.com/rs/210-BFY-977/images/TMC-WP-App-Store-Optimization-How-People-Make-Download-Decisions-on-Google-Play-and-the-App-Store.pdf, accessed June 2018, 7.

61. Ibid.

62. "How to manage your Brand's Reputation on Mobile", AppTentive, 2016, downloaded from https://go.apptentive.com/2016-03MobileBrandRepMgmt_ThankYouLandingPage.html?aliId=2532340, accessed July 2018, 3.

63. Paul Medrano, "How Much Your App Ratings & Reviews Affect Your Conversion Rate", Noteworthy – The Journal Blog (blog), Februar 19, 2018, https://blog.usejournal.com/how-much-your-app-ratings-reviews-affect-your-conversion-rate-4dfa458c1c2e, accessed June 2018.

64. "How to manage your Brand's Reputation on Mobile", AppTentive, 2016, downloaded from https://go.apptentive.com/2016-03MobileBrandRepMgmt_ThankYouLandingPage.html?aliId=2532340, accessed July 2018, 3.

65. "What is the Social Proof Theory?", The Psychology Notes HQ, August 31, 2015, https://www.psychologynoteshq.com/social-proof/, accessed June 2018.

66. Ibid.

67. "The Story of the George Foreman Grill", Foreman Grill Recipes, https://foremangrillrecipes.com/the-story/, accessed June 2018.

68. Ashley Sefferman, "The Average Mobile Apps' Ratings and Reviews, by Category", The Being Apptentive Blog (blog), October 20, 2016, https://www.apptentive.com/blog/2016/10/20/average-mobile-apps-ratings-and-reviews-by-category/, accessed June 2018.

69. "Bell Agrees To $1.25 Million Fine After Fake Company App Reviews", HuffPost Canada, October 15, 2015, https://www.huffingtonpost.ca/2015/10/14/bell-employees-post-positive-review_fine_n_8297458.html, accessed June 2018.

70. "How to manage your Brand's Reputation on Mobile", AppTentive, 2016, downloaded from https://go.apptentive.com/2016-03MobileBrandRepMgmt_ThankYouLandingPage.html?aliId=2532340, accessed July 2018, 5-6.

71. "Store Listing and Promotion", Google Play Developer Policy Center, https://play.google.com/intl/en_ALL/about/storelisting-promotional/ratings-reviews-installs/, accessed June 2018.

72. "97% of Google Play app reviews go unanswered", Appbot Support, https://support.appbot.co/help-docs/97-google-play-app-reviews-go-unanswered/, accessed June 2018.

73. Ashley Sefferman: "The 10-Step Checklist to Managing Negative App Reviews", The Being AppTentive Blog (blog), December 6, 2016, downloaded from http://cdn2.hubspot.net/hubfs/232559/The%2010%20Step%20Checklist%20to%20Managing%20Negative%20App%20Reviews.pdf?t=1480985822031, accessed June 2018.

74. John Koetsier, "How People Make Download Decisions on Google Play and the App Store", TUNE, 2018, downloaded from https://mkt.tune.com/rs/210-BFY-977/images/TMC-WP-App-Store-Optimization-How-People-Make-Download-Decisions-on-Google-Play-and-the-App-Store.pdf, accessed June 2018, 7.

75. Ibid.

76. "App Store Optimization Case Study by StoreMaven - Lift Conversions by 66%", StoreMaven, August 1, 2016, https://www.slideshare.net/maorgad/app-store-optimization-case-study-by-storemaven-lift-conversions-by-66, accessed June 2018, 27.

77. "Six Pack in 30 Days - Abs Workout", Apps on Google Play, https://play.google.com/store/apps/details?id=sixpack.sixpackabs.absworkout&hl=en, accessed December 2018.

78. "Fiverr — Freelance Services", Apps on Google Play, https://play.google.com/store/apps/details?id=com.fiverr.fiverr&hl=en, accessed December 2018.

79. "Babbel — Learn Languages", Apps on Google Play, https://play.google.com/store/apps/details?id=com.babbel.mobile.android.en&hl=en, accessed December 2018.

80. "Instant Gaming", Apps on Google Play, https://play.google.com/store/apps/details?id=com.instantgaming.android&hl=en, accessed December 2018.

81. "Remente - Self Improvement", Apps on Google Play, https://play.google.com/store/apps/details?id=com.remente.app&hl=en, accessed December 2018.

82. "Uber", Apps on Google Play, https://play.google.com/store/apps/details?id=com.ubercab&hl=en, accessed December 2018.

83. "Grow Empire: Rome", Apps on Google Play, https://play.google.com/store/apps/details?id=com.empire.grow.rome&hl=en, accessed December 2018.

84. "Naviki — the bicycle satnav", Apps on Google Play, https://play.google.com/store/apps/details?id=org.naviki&hl=en, accessed December 2018.

85. "Komoot – Cycling, Hiking & Mountain Biking Maps", Apps on Google Play, https://play.google.com/store/apps/details?id=de.komoot.android&hl=en, accessed December 2018.

86. "Runtastic Running App & Mile Tracker", Apps on Google Play, https://play.google.com/store/apps/details?id=com.runtastic.android&hl=en, accessed December 2018.

87. "Walmart Grocery Shopping", iTunes, https://itunes.apple.com/us/app/walmart-grocery-shopping/id998754894?mt=8, accessed December 2018.

88. "Store Listing and Promotion", Google Play Developer Policy Center, https://play.google.com/about/storelisting-promotional/metadata/, accessed June 2018.

89. "Clash of Lords 2: Guild Castle", iTunes, https://itunes.apple.com/us/app/clash-of-lords-2-guild-castle/id867427452?mt=8, accessed December 2018.

90. "OpenTable", iTunes, https://itunes.apple.com/us/app/id296581815?mt=8, accessed December 2018.

91. "Duolingo: Learn Languages Free", Apps on Google Play, https://play.google.com/store/apps/details?id=com.duolingo&hl=en, accessed December 2018.

92. Katerina Zolotareva, "How to Use HTML & Emoji in your Google Play Store App Listing", ASO Blog (blog), TheTool.io, July 11, 2017, https://thetool.io/2017/how-to-use-html-emoji-googleplay, accessed June 2018.

93. Ibid.

94. "Shoot Goal — Soccer Games 2019", Apps on Google Play, https://play.google.com/store/apps/details?id=com.bambo.shootgoal&hl=de, accessed July 2018.

95. "Move Well - Mobility Routines", iTunes, https://itunes.apple.com/us/app/id957563124?mt=8, accessed July 2018.

96. "Home Street — Home Design Game", Apps on Google Play, https://play.google.com/store/apps/details?id=com.supersolid.spark&hl=en, accessed July 2018.

97. "Bikemap - GPS Bike Route Tracker & Map for Cycling", Apps on Google Play, https://play.google.com/store/apps/details?id=com.toursprung.bikemap&hl=en, accessed July 2018.

98. "Daily Horoscope - Zodiac Signs and Palmistry", Apps on Google Play, https://play.google.com/store/apps/details?id=daily.zodiac.horoscope.palmistry&hl=en, accessed July 2018.

99. "Affinity Photo", iTunes, https://itunes.apple.com/app/id1117941080?mt=8, accessed July 2018.

100. "Forex Calendar, Market & News", Apps on Google Play, https://play.google.com/store/apps/details?id=com.myfxbook.forex&hl=en, accessed July 2018.

101. John Koetsier, "How People Make Download Decisions on Google Play and the App Store", TUNE, 2018, downloaded from https://mkt.tune.com/rs/210-BFY-977/images/TMC-WP-App-Store-Optimization-How-People-Make-Download-Decisions-on-Google-Play-and-the-App-Store.pdf, accessed June 2018, 7-8.

102. Ibid., 7.

103. "App Store Optimization Case Study by StoreMaven - Lift Conversions by 66%", StoreMaven, August 1, 2016, https://www.slideshare.net/maorgad/app-store-optimization-case-study-by-storemaven-lift-conversions-by-66, accessed June 2018, 26.

104. "TimeTune - Optimize Your Time", Apps on Google Play, https://play.google.com/store/apps/details?id=com.gmail.jmartindev.timetune&hl=en, accessed December 2018.

105. "Marketing Resources and Identity Guidelines", Apple Developer, https://developer.apple.com/app-store/marketing/guidelines/#photography, accessed July 2018.

106. "CacheToolBox", iTunes, https://itunes.apple.com/us/app/id558528399?mt=8, accessed December 2018.

107. "mytaxi: Tap & Move Freely", iTunes, https://itunes.apple.com/us/app/id357852748?mt=8, accessed December 2018.

108. "Pill Alert - Med, Prescriptions Reminder & Tracker", iTunes, https://itunes.apple.com/us/app/id889581369?mt=8, accessed December 2018.

109. "Bumble - Meet New People", iTunes, https://itunes.apple.com/us/app/id930441707?mt=8, accessed December 2018.

110. "Todoist: Organize your life", iTunes, https://itunes.apple.com/us/app/id572688855?mt=8, accessed December 2018.

111. "wetter.com", iTunes, https://itunes.apple.com/us/app/id1020581825?mt=8, accessed December 2018.

112. "Hootsuite - Social Media Tools", iTunes, https://itunes.apple.com/us/app/id341249709?mt=8, accessed December 2018.

113. "SumUp - Credit Card Reader", iTunes, https://itunes.apple.com/us/app/id514879214?mt=8, accessed December 2018.

114. "Salesforce Authenticator", iTunes, https://itunes.apple.com/us/app/id782057975?mt=8, accessed December 2018.

115. "Joom", iTunes, https://itunes.apple.com/gb/app/id1117424833?mt=8, accessed December 2018.

116. "VivaVideo - Best Video Editor", iTunes, https://itunes.apple.com/us/app/id738897668?mt=8, accessed December 2018.

117. "Gmail - Email by Google", iTunes, https://itunes.apple.com/us/app/id422689480?mt=8, accessed December 2018.

118. "WordWhizzle Search", Apps on Google Play, https://play.google.com/store/apps/details?id=com.apprope.wordsearch&hl=en, accessed December 2018.

119. "Google Translate", Apps on Google Play, https://play.google.com/store/apps/details?id=com.google.android.apps.translate&hl=en, accessed December 2018.

120. "EVVA AirKey", iTunes, https://itunes.apple.com/us/app/id1167529896?mt=8, accessed December 2018.

121. "Heads Up!", iTunes, https://itunes.apple.com/us/app/id623592465?mt=8, accessed December 2018.

122. "Guitar Lessons Fender Play", iTunes, https://itunes.apple.com/us/app/id1226057939?mt=8, accessed December 2018.

123. "Pillow Automatic Sleep Tracker", iTunes, https://itunes.apple.com/us/app/id878691772?mt=8, accessed December 2018.

124. "Uber", iTunes, https://itunes.apple.com/gb/app/id368677368?mt=8, accessed December 2018.

125. "Tribal Wars", iTunes, https://itunes.apple.com/us/app/id435365767?mt=8, accessed December 2018.

126. "Pacifica for Stress & Anxiety", iTunes, https://itunes.apple.com/us/app/id922968861?mt=8, accessed December 2018.

127. "uSwitch: Switching Made Simple", iTunes, https://itunes.apple.com/gb/app/uswitch-switching-made-simple/id935325621, accessed December 2018.

128. "South Western Railway", iTunes, https://itunes.apple.com/us/app/id1104215511?mt=8, accessed December 2018.

129. "Budget Planner - Control Your Finances", iTunes, https://itunes.apple.com/us/app/id963763360?mt=8, accessed December 2018.

130. "Takeaway.com", iTunes, https://itunes.apple.com/us/app/id333214491?mt=8, accessed December 2018.

131. "Butt & Leg 101 Fitness - Free workout trainer", iTunes, https://itunes.apple.com/us/app/id1206739187?mt=8, accessed December 2018.

132. "AudioBook - Audio Books Player", iTunes, https://itunes.apple.com/us/app/id1010620060?mt=8, accessed December 2018.

133. "Ab Workout Trainer HD Sit-Up Crunch Exercise", iTunes, https://itunes.apple.com/us/app/id576230029?mt=8, accessed December 2018.

134. "Raw Food Diet Free - Healthy Organic Food Recipes and Diet Tracker", iTunes, https://itunes.apple.com/us/app/id575882091, accessed December 2018.

135. "Shpock - Sell & Buy Used Stuf", iTunes, https://itunes.apple.com/us/app/id557153158?mt=8, accessed December 2018.

136. "Unit Converter", Apps on Google Play, https://play.google.com/store/apps/details?id=com.androidapps.unitconverter&hl=en, accessed December 2018.

137. "World Explorer - Tour guide", iTunes, https://itunes.apple.com/us/app/id381581095?mt=8, accessed December 2018.

138. "10 Day UK Weather forecast", iTunes, https://itunes.apple.com/gb/app/id859015438?mt=8, accessed December 2018.

139. "Google Earth", iTunes, https://itunes.apple.com/us/app/id293622097?mt=8, accessed December 2018.

140. "TicTok - Productivity Tracker", iTunes, https://itunes.apple.com/us/app/id1360997148?mt=8, accessed December 2018.

141. "AirBrush - Der einfache Foto-Editor", Apps on Google Play, https://play.google.com/store/apps/details?id=com.magicv.airbrush&hl=de, accessed December 2018.

142. "Out of Milk - Shopping List", iTunes, https://itunes.apple.com/us/app/id564974992?mt=8, accessed December 2018.

143. "SoundHound – Music Discovery", iTunes, https://itunes.apple.com/us/app/id355554941?mt=8, accessed December 2018.

144. "Alpha Trainer : Get Customized Fitness Programs", iTunes, https://itunes.apple.com/us/app/id616360484?mt=8, accessed December 2018.

145. "Lose It! – Calorie Counter", iTunes, https://itunes.apple.com/us/app/id297368629?mt=8, accessed December 2018.

146. "Celtic Tribes - Strategy MMO", iTunes, https://itunes.apple.com/us/app/id564769273?mt=8, accessed December 2018.

147. "Lords & Knights - Medieval MMO", iTunes, https://itunes.apple.com/us/app/id421864154?mt=8, accessed December 2018.

148. "Amazon – Shopping made easy", iTunes, https://itunes.apple.com/us/app/id297606951?mt=8, accessed December 2018.

149. "Doodle Jump", iTunes, https://itunes.apple.com/us/app/id307727765?mt=8, accessed December 2018.

150. "Cookpad - Recipe Sharing App", Apps on Google Play, https://play.google.com/store/apps/details?id=com.mufumbo.android.recipe.search&hl=en, accessed December 2018.

151. "LootBoy - Grab your loot!", Apps on Google Play, https://play.google.com/store/apps/details?id=com.lootboy.app&hl=en, accessed December 2018.

152. "Real Madrid Fantasy Manager 19", iTunes, https://itunes.apple.com/us/app/id930794252?mt=8, accessed December 2018.

153. "Fit Men Cook - Healthy Recipes", iTunes, https://itunes.apple.com/us/app/id980368562?mt=8, accessed December 2018.

154. "Sweat: Kayla Itsines Fitness", iTunes, https://itunes.apple.com/us/app/id1049234587?mt=8, accessed December 2018.

155. "Battle Hordes - Building MMO", iTunes, https://itunes.apple.com/us/app/id1137986593?mt=8, accessed December 2018.

156. "Sports Direct", Apps on Google Play, https://play.google.com/store/apps/details?id=com.sportsdirect.sdapp&hl=en, accessed December 2018.

157. "Productivity Helper Dezide+", Apps on Google Play, https://play.google.com/store/apps/details?id=com.dezideplus.productivityhelper&hl=en, accessed December 2018.

158. "Mollie Makes", iTunes, https://itunes.apple.com/us/app/id911319779, accessed December 2018.

159. "Photobox.", iTunes, https://itunes.apple.com/gb/app/id574408353?mt=8, accessed December 2018.

160. "Launch Center Pro", iTunes, https://itunes.apple.com/us/app/id532016360?mt=8, accessed December 2018.

161. "Fudget: Budget Planner Tracker", iTunes, https://itunes.apple.com/us/app/id897849266/, accessed December 2018.

162. "Battleships: Blood & Sea", Apps on Google Play, https://play.google.com/store/apps/details?id=com.joyfun.battleship.google&hl=en, accessed December 2018.

163. "Complete Guide to Product Page Creative Requirements", StorenMaven Academy, December 6, 2018, https://www.storemaven.com/app-store-product-page-promotional-artwork-requirements/, assessed December 2018.

APPENDIX

164. "Chem Pro: Chemistry Tutor", iTunes, https://itunes.apple.com/us/app/id509384060?mt=8, accessed December 2018.

165. Gilad Bechar, "Creative Guide for iPhone X & iOS 11", Moburst, January 11, 2018, https://www.moburst.com/creative-guide-ios-11-iphone-x/, accessed December 2018.

166. Ibid.

167. John Koetsier, "How People Make Download Decisions on Google Play and the App Store", TUNE, 2018, downloaded from https://mkt.tune.com/rs/210-BFY-977/images/TMC-WP-App-Store-Optimization-How-People-Make-Download-Decisions-on-Google-Play-and-the-App-Store.pdf, accessed June 2018, 7-8.

168. Ibid., 7.

169. "App Store Optimization Case Study by StoreMaven - Lift Conversions by 66%", StoreMaven, August 1, 2016, https://www.slideshare.net/maorgad/app-store-optimization-case-study-by-storemaven-lift-conversions-by-66, accessed June 2018, 25.

170. John Koetsier, "How People Make Download Decisions on Google Play and the App Store", TUNE, 2018, downloaded from https://mkt.tune.com/rs/210-BFY-977/images/TMC-WP-App-Store-Optimization-How-People-Make-Download-Decisions-on-Google-Play-and-the-App-Store.pdf, accessed June 2018, 13.

171. "Graphic assets, screenshots, & video", Play Console Help, https://support.google.com/googleplay/android-developer/answer/1078870?hl=en, accessed July 2018.

172. "Age-restricted content", YouTube Help, https://support.google.com/youtube/answer/2802167?hl=en, accessed July 2018.

173. "Show More with App Previews", Apple Developer, https://developer.apple.com/app-store/app-previews/, accessed July 2018.

174. Liza Knotko, "10 Insights into Creating Pitch-Perfect App Preview for Apple App Store", App Store Optimization Blog (blog), May 2, 2018, https://splitmetrics.com/blog/create-app-preview-video-app-store-ios/, accessed July 2018.

175. "Minimon: Adventure of Minions", iTunes, https://itunes.apple.com/us/app/id1149841223?mt=8, accessed December 2018.

176. "Panzer Sturm", iTunes, https://itunes.apple.com/us/app/id840755742?mt=8, accessed December 2018.

177. "App Store Optimization Case Study by StoreMaven - Lift Conversions by 66%", StoreMaven, August 1, 2016, https://www.slideshare.net/maorgad/app-store-optimization-case-study-by-storemaven-lift-conversions-by-66, accessed June 2018, 25.

178. Dan Griego, "Basic Video Production Terms: The Shot, Scene and Sequence", VideoEditingSage.com, https://www.videoeditingsage.com/basic-video-production-terms-shot-scene-sequence.html, accessed July 2018.

179. "Skoove - Piano Lessons", iTunes, https://itunes.apple.com/us/app/id1160668178?mt=8, accessed December 2018.

180. "Bookly - Read More", iTunes, https://itunes.apple.com/us/app/id1085047737?mt=8, accessed December 2018.

181. "Where To?", iTunes, https://itunes.apple.com/us/app/id903955898?mt=8, accessed December 2018.

182. "Linea Sketch", iTunes, https://itunes.apple.com/us/app/id1094770251?mt=8, accessed December 2018.

183. "Scientific Calculator +", iTunes, https://itunes.apple.com/au/app/scientific-calculator/id367164379, accessed February 2019.

184. "App Store Optimization Case Study by StoreMaven - Lift Conversions by 66%", StoreMaven, August 1, 2016, https://www.slideshare.net/maorgad/app-store-optimization-case-study-by-storemaven-lift-conversions-by-66, accessed June 2018, 12-17.

185. "7mind Meditation", iTunes, https://itunes.apple.com/us/app/id943347681?mt=8, accessed December 2018.

186. "TikTok - Real Short Videos", iTunes, https://itunes.apple.com/us/app/id835599320?mt=8, accessed December 2018.

187. "ViewRanger: Hike, Ride or Walk", iTunes, https://itunes.apple.com/us/app/id404581674?mt=8, accessed December 2018.

188. "Blinkist: Books in 15 minutes", iTunes, https://itunes.apple.com/us/app/id568839295?mt=8, accessed December 2018.

189. "Where To?", iTunes, https://itunes.apple.com/us/app/id903955898?mt=8, accessed December 2018.

190. "Mondly: Learn 33 Languages", iTunes, https://itunes.apple.com/us/app/id987873536?mt=8, accessed December 2018.

191. "Tandem - Language Exchange", iTunes, https://itunes.apple.com/us/app/id959001619?mt=8, accessed December 2018.

192. "Calzy 3", iTunes, https://itunes.apple.com/us/app/id623690732?mt=8, accessed December 2018.

193. "happn — Dating app", iTunes, https://itunes.apple.com/us/app/id489185828?mt=8, accessed December 2018.

194. "Rodeo Stampede: Sky Zoo Safari", iTunes, https://itunes.apple.com/us/app/id1047961826?mt=8, accessed December 2018.

195. "Restaurant DASH: Gordon Ramsay", iTunes, https://itunes.apple.com/us/app/id1089048531?mt=8, accessed December 2018.

196. "Flightscom - Cheap Flights", iTunes, https://itunes.apple.com/us/app/id1330972683?mt=8, accessed December 2018.

197. "Elk Travel Currency Converter", iTunes, https://itunes.apple.com/us/app/id1189748820?mt=8, accessed December 2018.

198. "My Scans PRO, pdf scanner app", iTunes, https://itunes.apple.com/us/app/id948216105?mt=8, accessed December 2018.

199. "Hippie Lane", iTunes, https://itunes.apple.com/us/app/id956049398?mt=8, accessed December 2018.

200. "SimCity BuildIt", iTunes, https://itunes.apple.com/us/app/id913292932?mt=8, accessed December 2018.

201. "Asphalt 9: Legends", iTunes, https://itunes.apple.com/us/app/id805603214?mt=8, accessed December 2018.

202. "Pacing & Rhythm", Advanced Video Camera and Editing, http://www.cuvideoedit.com/pacing-and-rhythm.php, accessed July 2018.

203. "Hungry Shark World", iTunes, https://itunes.apple.com/us/app/id1046846443?mt=8, accessed December 2018.

204. "Wildfulness 2 - Nature Sounds", iTunes, https://itunes.apple.com/us/app/id1173056260?mt=8, accessed December 2018.

205. "Thunderdogs", iTunes, https://itunes.apple.com/us/app/id1394454716?mt=8, accessed December 2018.

206. "AirPano Travel Book", iTunes, https://itunes.apple.com/us/app/id887138564?mt=8, accessed December 2018.

207. "Pacing & Rhythm", Advanced Video Camera and Editing, http://www.cuvideoedit.com/pacing-and-rhythm.php, accessed July 2018.

208. "Iron Throne", iTunes, https://itunes.apple.com/us/app/id1124752613?mt=8, accessed December 2018.

209. "Donut County", iTunes, https://itunes.apple.com/us/app/id1292099839?mt=8, accessed December 2018.

210. "Pacing & Rhythm", Advanced Video Camera and Editing, http://www.cuvideoedit.com/pacing-and-rhythm.php, accessed July 2018.

211. Ibid.

212. Amir Farooq, "Jump Cut (Technique)", Filming and Editing Blog (blog), http://amirediting.blogspot.com/p/jump-cut-technique.html, accessed July 2018.

213. "Dawn of Titans", iTunes, https://itunes.apple.com/us/app/id911800950?mt=8, accessed December 2018.

214. Logan Baker, "The Secrets to Using a Dissolve Transition Effectively", The Beat (blog), August 16, 2016, https://www.premiumbeat.com/blog/secret-of-dissolve-transition/, accessed July 2018.

215. "CSI: Hidden Crimes", iTunes, https://itunes.apple.com/us/app/id762131394?mt=8, accessed July 2018.

216. "Types of Video Transition", MediaCollege.com, https://www.mediacollege.com/video/editing/transition/types.html, accessed July 2018.

217. "Apollo Justice Ace Attorney", iTunes, https://itunes.apple.com/us/app/id1136993233?mt=8, accessed December 2018.

218. "Types of Video Transition", MediaCollege.com, https://www.mediacollege.com/video/editing/transition/types.html, accessed July 2018.

219. "Scanbot Scanner App - Scan PDF", iTunes, https://itunes.apple.com/us/app/id834854351?mt=8, accessed December 2018.

220. "Blade Reborn", iTunes, https://itunes.apple.com/us/app/id1317240781?mt=8, accessed December 2018.

221. "Asphalt Xtreme", iTunes, https://itunes.apple.com/us/app/id971233157?mt=8, accessed December 2018.

222. Doris Berger-Grabner, "Wissenschaftliches Arbeiten in den Wirtschafts- und Sozialwissenschaften" (Wiesbaden: Springer Gabler Verlag, 2010), 4.

223. "Todoist: Organize your life", iTunes, https://itunes.apple.com/us/app/id572688855?mt=8, accessed December 2018.

224. Michelle Trudeau, "You Had Me At Hello: The Science Behind First Impressions", National Public Radio, May 5, 2014, https://www.npr.org/sections/health-shots/2014/05/05/308349318/you-had-me-at-hello-the-science-behind-first-impressions?t=1540562330000, accessed July 2018.

225. Debbie Grattan, "The Big Voice-Over Decision: Male vs. Female Voice-Over Talent", LinkedIn, April 21, 2016, https://www.linkedin.com/pulse/big-voice-over-decision-male-vs-female-talent-debbie-grattan/, accessed July 2018.

226. Izzy Hyman, "How to Record a Quality Voice-Over (and Why You Should Do It)", IzzyVideo.com, January 8, 2015, https://www.izzyvideo.com/voice-over/, accessed July 2018.

227. Peter Robins, "10 Tips For Recording High Quality Video Voice Overs", Vidyard Blog (blog), November 25, 2013, https://www.vidyard.com/blog/recording-high-quality-video-voice-overs/, accessed July 2018.

228. Ibid.

229. Izzy Hyman, "How to Record a Quality Voice-Over (and Why You Should Do It)", IzzyVideo.com, January 8, 2015, https://www.izzyvideo.com/voice-over/, accessed July 2018.

230. Peter Robins, "10 Tips For Recording High Quality Video Voice Overs", Vidyard Blog (blog), November 25, 2013, https://www.vidyard.com/blog/recording-high-quality-video-voice-overs/, accessed July 2018.

231. "2048", Apps on Google Play, https://play.google.com/store/apps/details?id=com.androbros.puzzle2048eng&hl=en, accessed December 2018.

232. "DAZN Live Fight Sports: Boxing, MMA & More", Apps on Google Play, https://play.google.com/store/apps/details?id=com.dazn&hl=en, accessed December 2018.

233. "Fallout Shelter", Apps on Google Play, https://play.google.com/store/apps/details?id=com.bethsoft.falloutshelter&hl=en, accessed December 2018.

234. "UFC", Apps on Google Play, https://play.google.com/store/apps/details?id=com.ea.game.easportsufc_row&hl=en, accessed December 2018.

235. "Journi Print: Photobook", iTunes, https://itunes.apple.com/us/app/id1359161090?mt=8, accessed December 2018.

236. "Food Street – Restaurant Game", iTunes, https://itunes.apple.com/us/app/id935623337?mt=8, accessed December 2018.

237. "App preview specifications", App Store Connect Help, https://help.apple.com/app-store-connect/?lang=en/#/dev4e413fcb8, accessed August 2018.

238. "Graphic assets, screenshots, & video", Play Console Help, https://support.google.com/googleplay/android-developer/answer/1078870?hl=en, accessed July 2018.

239. Sylvain Gauchet, "Differences between Video on the iOS App Store and the Google Play Store", The Boost: Mobile Growth and Creatives (blog), January 12, 2018, https://www.apptamin.com/blog/videos-app-store-vs-play-store/, accessed August 2018.

240. "How to show touches (tap signs) while recording iPhone's Screen", TechGrapple.com, June 26, 2016, https://www.techgrapple.com/record-iphone-ios-screen-showing-touches-tap-signs, accessed August 2018.

241. "Fingertips", GitHub, July 27, 2017, https://github.com/mapbox/Fingertips, accessed December 2018.

242. "Touchpose", GitHub, March 26, 2017, https://github.com/toddreed/Touchpose, accessed December 2018.

243. Karen Haslam, "How to record your iPhone screen", MacWorld, June 27, 2018, https://www.macworld.co.uk/how-to/iphone/record-iphone-screen-video-3522253/, accessed August 2018.

244. Sylvain Gauchet, "iOS 11 App Previews – How to leverage Video on the latest iOS App Store", The Boost: Mobile Growth and Creatives (blog), August 15, 2017, https://www.apptamin.com/blog/ios-11-app-previews/, accessed August 2018.

245. "App preview specifications", App Store Connect Help, https://help.apple.com/app-store-connect/?lang=en/#/dev4e413fcb8, accessed August 2018.

246. "Recommended upload encoding settings", YouTube Help, https://support.google.com/youtube/answer/1722171?hl=en, accessed August 2018.

247. John Koetsier, "How People Make Download Decisions on Google Play and the App Store", TUNE, 2018, downloaded from https://mkt.tune.com/rs/210-BFY-977/images/TMC-WP-App-Store-Optimization-How-People-Make-Download-Decisions-on-Google-Play-and-the-App-Store.pdf, accessed June 2018, 6.

248. "trivago: Hotels & Travel", Apps on Google Play, https://play.google.com/store/apps/details?id=com.trivago&hl=en, accessed December 2018.

249. "Duolingo: Learn Languages Free", Apps on Google Play, https://play.google.com/store/apps/details?id=com.duolingo&hl=en, accessed December 2018.

250. "Learn Russian Free", Apps on Google Play, https://play.google.com/store/apps/details?id=com.metalanguage.learnrussianfree&hl=en, accessed December 2018.

251. "McDonald's", Apps on Google Play, https://play.google.com/store/apps/details?id=com.mcdonalds.mobileapp&hl=en, accessed December 2018.

252. "Netflix", Apps on Google Play, https://play.google.com/store/apps/details?id=com.netflix.mediaclient&hl=en, accessed December 2018.

253. "Zalando – Shopping & Fashion", Apps on Google Play, https://play.google.com/store/apps/details?id=de.zalando.mobile&hl=en, accessed December 2018.

254. "Flush - Crowdsourced Toilets", Apps on Google Play, https://play.google.com/store/apps/details?id=toilet.samruston.com.toilet&hl=en, accessed December 2018.

255. "Toilet Paper", Apps on Google Play, https://play.google.com/store/apps/details?id=com.aemobile.toiletPaper&hl=en, accessed December 2018.

256. "Toilet Paper Racing", Apps on Google Play, https://play.google.com/store/apps/details?id=com.gsoftteam.toiletpaperracing&hl=en, accessed December 2018.

257. "Swiss Dating & Chat", Apps on Google Play, https://play.google.com/store/apps/details?id=com.narchat.switzerland&hl=en, accessed December 2018.

258. "Lieferando.de - Order Food", Apps on Google Play, https://play.google.com/store/apps/details?id=com.yopeso.lieferando&hl=en, accessed December 2018.

259. "Skyscanner - Cheap Flights, Hotels and Car Rental", Apps on Google Play, https://play.google.com/store/apps/details?id=net.skyscanner.android.main&hl=en, accessed December 2018.

260. "Guitar Lessons Fender Play", iTunes, https://itunes.apple.com/app/id1226057939?mt=8, accessed December 2018.

261. "Deezer Music Player: Songs, Radio & Podcasts", Apps on Google Play, https://play.google.com/store/apps/details?id=deezer.android.app&hl=en, accessed December 2018.

262. "Banggood - Easy Online Shopping", Apps on Google Play, https://play.google.com/store/apps/details?id=com.banggood.client&hl=en, accessed December 2018.

263. "Instagram", Apps on Google Play, https://play.google.com/store/apps/details?id=com.instagram.android&hl=en, accessed December 2018.

264. "Inst Download - Video & Photo", Apps on Google Play, https://play.google.com/store/apps/details?id=com.znstudio.instadownload&hl=en, accessed December 2018.

265. "Photo Grid for Instagram", Apps on Google Play, https://play.google.com/store/apps/details?id=photo.grid.instagram&hl=en, accessed December 2018.

266. "Follower Analyzer (Instagram)", Apps on Google Play, https://play.google.com/store/apps/details?id=com.maximolab.followeranalyzer&hl=en, accessed December 2018.

267. "PanoramaCrop for Instagram", Apps on Google Play, https://play.google.com/store/apps/details?id=pt.muffin.instapanorama&hl=en, accessed December 2018.

268. "Leap Fitness Group", Apps on Google Play, https://play.google.com/store/apps/developer?id=Leap+Fitness+Group, accessed December 2018.

269. "Six Pack in 30 Days - Abs Workout", Apps on Google Play, https://play.google.com/store/apps/details?id=sixpack.sixpackabs.absworkout&hl=en, accessed December 2018.

270. "Lose Belly Fat in 30 Days - Flat Stomach", Apps on Google Play, https://play.google.com/store/apps/details?id=losebellyfat.flatstomach.absworkout.fatburning&hl=en, accessed December 2018.

271. "Stretching Exercises - Flexibility Training", Apps on Google Play, https://play.google.com/store/apps/details?id=stretching.stretch.exercises.back&hl=en, accessed December 2018.

272. "Arm Workout - Biceps Exercise", Apps on Google Play, https://play.google.com/store/apps/details?id=armworkout.armworkoutformen.armexercises&hl=en, accessed December 2018.

273. "Leg Workouts for Women - Slim Leg & Burn Thigh Fat", Apps on Google Play, https://play.google.com/store/apps/details?id=legsworkout.slimlegs.fatburning.stronglegs&hl=en, accessed December 2018.

274. "Adobe", Apps on Google Play, https://play.google.com/store/apps/dev?id=4734916851270416020, accessed December 2018.

275. "Adobe Illustrator Draw", Apps on Google Play, https://play.google.com/store/apps/details?id=com.adobe.creativeapps.draw&hl=en, accessed December 2018.

276. "Adobe Premiere Clip", Apps on Google Play, https://play.google.com/store/apps/details?id=com.adobe.premiereclip&hl=en, accessed December 2018.

277. "Adobe Connect", Apps on Google Play, https://play.google.com/store/apps/details?id=air.com.adobe.connectpro&hl=en, accessed December 2018.

278. "Adobe Scout", Apps on Google Play, https://play.google.com/store/apps/details?id=com.adobe.monocle.companion&hl=en, accessed December 2018.

279. "Adobe Photoshop Express:Photo Editor Collage Maker", Apps on Google Play, https://play.google.com/store/apps/details?id=com.adobe.psmobile&hl=en, accessed December 2018.

280. "Google Chrome: Fast & Secure", Apps on Google Play, https://play.google.com/store/apps/details?id=com.android.chrome&hl=en, accessed December 2018.

281. "Google Maps Go - Directions, Traffic & Transit", Apps on Google Play, https://play.google.com/store/apps/details?id=com.google.android.apps.mapslite&hl=en, accessed December 2018.

282. "Google Photos", Apps on Google Play, https://play.google.com/store/apps/details?id=com.google.android.apps.photos&hl=en, accessed December 2018.

283. "Google News", Apps on Google Play, https://play.google.com/store/apps/details?id=com.google.android.apps.magazines&hl=en, accessed December 2018.

284. "Google Home", Apps on Google Play, https://play.google.com/store/apps/details?id=com.google.android.apps.chromecast.app&hl=en, accessed December 2018.

285. "Need for Speed™ No Limits", Apps on Google Play, https://play.google.com/store/apps/details?id=com.ea.game.nfs14_row&hl=en, accessed December 2018.

286. "The Sims FreePlay", Apps on Google Play, https://play.google.com/store/apps/details?id=com.ea.games.simsfreeplay_row&hl=en, accessed December 2018.

287. "TETRIS", Apps on Google Play, https://play.google.com/store/apps/details?id=com.ea.game.tetris2011_row&hl=en, accessed December 2018.

288. "Real Racing 3", Apps on Google Play, https://play.google.com/store/apps/details?id=com.ea.games.r3_row&hl=en, accessed December 2018.

289. "The Sims™ Mobile", Apps on Google Play, https://play.google.com/store/apps/details?id=com.ea.gp.simsmobile&hl=en, accessed December 2018.

290. "ELECTRONIC ARTS", Apps on Google Play, https://play.google.com/store/apps/dev?id=6605125519975771237&hl=en, accessed December 2018.

291. "Gameloft", Apps on Google Play, https://play.google.com/store/apps/dev?id=6258770168633898802&hl=en, accessed December 2018.

292. "Dragon Mania Legends", Apps on Google Play, https://play.google.com/store/apps/details?id=com.gameloft.android.ANMP.GloftDOHM&hl=en, accessed December 2018.

293. "Asphalt Xtreme: Rally Racing", Apps on Google Play, https://play.google.com/store/apps/details?id=com.gameloft.android.ANMP.GloftMOHM&hl=en, accessed December 2018.

294. "Gangstar New Orleans OpenWorld", Apps on Google Play, https://play.google.com/store/apps/details?id=com.gameloft.android.ANMP.GloftOLHM&hl=en, accessed December 2018.

295. "Iron Blade: Medieval Legends RPG", Apps on Google Play, https://play.google.com/store/apps/details?id=com.gameloft.android.ANMP.GloftHFHM&hl=en, accessed December 2018.

296. "N.O.V.A. Legacy", Apps on Google Play, https://play.google.com/store/apps/details?id=com.gameloft.android.ANMP.GloftNOHM&hl=en, accessed December 2018.

297. "Amazon Mobile LLC", Apps on Google Play, https://play.google.com/store/apps/developer?id=Amazon+Mobile+LLC&hl=en, accessed December 2018.

298. "Amazon Go", Apps on Google Play, https://play.google.com/store/apps/details?id=com.amazon.ihm.richard&hl=en, accessed December 2018.

299. "Amazon Prime Video", Apps on Google Play, https://play.google.com/store/apps/details?id=com.amazon.avod.thirdpartyclient&hl=en, accessed December 2018.

300. "Amazon Music", Apps on Google Play, https://play.google.com/store/apps/details?id=com.amazon.mp3&hl=en, accessed December 2018.

301. "Amazon Photos", Apps on Google Play, https://play.google.com/store/apps/details?id=com.amazon.clouddrive.photos&hl=en, accessed December 2018.

302. "Amazon Drive", Apps on Google Play, https://play.google.com/store/apps/details?id=com.amazon.drive&hl=en, accessed December 2018.

303. Laurie Galazzo, "9 Tips to Make Your App Icon Stand Out", Aso Blog (blog), May 5, 2014, https://www.apptweak.com/aso-blog/9-tips-to-make-your-app-icon-stand-out, accessed August 2018.

304. "The Simpsons: Tapped Out", WikiSimpsons, https://simpsonswiki.com/wiki/The_Simpsons:_Tapped_Out, accessed December 2018

305. "The Simpsons™: Tapped Out", Apps on Google Play, https://play.google.com/store/apps/details?id=com.ea.game.simpsons4_na&hl=de, accessed December 2018 & August 2018.

306. "Fleet Battle - Sea Battle", Apps on Google Play, https://play.google.com/store/apps/details?id=de.smuttlewerk.fleetbattle&hl=en, accessed December 2018.

307. "Minesweeper", Apps on Google Play, https://play.google.com/store/apps/details?id=Draziw.Button.Mines&hl=en, accessed December 2018.

308. "Art of War 3: PvP RTS modern warfare strategy game", Apps on Google Play, https://play.google.com/store/apps/details?id=com.geargames.aow&hl=en, accessed December 2018.

309. "Accurate Altimeter", Apps on Google Play, https://play.google.com/store/apps/details?id=com.arlabsmobile.altimeterfree&hl=en, accessed December 2018.

310. "Ghost in Photo", Apps on Google Play, https://play.google.com/store/apps/details?id=com.prankdesk.ghostinphotoprank&hl=en, accessed December 2018.

311. "Photo Editor Collage Maker Pro: Filters & Stickers", Apps on Google Play, https://play.google.com/store/apps/details?id=com.lyrebirdstudio.montagenscolagem&hl=en, accessed December 2018.

312. "Vivitar Smart Home Security", Apps on Google Play, https://play.google.com/store/apps/details?id=itdim.shsm&hl=en, accessed December 2018.

313. "Boxing Round Interval Timer", Apps on Google Play, https://play.google.com/store/apps/details?id=com.netincome.boxingroundintervaltimer&hl=en, accessed December 2018.

314. "Boxing Round", Apps on Google Play, https://play.google.com/store/apps/details?id=com.boxs.craft.boxinground&hl=en, accessed December 2018.

315. John Koetsier, "How People Make Download Decisions on Google Play and the App Store", TUNE, 2018, downloaded from https://mkt.tune.com/rs/210-BFY-977/images/TMC-WP-App-Store-Optimization-How-People-Make-Download-Decisions-on-Google-Play-and-the-App-Store.pdf, accessed June 2018, 7.

316. Ibid.

317. "Badoo - The Dating App", iTunes, https://itunes.apple.com/us/app/id351331194?mt=8, accessed July 2018.

318. "FOOBY: Recipes & More", iTunes, https://itunes.apple.com/us/app/id1189007291?mt=8, accessed July 2018.

319. "Simply Piano by JoyTunes", iTunes, https://itunes.apple.com/us/app/id1019442026?mt=8, accessed July 2018.

320. "Shop top brands at eBay", iTunes, https://itunes.apple.com/us/app/id282614216?mt=8, accessed March 2019.

321. "CodeCheck: Food & Cosmetics", iTunes, https://itunes.apple.com/us/app/id359351047?mt=8, accessed July 2018.

322. "8fit Workouts & Meal Planner", iTunes, https://itunes.apple.com/us/app/id866617777?mt=8, accessed July 2018.

323. Jason Oxenham, "The 15 Most Spoken Languages in the World", Rocket Languages Blog (blog), July 6, 2016, https://www.rocketlanguages.com/blog/the-15-most-spoken-languages-in-the-world/, accessed September 2018.

324. "Google Maps - Transit & Food", iTunes, https://itunes.apple.com/app/id585027354?mt=8, accessed December 2018.

325. Jason Oxenham, "The 15 Most Spoken Languages in the World", Rocket Languages Blog (blog), July 6, 2016, https://www.rocketlanguages.com/blog/the-15-most-spoken-languages-in-the-world/, accessed September 2018.

326. Sue Layman Lightman, "Brand Identity: The Importance of Color", Memphis Daily News, October 19, 2016, https://www.memphisdailynews.com/news/2016/oct/19/brand-identity-the-importance-of-color/, accessed September 2018.

327. Collins English Dictionary, s.v. "colour", https://www.collinsdictionary.com/dictionary/english/colour, accessed September 2018.

328. Richard Lackey, "What Is Color Temperature?", Cinema5D.com, February 16, 2016, https://www.cinema5d.com/what-is-color-temperature/, accessed September 2018.

329. Oxford Dictionaries, s.v. "hue", https://en.oxforddictionaries.com/definition/hue, accessed September 2018.

330. "The basics of the color wheel for presentation design (Part I)", Presentitude, September 28, 2015, http://presentitude.com/color-theory-part-1/, accessed December 2018.

331. Bonnie Skaalid, "Elements of Design: Value & Color", Web Design for Instruction, April 5, 1999, https://etad.usask.ca/skaalid/theory/cgdt/color.htm, accessed September 2018.

332. Ibid.

333. "The basics of the color wheel for presentation design (Part I)", Presentitude, September 28, 2015, http://presentitude.com/color-theory-part-1/, accessed December 2018.

334. Shirley Williams, "Primary Colors, Secondary and Tertiary Explained", Color Wheel Artists (blog), February 15, 2017, https://color-wheel-artist.com/primary-colors/, accessed September 2018.

335. "The basics of the color wheel for presentation design (Part I)", Presentitude, September 28, 2015, http://presentitude.com/color-theory-part-1/, accessed December 2018.

336. "Color Basics", Usability.gov, Februar 11, 2015, https://www.usability.gov/how-to-and-tools/methods/color-basics.html, accessed September 2018.

337. Jacci Howard Bear, "What Meanings Are Associated With the Various Colors", Lifewire.com, October 26, 2018, https://www.lifewire.com/color-symbolism-information-1073947, accessed October 2018.

338. Jennifer Bourn, "Color Meaning: Meaning of The Color Blue", BournCreative.com (blog), January 15, 2011, https://www.bourncreative.com/meaning-of-the-color-blue/, accessed October 2018.

339. Jennifer Bourn, "Color Meaning: Meaning of The Color Red", BournCreative.com (blog), February 25, 2011, https://www.bourncreative.com/meaning-of-the-color-red/, accessed October 2018.

340. Jennifer Bourn, "Color Meaning: Meaning of The Color Yellow", BournCreative.com (blog), February 5, 2011, https://www.bourncreative.com/meaning-of-the-color-yellow/, accessed October 2018.

341. Jennifer Bourn, "Color Meaning: Meaning of The Color Purple", BournCreative.com (blog), January 5, 2011, https://www.bourncreative.com/meaning-of-the-color-purple/, accessed October 2018.

342. Joe Sabin, "23 Famous Purple Brands with the Color Purple in their Logo", Design Blog (blog), DesignCrowd.com, February 20, 2014, https://blog.designcrowd.com/article/447/-23-purple-power-brands-, accessed October 2018.

343. Jennifer Bourn, "Color Meaning: Meaning of The Color Orange", BournCreative.com (blog), February 16, 2011, https://www.bourncreative.com/meaning-of-the-color-orange/, accessed October 2018.

344. Jennifer Bourn, "Color Meaning: Meaning of The Color Green", BournCreative.com (blog), January 25, 2011, https://www.bourncreative.com/meaning-of-the-color-green/, accessed October 2018.

345. Jennifer Bourn, "Color Meaning: Meaning of The Color Black", BournCreative.com (blog), December 15, 2010, https://www.bourncreative.com/meaning-of-the-color-black/, accessed October 2018.

346. Jennifer Bourn, "Color Meaning: Meaning of The Color White", BournCreative.com (blog), December 5, 2010, https://www.bourncreative.com/meaning-of-the-color-white/, accessed October 2018.

347. Jennifer Bourn, "Color Meaning: Meaning of The Color Grey", BournCreative.com (blog), December 27, 2010, https://www.bourncreative.com/meaning-of-the-color-grey/, accessed October 2018.

348. Jennifer Bourn, "Color Meaning: Meaning of The Color Brown", BournCreative.com (blog), October 25, 2010, https://www.bourncreative.com/meaning-of-the-color-brown/, accessed October 2018.

349. Jennifer Bourn, "Color Meaning: Meaning of The Color Gold", BournCreative.com (blog), November 5, 2010, https://www.bourncreative.com/meaning-of-the-color-gold/, accessed October 2018.

350. Jennifer Bourn, "Color Meaning: Meaning of The Color Silver", BournCreative.com (blog), October 30, 2010, https://www.bourncreative.com/meaning-of-the-color-silver/, accessed October 2018.

351. "Colours of mourning around the world", FuneralZone.com (blog), October 26, 2017, https://www.funeralzone.com.au/blog/mourning-colours, accessed October 2018.

352. "Colors Across Cultures – Color Psychology", globalme.net, https://www.globalme.net/blog/colours-across-cultures, accessed December 2018.

353. Joe Hallock, "Preferences - Favorite Color", JoeHallock.com, http://www.joehallock.com/edu/COM498/preferences.html#favcolour, accessed October 2018.

354. Ibid.

355. Ibid.

356. Ibid.

357. "Colors for living and learning", Resene.co.nz, https://www.resene.co.nz/homeown/use_colr/colours-for-living.htm, accessed October 2018.

358. Ibid.

359. Charlotte Meyer, "Die Lieblingsfarbe – eine unstete Sache", Uni.de, September 11, 2015, https://uni.de/redaktion/lieblingsfarbe, accessed October 2018.

360. "Age-Related Color Bias", Sherwin-Williams.com, https://www.sherwin-williams.com/home-builders/color/color-education/sw-article-pro-agerelatedcolor, accessed October 2018.

361. Charlotte Meyer, "Die Lieblingsfarbe – eine unstete Sache", Uni.de, September 11, 2015, https://uni.de/redaktion/lieblingsfarbe, accessed October 2018.

362. "Basic Color Theory", ColorMatters.com, https://www.colormatters.com/color-and-design/basic-color-theory, accessed October 2018.

363. Justin Baker, "The Science of Color Contrast—An Expert Designer's Guide", Medium.com, June 25, 2018, https://medium.muz.li/the-science-of-color-contrast-an-expert-designers-guide-33e84c41d156, accessed December 2018.

364. "Color contrast", Khan Academy, https://www.khanacademy.org/partner-content/pixar/color/color-101/v/color4-master, accessed December 2018.

365. Bonnie Skaalid, "Elements of Design: Value & Color", Web Design for Instruction, April 5, 1999, https://etad.usask.ca/skaalid/theory/cgdt/color.htm, accessed September 2018.

366. "Monochromatic color scheme", Colorpedia by Paletton, April 25, 2016, http://www.paletton.com/wiki/index.php?title=Monochromatic_color_scheme, accessed October 2018.

367. Online Logo Maker, "Complementary Colors on Logo Design", Medium.com, March 8, 2017, https://medium.com/@onlinelogomaker/complementary-colors-on-logo-design-85a3027c07b4, accessed October 2018.

368. "Basic color schemes - Introduction to Color Theorys", TigerColor.com, http://www.tigercolor.com/color-lab/color-theory/color-theory-intro.htm#color_harmonies, accessed February 2019.

369. "The basics of the color wheel for presentation design (Part I)", Presentitude, September 28, 2015, http://presentitude.com/color-theory-part-1/, accessed December 2018.

370. "Basic color schemes - Introduction to Color Theorys", TigerColor.com, http://www.tigercolor.com/color-lab/color-theory/color-theory-intro.htm#color_harmonies, accessed February 2019.

371. Ibid.

372. "Split complementary color scheme", Colorpedia by Paletton, April 26, 2016, http://www.paletton.com/wiki/index.php?title=Split_complementary_color_scheme, accessed October 2018.

373. "Triadic color scheme", Colorpedia by Paletton, April 25, 2016, http://www.paletton.com/wiki/index.php?title=Triadic_color_scheme, accessed October 2018.

374. "Basic color schemes - Introduction to Color Theorys", TigerColor.com, http://www.tigercolor.com/color-lab/color-theory/color-theory-intro.htm#color_harmonies, accessed February 2019.

375. "The basics of the color wheel for presentation design (Part I)", Presentitude, September 28, 2015, http://presentitude.com/color-theory-part-1/, accessed December 2018.

376. "Dual color scheme", Colorpedia by Paletton, April 26, 2016, http://www.paletton.com/wiki/index.php?title=Dual_color_scheme, accessed October 2018.

377. Online Logo Maker, "Complementary Colors on Logo Design", Medium.com, March 8, 2017, https://medium.com/@onlinelogomaker/complementary-colors-on-logo-design-85a3027c07b4, accessed October 2018.

378. "Basic color schemes - Introduction to Color Theorys", TigerColor.com, http://www.tigercolor.com/color-lab/color-theory/color-theory-intro.htm#color_harmonies, accessed February 2019.

379. "The basics of the color wheel for presentation design (Part I)", Presentitude, September 28, 2015, http://presentitude.com/color-theory-part-1/, accessed December 2018.

380. "Basic color schemes - Introduction to Color Theorys", TigerColor.com, http://www.tigercolor.com/color-lab/color-theory/color-theory-intro.htm#color_harmonies, accessed February 2019.

381. Cameron Chapman, "Color Theory for Designers: How To Create Your Own Color Schemes", SmashingMagazine.com, February 8, 2010, https://www.smashingmagazine.com/2010/02/color-theory-for-designer-part-3-creating-your-own-color-palettes/, accessed October 2018.

382. Ben Gremillion, "Hex Color – The Code Side Of Color", SmashingMagazine.com, October 4, 2012, https://www.smashingmagazine.com/2012/10/the-code-side-of-color/, accessed October 2018.

383. Cristina Stefanova, "Black Hat ASO for Mobile Apps & Games: What is It and How It Works (and Why you Shouldn't Do It)", ASO Blog (blog), TheTool.io, August 2, 2018, https://thetool.io/2018/black-hat-aso, accessed October 2018.

384. Regina Leuwer, "Black Hat ASO—Where to Draw the Line", ASO Stack, March 21, 2017, https://asostack.com/black-hat-aso-where-to-draw-the-line-eef10df05d0a, accessed October 2018.

385. Lukas Stefanko, Twitter Post, August 21, 2018, https://twitter.com/LukasStefanko/status/1032144355413446656, accessed December 2018.

386. Sebastian Knopp, "7 Black-Hat-ASO-Taktiken die man kennen sollte", Mobile Marketing Review, June 6, 2018, http://mobilemarketingreview.de/7-black-hat-aso-taktiken-die-man-kennen-sollte/, accessed October 2018.

387. Cristina Stefanova, "Black Hat ASO for Mobile Apps & Games: What is It and How It Works (and Why you Shouldn't Do It)", ASO Blog (blog), TheTool.io, August 2, 2018, https://thetool.io/2018/black-hat-aso, accessed October 2018.

388. Sebastian Knopp, "7 Black-Hat-ASO-Taktiken die man kennen sollte", Mobile Marketing Review, June 6, 2018, http://mobilemarketingreview.de/7-black-hat-aso-taktiken-die-man-kennen-sollte/, accessed October 2018.

389. Regina Leuwer, "Black Hat ASO—Where to Draw the Line", ASO Stack, March 21, 2017, https://asostack.com/black-hat-aso-where-to-draw-the-line-eef10df05d0a, accessed October 2018.

390. Cristina Stefanova, "Black Hat ASO for Mobile Apps & Games: What is It and How It Works (and Why you Shouldn't Do It)", ASO Blog (blog), TheTool.io, August 2, 2018, https://thetool.io/2018/black-hat-aso, accessed October 2018.

391. Lukas Stefanko, Twitter Post, May 28, 2018, https://twitter.com/LukasStefanko/status/1001039354414944258, accessed December 2018.

392. "DU Recorder – Screen Recorder, Video Editor, Live", Apps on Google Play, https://play.google.com/store/apps/details?id=com.duapps.recorder, accessed August 2018.

393. "AZ Screen Recorder - No Root", Apps on Google Play, https://play.google.com/store/apps/details?id=com.hecorat.screenrecorder.free, accessed August 2018.

394. "Mobizen Screen Recorder - Record, Capture, Edit", Apps on Google Play, https://play.google.com/store/apps/details?id=com.rsupport.mvagent, accessed August 2018.

395. "KineMaster – Pro Video Editor", Apps on Google Play, https://play.google.com/store/apps/details?id=com.nexstreaming.app.kinemasterfree, accessed August 2018.

396. "KineMaster - Pro Video Editor", iTunes, https://itunes.apple.com/app/id1223932558?mt=8, accessed August 2018.

397. "PowerDirector - Video Editor App, Best Video Maker", Apps on Google Play, https://play.google.com/store/apps/details?id=com.cyberlink.powerdirector.DRA140225_01, accessed August 2018.

398. "iMovie", iTunes, https://itunes.apple.com/app/id377298193?mt=8, accessed August 2018.

399. "Adobe Capture CC", iTunes, https://itunes.apple.com/us/app/id1040200189?mt=8, accessed October 2018.

400. "Adobe Capture CC", Apps on Google Play, https://play.google.com/store/apps/details?id=com.adobe.creativeapps.gather&hl=en, accessed October 2018.

401. Gabe Kwakyi, "The App Store Optimization Activities Impact Chart", June 05, 2017, Incipia Blog (blog), https://incipia.co/post/app-marketing/the-app-store-optimization-activities-impact-chart-2/, accessed December 2018.

402. Ibid.

Made in the USA
Middletown, DE
02 January 2020